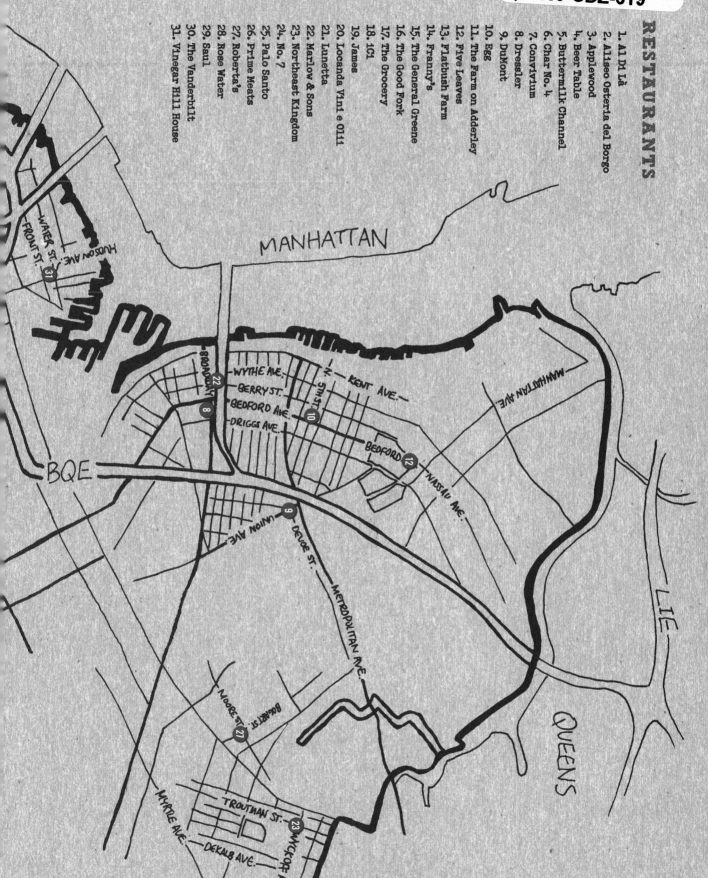

RESTAURANTS

THE NEW
BROOKLYN
COOKBOOK

THE NEW BROOKLYN COOKBOOK

RECIPES AND STORIES FROM **31** RESTAURANTS THAT PUT BROOKLYN ON THE CULINARY MAP

MELISSA VAUGHAN & BRENDAN VAUGHAN

PHOTOGRAPHS BY MICHAEL HARLAN TURKELL

WILLIAM MORROW

An Imprint of HarperCollinsPublishers

HarperCollins books may be purchased for educational, business, or sales promotional use. For information please write: Special Markets Department, HarperCollins Publishers, 10 East 53rd Street, New York, NY 10022.

FIRST EDITION

Designed by Kris Tobiassen

Library of Congress Cataloging-in-Publication Data

Vaughan, Melissa.
    The new Brooklyn cookbook : recipes and stories from 31 restaurants that put Brooklyn on the culinary map / Melissa Vaughan and Brendan Vaughan ; photographs by Michael Harlan Turkell. — 1st ed.
        p.   cm.
    Includes index.
    ISBN 978-0-06-195622-5
    1. Cookery, American.   2. Cookery—New York (State)—New York.   3. Brooklyn (New York, N.Y.)—Social life and customs.   I. Vaughan, Brendan.   II. Title.
    TX715.V3476   2010
    641.59747'23—dc22
                                                                2010007139

10   11   12   13   14   ID4/QG   10   9   8   7   6   5   4   3   2   1

FOR ROAN AND DORY

CONTENTS

(In chronological order)

INTRODUCTION

Greetings, eater, and welcome to *The New Brooklyn Cookbook*.

First, a word about the "old" Brooklyn. We love the old Brooklyn. We eat there all the time: Di Fara's Pizza in Midwood, where the legendary Dom DeMarco labors over every pie like it's the last he'll ever make; Primorski in Brighton Beach for herring with onions, too much vodka, and way too much Lady Gaga; Peter Luger in Williamsburg for the porterhouse, of course, but also for the starter of thick-cut bacon; Tanoreen in Bay Ridge, which is not even that old (it opened in 1998) but is undeniably the reigning Middle Eastern restaurant in all of Kings County; and Nathan's in Coney Island for dogs and fries before the Brooklyn Cyclones take the field (not recommended before a ride on the original Cyclone).

Thank God and Marty Markowitz for all that. Due respect. But this book is about something else. It's about the surge of culinary energy that has coursed through Brooklyn in the past decade or so, generating dozens of excellent neighborhood restaurants, many of which have become destination restaurants. It's about the people who pulled it off, too, the dice-rollers who many called crazy for trying to sell calf's tongue salad and ricotta beignets in the borough of pizza, bagels, and ethnic takeout of every conceivable flavor. And it's about the community of Brooklyn-based food entrepreneurs many of these chefs buy from—the coffee-roasters, picklers, granola makers, brewers, bearded Willy Wonkas, and kimchee-making deejays who peddle their products at markets like the Brooklyn Flea and specialty shops throughout the city and beyond.

The social and economic forces that transformed Brooklyn have been gathering momentum for decades. Food-wise, though, it's easy to pinpoint the beginning of today's thriving scene: late 1998. True, there were a few trailblazers before, since closed. Remember Cucina on Fifth Avenue in Park Slope? Or Oznot's Dish in Williamsburg? Due respect to them, too. Ahead of their time. But for all the dynamism that characterizes Brooklyn's dining scene today, you can trace it all back to two restaurants: Al Di Là, which opened in November 1998, and Diner, born less than two months later, on New Year's Eve. These restaurants have little in common. Al Di Là is a traditional Venetian trattoria that pays loving homage to dishes, not their component parts; Diner was an early advocate of the local-seasonal-sustainable approach, spreading the gospel of organic produce and humanely raised meat and helping to create a whole new framework for doing good by eating well. But from the beginning, both demonstrated that there was a vastly underserved market for ambitious, Manhattan-level cooking at Brooklyn prices. The Grocery and Saul, a pair of high-end French-inspired New American restaurants (both more expensive and fancier, culinarily, than either Al Di Là or Diner), stress-tested that notion further when they opened in the fall of 1999 on Smith Street.

This was no "scene" yet, just a smattering of believers who placed a big bet on Brooklyn. But over the next few years, this initial diversity morphed into something like a movement. Rose Water, Franny's, iCi, Applewood, the Farm on Adderley—these restaurants, building on the ideas of Alice Waters at Chez Panisse in Berkeley and Peter Hoffman at Savoy in SoHo and, yes, Caroline Fidanza at Diner, formed the foundation of the so-called New Brooklyn Cuisine, "a very specific subgenre of the more familiar New American Cuisine," wrote Robin Raisfeld and Rob Patronite, *New York* magazine's influential Underground Gourmet critics, in an ecstatic four-star review of the General Greene. "It flourishes in the bucolic hinterlands of Boerum Hill and Prospect Heights, the low country of Carroll Gardens and Williamsburg, and the great plains of Park Slope, and has as its common denominator a very New York culinary sophistication melded with a wistfully agrarian passion for the artisanal, the sustainably grown, and the homespun."

That review, headlined "Best of Breed" and published in August 2008, might have been the high point for that particular conception of a New Brooklyn restaurant. When you talk to people about Brooklyn food these days, it's not hard to detect fatigue with the farm-to-table, local-seasonal-sustainable thing, even among those who fully subscribe. "I'm not here to preach *at all,*" Catherine Saillard, owner of iCi, told us. "I want to make it stronger, the attachment and philosophy that I have here, but I never want to preach, and to be like, *What?! What do you mean? You don't eat organic?! Oh my God, that's why the earth's not turning!* No." We'll stop short of calling it a backlash. Chefs still believe in these ideals, after all. So does everyone else. By now, we just *expect* ingredients at a certain type of restaurant to be responsibly sourced. And we appreciate it. But let's declare a thousand-year-ban on the buzzwords, shall we?

Another occasional quibble with the new Brooklyn is that it's thriving at the expense of the old Brooklyn—the slice counters, red-sauce Italian joints, and Irish bars that defined the borough for decades. And yes, that world is losing ground, at least in so-called brownstone Brooklyn. No point in denying that gentrification has been a huge factor in the creation of the borough's dining scene. (Fifteen years ago, the core clientele for these restaurants would have lived in Manhattan.) But the curious thing is these new restaurants represent a modern-day version of the prototypical Old World establishment where the owner's always there, the customers know each other by face if not name, and the specials are scrawled on a chalkboard. In this sense, at least, these *are* the good old days.

Always evolving and obsessed with maintaining their own freshness and vitality, Brooklyn's new wave of restaurants have nevertheless been around long enough to have produced a repertoire of well-known dishes, from The Good Fork's steak and eggs Korean-style (page 108) to Marlow & Sons' brick chicken (page 65) to Al Di Là's braised rabbit with black olives and polenta (page 8). *The New Brooklyn Cookbook* has plenty of these signature recipes. Yet we're just as proud to include many lesser-known creations, those hidden gems and occasional specials you might not order until your fourth or fifth visit. We'll single out the General Greene's soft tofu with broad beans and chili paste (page 165), Egg's duck legs and dirty rice (page 94), and Locanda Vini a Olii's spicy seafood guazzetto (page 45) as prime examples. After all, every dish in this book was carefully selected by the chef who created it. We consulted with them, sometimes suggesting that, say, a pasta might be nice for the mix, but the final choices were theirs. Which means these recipes all convey something essential about how the chefs perceive their restaurants.

We'd like to stress: *This book is not meant to be comprehensive.* Brooklyn's dining scene is constantly expanding. There are plenty of very good restaurants we couldn't include because we just didn't have the space, and others that have opened since our deadline. We're not saying these are the thirty-one "best" restaurants in Brooklyn. (The Michelin guide would probably agree: There are only four Michelin-starred restaurants in the borough, and two of them, Peter Luger and the River Café, wouldn't make sense in this collection.) We're just saying they best embody the food culture we're celebrating between these covers.

To stay fresh, to stay exciting, Brooklyn's restaurant culture needs to expand and evolve. And it is. *The New Brooklyn Cookbook* is organized in chronological order, and this ongoing evolution reveals itself as the book progresses. Later entries include Prime Meats, an "American-German" restaurant, to borrow the owners' term; No. 7, where chef Tyler Kord dabbles in all kinds of kitchen craziness; and the Vanderbilt, a surprisingly Manhattan-ish restaurant on a vast (for Brooklyn) corner space in Prospect Heights. All of which hint at the future of great eating in Brooklyn—an increasingly diverse and vital future, in which the dining choices rival Manhattan's not just in quality, but in range. Amen.

AL DI LÀ

PARK SLOPE

It begins—where else?—with Al Di Là.

Back in 1997 Anna Klinger was cooking at Lespinasse, the storied, staid, and now defunct French restaurant in the St. Regis hotel in midtown Manhattan. She worked nights, her husband worked days, and they never saw each other. This, they realized, was no way to live. So the couple decided to open a restaurant in their Park Slope neighborhood. Al Di Là—the name means "over there"—would be an intimate Venetian trattoria specializing in the simple, soulful cuisine that Emiliano Coppa (right), the chef's Italian husband, grew up on. They leased a space on Fifth Avenue ("a bit dicey at night back then," Klinger recalls), ripped out the nine-foot wok in the kitchen (it had been a Chinese takeout place), scavenged mismatched plates and glasses at flea markets, and opened in November 1998. The neighborhood was hungry.

"I was telling my husband, 'Take tables out of the dining room; I can't handle it!'" Klinger says now, laughing at the heart-pounding blur of those early months. One night soon after opening, she sent some extras out to a friend who'd come in for dinner. But the waiters hadn't mastered the table-numbering system, so the freebies went to the wrong diner—who happened to be an influential food critic. "He was delighted he was being taken care of," she says drily. "Soon he was talking up a storm on the radio, and we got a million phone calls."

But Al Di Là doesn't take reservations—not then, not now. Instead there's a nightly waiting list that always seems to be an hour long. You just shrug and say okay. You're willing to wait for your favorites: *malfatti* with Swiss chard, ricotta, brown butter and sage; *trippa alla Toscana;* and the braised rabbit on page 8, Klinger's most beloved dish. ("I can't take it off the menu. I try to every once in a while, but people yell at me.") To make the wait a bit more bearable, Coppa and Klinger added a wine bar directly behind the restaurant in 2003.

By then it was clear that the couple had pioneered—and to some degree inspired—a food scene that would grow much larger and more dynamic. Not that they realized it back in 1998. "We just had our heads down and were doing our thing," she says. "It was all-encompassing."

It still is, which means the wine bar is probably the extent of their expansion plans. "I don't know how people do two restaurants without losing control of the first one," Klinger says. "I'm perfectly happy with the way things are going. It's still very personal, and I like that."

Spaghetti alle Vongole / AL DI LÀ

SERVES 4

2 dozen Manila clams

Coarse salt

12 ounces spaghetti

½ cup extra-virgin olive oil

1 large shallot, finely diced

4 tablespoons finely chopped garlic

1 teaspoon crushed red pepper flakes

1 tablespoon dried oregano

1 cup dry white wine

2 tablespoons chopped fresh flat-leaf parsley

Freshly ground black pepper

"Every hand that makes this makes it slightly differently," says chef Anna Klinger of this classic dish, a perfectly balanced blend of briny, garlicky, spicy flavors. The shallots, for example, are controversial. "My husband and I argue about whether or not we should put shallots in," she says, laughing. "Traditionally, there aren't any. But I win." Klinger uses Manila clams, but you can also go with Littlenecks or cockles.

1. Fill a large bowl with salted water. Add the clams and soak for 10 minutes. Drain, then scrub the clams with a brush to remove any remaining grit.

2. Discard any clams that have broken, cracked, or open shells that do not close when tapped firmly.

3. Bring a large pot of salted water to a boil. Add the spaghetti and cook until just al dente, about 9 minutes.

4. Heat the olive oil in a 12-inch sauté pan. Add the shallots, garlic, red pepper flakes, and oregano. Sauté until the garlic is just beginning to turn a light golden brown and the mixture is very aromatic, about 2 minutes. Add the clams to the pan and mix well. Add the wine and cook over high heat until the clams begin to open, shaking the pan occasionally to cook the clams evenly. As each clam starts to open, transfer it to a large plate, leaving the liquid in the pan; the clams will finish opening and won't be overcooked. Discard any clams that do not open. Bring the pan liquid to a boil over high heat and cook until reduced by half. The sauce should be reduced enough to cling to the pasta, with a little extra for mopping up with bread.

5. Drain the pasta and add it to the reduced liquid. Top it with the reserved clams and the parsley and season with salt and freshly ground black pepper to taste. Toss well, then divide among 4 plates and serve immediately.

Braised Rabbit with Black Olives and Creamy Polenta / AL DI LÀ

For the rabbit

2 3-pound rabbit fryers, cut into 7 pieces: 2 forelegs, 2 hind legs, and the loin cut across the saddle into 3 pieces (have the butcher do this for you)

Coarse salt and freshly ground black pepper

2 tablespoons extra-virgin olive oil

¼ cup canola oil

1 cup dry white wine

10 garlic cloves, minced

4 fresh rosemary sprigs

6 cups hot homemade chicken stock or prepared low-sodium chicken broth

6 tablespoons (¾ stick) unsalted butter

24 oil-cured black olives

2 large tomatoes, seeded and cut into ¼-inch dice (about 3½ cups)

For the polenta

1½ cups heavy cream

2 teaspoons coarse salt

1½ cups polenta (cornmeal)

This dish has been an anchor of Al Di Là's menu since day one, but chef Anna Klinger almost talked herself out of serving it at all. Rabbit is popular in Northern Italy, and her Italian husband and partner pushed for it, but Klinger had her doubts about its potential in Brooklyn. Those doubts were unfounded. "There are people who have been coming since we opened who have *only* had the rabbit," she says. It's a visually striking dish, too, with an upturned bone that makes it look rustic and theatrical at the same time.

1. Preheat the oven to 375°F.

2. **To braise the rabbit,** pat the rabbit dry with a paper towel and season liberally with salt and pepper. Heat 1 tablespoon of the olive oil and 2 tablespoons of the canola oil in a large heavy-bottomed casserole or Dutch oven over medium-high heat until hot but not smoking. Working in batches, place the rabbit in the oil and brown on all sides, 8 to 10 minutes in all, adding more olive oil and canola oil as needed. Transfer the rabbit to a plate lined with a paper towel and drain the cooking oil from the pan.

3. Return the pan to the stove. Add the wine, garlic, and rosemary and increase the heat to high; simmer, scraping up browned bits from the bottom of the pot. Cook until 1 tablespoon of the wine remains.

4. Add the rabbit back to the pot. Add the hot stock and cover the pot with a tight-fitting lid or aluminum foil and place it in the oven. Roast until the rabbit is fork tender, about 1 hour. Transfer the rabbit to a serving plate and tent it with foil to keep it warm.

5. **To cook the polenta,** in a heavy pot or large saucepan, bring the cream, 3½ cups water, and the salt to a boil. Whisking constantly, pour the polenta into the pan in a thin stream. Cook the polenta, still whisking constantly, until the mixture has thickened, about 3 minutes. Reduce

the heat to low and cook for 45 minutes, stirring as frequently as possible with a wooden spoon. Remove the pan from the heat and cover to keep warm. Stir the polenta just before serving. The polenta will keep warm, covered, for about 20 minutes.

6. While the polenta cooks, prepare the sauce. Add the butter, olives, and tomatoes to the braising liquid. Reduce over medium-high heat until the sauce thickens enough to cling to the rabbit, 15 to 20 minutes. Adjust the seasoning. Return the rabbit to the pot and spoon the sauce over the rabbit to coat.

7. To serve, divide the polenta among 6 serving plates. Place the rabbit on the polenta and spoon the sauce on top.

THE GROCERY
CARROLL GARDENS

Way too early on the morning of October 20, 2003, Sharon Pachter, the co-chef and -owner of the Grocery, got a phone call from her father. She was awake. Kind of. Then she heard him say something about "the front page." Okay, *now* she was awake. She grabbed the paper and there it was, an A1 story in the *New York Times* that began like this: "Here, in order, are the seven best restaurants in New York City, according to food ratings in the 2004 Zagat Survey published today: Le Bernardin, Daniel, Peter Luger, Nobu, Bouley, Jean Georges and the Grocery. The Grocery? You may be forgiven for asking."

How could a storefront restaurant in the remote province of Carroll Gardens, a tiny, thirty-seat dining room with no hostess, no coat check, no sommelier—and, in the view of many, no business being in such elite company—have cracked the top-ten list of the most influential restaurant guide in New York? The *Times* article went on to explore that question in ludicrous detail, picking apart Zagat's scoring methodology and parsing the mathematical jujitsu that would allow such a low-profile neighborhood restaurant to outrank Alain Ducasse, Babbo, Gramercy Tavern, and so on. But the bottom line was this: The Grocery had the votes, the ranking was legit (twenty-eight out of a possible thirty points for food), and the New York restaurant world had no choice but

to pay attention. The Grocery may have opened four years earlier, but that day in October 2003 was the day it arrived.

The restaurant's big news wasn't news at all to its regulars. When the Grocery opened in September 1999, it was the first "serious" restaurant in the neighborhood. (Saul, profiled on page 18, would open two months later.) Pachter and Charlie Kiely (her partner in business and in life) had both worked in the kitchens of Savoy and Gotham Bar and Grill, and the locals responded immediately to their market-driven New American cooking. (A few early favorites: seared tuna with beet relish and cumin yogurt, duck breast with warm bulgur salad, and baked halibut with fava beans and bacon.) But Pachter and Kiely—a perpetually harried, lovable crank who's always saying things like "I wear way too many hats and none of them fit"— never took themselves all that seriously. Nor did they have much of a plan. "We didn't design our menu in expectation of what people were looking for," Pachter says. "It was all very selfishly driven. We wanted to make the food that we wanted to make, the food that *we* were hungry for."

And that's more or less what they still do. Things have settled down since that insane period after the *Times* story, when every ratings slave in Manhattan made the pilgrimage to

Carroll Gardens, crossed the Grocery off their list, and headed back over the bridge. The restaurant's business doubled in 2004, but its Zagat rating slipped a bit—the result, no doubt, of all those new voters with stratospheric expectations. For the last couple years, its food rating has been twenty-seven. That keeps the Grocery in Zagat's top-forty citywide, and in Brooklyn second only to legendary Di Fara Pizza in Midwood. As even Charlie Kiely would concede, that's solid company.

Pan-Roasted Chicken with Sweet Potato Strudel, Adobo, and Brussels Sprouts / THE GROCERY

SERVES 4

For the sweet potato strudel dough*

12 tablespoons (1½ sticks) unsalted butter, melted

1 cup boiling water

1 tablespoon freshly squeezed lemon juice

2 tablespoons vegetable oil

3 cups all-purpose flour

For the chicken gizzard adobo

1 pound chicken gizzards, cleaned and halved

2 cups distilled vinegar

¼ cup soy sauce

13 garlic cloves

1 tablespoon whole black peppercorns

1 bay leaf

For the sweet potato strudel filling

1½ pounds sweet potatoes, washed and dried

1 to 2 tablespoons extra-virgin olive oil

2 tablespoons unsalted butter

Coarse salt and freshly ground black pepper

This strudel dough is suitable for a multitude of savory and sweet fillings. Pachter suggests mushrooms and onions, ground meat, apples, jam, dried fruit and nuts, or farmer cheese. Just substitute sugar for salt when rolling sweet strudels.

This is a beautifully balanced plate of food. At the center is a juicy roasted chicken, surrounded by sweet strudel (via co-chef Sharon Pachter's grandmother), roasted sprouts, and a spectacular Filipino-style adobo that brings acidity (from the vinegar) and heat (from the peppercorns). It takes some effort, but verything except the chicken can be done ahead of time. Just warm the other components as the chicken's roasting, assemble while it's resting, and serve.

1. **To make the strudel dough,** pour the melted butter into a medium, heat-proof bowl and cover with the boiling water. Add the lemon juice and vegetable oil and stir to combine. Gradually add the flour, stirring gently with a fork, until a dough is formed.

2. Turn the dough out onto a lightly floured work surface and knead until the dough is uniform and no longer sticky, about 10 minutes. Divide the dough into 4 equal portions. Wrap separately in plastic wrap and freeze 3 pieces for future use. Refrigerate one portion for 3 hours or overnight.

3. **To make the adobo,** combine the gizzards, vinegar, and soy sauce in a small saucepan with just enough water to cover. Bring to a simmer over medium heat, skimming to remove the impurities. Add the garlic, peppercorns, and bay leaf and simmer gently until the gizzards are tender and the garlic cloves are soft, about 1 hour. Set the pan aside and allow the gizzards to cool in their cooking liquid.

4. **To make the strudel filling,** preheat the oven to 425°F. Coat the sweet potatoes with the olive oil, wrap them in aluminum foil, and roast until they are tender when pierced with the tip of a small, sharp knife, about 45 minutes. When they are cool enough to handle, scrape the flesh into a medium bowl, roughly mash the sweet potatoes with the butter, and season to taste. Cool the potatoes to room temperature or refrigerate if not using immediately.

5. To prepare the strudel, preheat the oven to 400°F with a rack in the center of the oven.

6. Lay a large clean dish towel on a clean work surface and dust the towel with flour. Roll the dough into an 18 x 12-inch rectangle (sized to fit a baking sheet). The dough should be thin and translucent. Brush off any excess flour and then carefully brush the dough with some of the melted brown butter or vegetable oil. Sprinkle the bread crumbs evenly across the surface of the dough and season with salt.

7. Form a 2-inch-thick snake of cooled sweet potato filling across the long front edge, just short of the ends of the dough. Start rolling the dough over the filling to enclose it, using the towel to facilitate rolling and tucking in the ends of the roll to close the tube. Finish by pinching the seam closed. Transfer the roll to a parchment-lined baking sheet, seam side down. Brush the top and sides with the remaining brown butter and sprinkle with salt.

8. Pierce the top and sides of the strudel every few inches with a sharp paring knife to allow the steam to escape and prevent the strudel from bursting. You can make these perforations as diagonal cut guidelines that will show you where to cut the strudel into 8 pieces when it's finished.

9. Bake, rotating the pan from front to back after 15 minutes, until the strudel is golden brown, about 35 minutes. If the bottom starts to darken too quickly, place the baking sheet on top of another baking sheet. Set the strudel aside to cool slightly.

10. To roast the chicken, season it to taste with salt and pepper, taking into account the salt in the soy sauce and the peppercorns in the adobo sauce.

11. Coat the bottom of a large, ovenproof sauté pan with olive oil and heat the pan over high heat until smoking. Place the chicken skin side down in the pan and sear until the skin is brown and crispy, 3 to 4 minutes. Turn the chicken over and cook on the flesh side for 5 minutes more. Place the chicken in the oven and roast until the juices from the thigh run clear, about 25 minutes. Transfer to a cutting board and tent the chicken with foil to allow it to rest and keep warm.

12. To prepare the Brussels sprouts, make a small cut across the stem of each Brussels sprout half. This will help the sprout to cook through without overcooking the leaves.

For composing the strudel

All-purpose flour, for dusting

2 tablespoons unsalted butter, melted and cooked until the solids are brown and nutty, then cooled to room temperature, or 2 tablespoons vegetable oil

2 tablespoons unseasoned bread crumbs

Coarse salt

*For the roasted chicken**

4 organic bone-in, skin-on chicken breasts, about 8 ounces each

4 organic bone-in, skin-on chicken thighs, about 4 ounces each

Coarse salt and freshly ground black pepper

2 to 3 tablespoons extra-virgin olive oil

For the Brussels sprouts

1 pound Brussels sprouts, trimmed and halved

2 tablespoons extra-virgin olive oil

Coarse salt and freshly ground black pepper

1 Macoun, Cortland, Cameo, or other hard, sweet-tart red-skinned apple, unpeeled and cut into ¼-inch dice

* Buy chicken in parts or butcher your own. Buy a 3½-pound chicken, use the breasts and thighs for this recipe, and roast the legs and wings separately for a snack.

13. Heat the olive oil in a medium sauté pan over medium heat. Add the sprouts and sauté them until lightly browned, 4 to 5 minutes. If the pan gets too hot, sprinkle it with a little water. Season to taste with salt and pepper. Add the apples and sauté for 2 minutes, or until the apples are heated through.

14. Meanwhile, reheat the chicken gizzard adobo in a small sauce pot over low heat until heated through. Discard the bay leaf.

15. Use a serrated knife to slice the strudel on the diagonal into 8 pieces.

16. To serve, remove the bones from the chicken thighs. Place the thighs skin side down on a cutting board. Cut on either side of the bone to release the thigh meat. Remove the bones from the breast. Place the breast skin side down on a cutting board. Gently remove the rib bones, then pull

the meat, in one piece, from the remaining bones. Slice the chicken pieces and divide among 4 plates (1 breast and 1 thigh per serving). Add 1 piece of strudel to each

plate (reserving the other pieces for seconds or for another meal), then add the Brussels sprouts and apples. Spoon the adobo around the chicken and serve.

Stuffed Squid with Ratatouille, Polenta Fries, and Balsamic Butter / THE GROCERY

Here's an updated version of a dish Charlie Kiely conceived back in 1992 in his first chef job at a (now closed) Manhattan restaurant called Abby. In those days he did it with an oven-dried-tomato garnish, but for the Grocery, his wife (and partner in the kitchen), Sharon Pachter, convinced him to swap that out for a parsley salad. "The lemon juice and olive oil gives it an acidic lift," she says, adding that the crispy polenta fries bring some crunch to an otherwise soft-textured dish. Stuffed squid is a Kiely favorite, and you can find it on the Grocery's menu (in a variety of preparations) every winter.

1. To make the polenta, combine the butter, salt, and 2¼ cups water in a medium saucepan and bring to a rapid boil over high heat. Gradually add the polenta, whisking until well combined. Lower the heat and simmer gently, stirring frequently with a wooden spoon to prevent the polenta from sticking to the bottom of the pan. Cook for 30 minutes, or until the polenta has thickened, and add salt and pepper to taste.

2. Line an 8 x 8-inch baking dish with plastic wrap and spread the polenta ½ inch thick over the plastic. Cover and refrigerate overnight or until firm.

3. To make the ratatouille, heat 2 tablespoons of the olive oil in a large heavy sauté pan or Dutch oven over medium-high heat. Add the eggplant and season with salt and pepper. Cook, stirring frequently, until the eggplant is softened, about 6 minutes. Remove the eggplant with a slotted spoon and transfer to a large bowl. Add the zucchini to the pan and season with salt and pepper. Cook, stirring frequently, until the zucchini is tender but still bright, about 4 minutes. Transfer to the bowl with the eggplant.

4. Heat 2 more tablespoons of olive oil, then add the red and green peppers; season with salt and pepper. Cook, stirring, until the peppers are softened, about 8 minutes. Transfer to the bowl with the other vegetables. Add the red onion and season with salt and pepper. Sauté until translucent, about 2 minutes. Combine with the other vegetables and set aside to cool.

SERVES 4

For the fried polenta

2 tablespoons unsalted butter

¾ teaspoon kosher salt

¾ cup coarse-ground polenta (cornmeal)

Freshly ground black pepper

Vegetable oil, for frying

For the ratatouille

5 tablespoons extra-virgin olive oil

½ small eggplant, skin on, cut into ¼-inch dice (about ¾ cup)

Coarse salt and freshly ground black pepper

½ medium zucchini, cut into ¼-inch dice (about ¾ cup)

½ red bell pepper, seeded and cut into ¼-inch dice (about ½ cup)

½ green bell pepper, seeded and cut into ¼-inch dice (about ½ cup)

½ small red onion, cut into ¼-inch dice (about ¼ cup)

3 garlic cloves, minced

½ cup dry white wine

6 canned peeled plum tomatoes (from one 28-ounce can), strained, stemmed, seeded, and cut into ¼-inch dice

1 tablespoon chopped fresh thyme leaves

For the squid and the balsamic butter

8 medium (4- to 5-inch-long) whole fresh cleaned squid, plus the tentacles (about 1½ pounds in total)*

Coarse salt and freshly ground black pepper

2 tablespoons canola oil

1 tablespoon extra-virgin olive oil

¼ cup dry white wine

¾ cup balsamic vinegar

1 tablespoon unsalted butter

For the fried tentacles

Vegetable oil, for frying

½ cup rice flour

½ to ¾ cup sparkling water or club soda

Coarse salt

For the parsley salad

1 tablespoon extra-virgin olive oil

1 teaspoon freshly squeezed lemon juice, strained

Coarse salt and freshly ground black pepper

2 cups fresh flat-leaf parsley leaves (from about 1 bunch parsley)

Many fish stores sell cleaned squid bodies and tentacles separately. But if you're shopping in Chinatown or other ethnic markets you'll save money by buying whole, uncleaned squid. To clean, remove everything from inside the body (or hood), including the plasticlike quill, by holding the squid tail in one hand and the head in the other. Twist and pull apart. Cut the tentacles off and reserve. Rinse the body under cold running water, then pull the thin gray membrane off the outside or scrape it off with the back of a small knife. Finally, remove the two wings on the side of the hood.

5. If the pan is dry, heat 1 tablespoon olive oil, then add the garlic and sauté over medium heat until it is fragrant and tender, about 5 minute. Add the wine, tomatoes, and thyme, reduce the heat to medium low, and simmer until the liquid is reduced by half, about 8 minutes. Remove from the heat. Add the tomato mixture to the vegetables and adjust the seasoning.

6. To make the squid, preheat the oven to 200°F. Rinse and dry the squid. Turn the tubes inside out by using your fingers to push the tip up through the tube and gently roll down the sides until the tube is inverted. Using a small spoon, stuff the tubes three-quarters full with about ¼ cup of ratatouille. Season the stuffed squid with salt and pepper.

7. Heat the canola oil and olive oil in a medium sauté pan over medium-high heat. Carefully lay the tubes in the pan and cook until they are golden brown on all sides, about 6 minutes total. Remove the squid from the pan and transfer to a rimmed baking sheet. Place in the oven to keep warm.

8. To make the balsamic butter, drain the fat from the pan and discard any loose burned bits of ratatouille. Add the wine and balsamic vinegar, scraping the bottom of the pan to release any browned bits, and simmer over medium heat until the mixture reduces and coats the back of a spoon, 8 to 9 minutes. Stir in the butter, swirling the pan, to emulsify. Season to taste with salt and pepper.

9. To fry the polenta, heat 1 inch of vegetable oil in a deep sauté pan over medium-high heat until it registers 375°F on a deep-fry thermometer. Line a plate with paper towels. Turn the firm polenta onto a large cutting board, remove the plastic wrap, and cut in half. Wrap and refrigerate half of the polenta for another use. Cut the remaining half into 8 triangles. Fry the polenta, turning once, until the outside is crispy and golden brown, about 6 minutes total. Remove the polenta from the oil with a slotted spoon and drain on the paper-towel-lined plate. Immediately season the polenta triangles with salt. Transfer the polenta to the baking sheet with the squid and return to the oven to keep warm.

10. To fry the tentacles, heat 3 inches of vegetable oil in a medium sauce pot over medium-high heat until it registers 375°F on a deep-fry thermometer. Line a plate with paper towels. Mound the rice flour in the bottom of a medium bowl and make a well. Pour the sparkling water into the well and whisk until the mixture is smooth and the consistency of melted ice cream; it should be just thick enough to coat the tentacles.

11. Pat the tentacles dry. Dip in the batter, then drain the excess batter back into the bowl. Working in batches, fry until the tentacles are crispy and lightly colored, about 1 minute. Remove the tentacles from the oil, drain on the paper-towel-lined plate, and immediately season with salt. Transfer to the baking sheet with the squid and polenta and return to the oven to keep warm.

(You can also sauté the tentacles rather than battering and frying. Heat 2 tablespoons olive oil in a medium sauté pan over medium-high heat. Season the tentacles with salt and pepper and sauté until they are opaque, about 3 minutes.)

12. To make the parsley salad, whisk together the olive oil, lemon juice, and salt and pepper to taste. Add the parsley leaves and toss to combine.

13. To serve, slice 4 of the stuffed tubes in half. Place 2 halves and 1 whole tube on each of 4 plates. Arrange the fried polenta and parsley salad around the squid. Spoon the balsamic butter sauce around the squid and garnish with a fried tentacle.

SAUL

BOERUM HILL

If Brooklyn restaurants were people, most would be a thirtysomething creative professional in head-to-toe Uniqlo. Saul, meanwhile, is the fiftyish law professor in a cashmere sweater. From the day he opened in November 1999, chef Saul Bolton has turned out "sophisticated" food, to quote his website, becoming one of only four Brooklyn restaurants to earn a Michelin star. (The other three are Dressler, page 114, Peter Luger steak house, and the River Café). For its tenth birthday, Saul got a big wet kiss of a review from the *New York Times,* which praised the restaurant for its sustained energy and inventiveness.

Sophisticated. That's a word that few other restaurants in this book would use to describe themselves. In fact, many would be vaguely embarrassed. But it's the perfect word for Saul, Brooklyn's version of a fancy restaurant. The dining room is warm, airy, and elegant. The clean-shaven maître d' wears a coat and tie. The white-shirted servers discreetly swap in new flatware between courses. (Mercifully, they do *not* do that architectural thing with your napkin when you go to the restroom.) And a typical meal goes something like this: *amuse-bouche* of pureed mushroom with white truffle oil and chives, rich and earthy,

wonderful right off the spoon, even better sopped up with a soft, crusty slice of bread; seafood chowder of Manila clams, mussels, shrimp, and crispy little nuggets of smoky bacon in a light broth flecked with fines herbes; oxtail ragù with poached egg, homemade tagliatelle, and Parmesan cheese, which comes in a high-sided conical bowl that collects the egg, cheese, and pasta in the bottom, making for some intensely flavored final bites; and perfectly cooked squab with wild arugula, *farro verde,* and tiny disks of brightly flavored pickled artichokes.

Bolton, a native Ohioan who owns the restaurant with his wife,

Lisa, came to New York in the early nineties because he wanted to work with David Bouley. He accomplished that goal, then went on to stints at Le Bernardin and Verbena (now closed) before landing his first executive-chef job at Grove, also defunct, in the West Village. He toiled there for three years before opening Saul in November 1999, just two months after the Grocery appeared eight blocks south.

"So many people said it wouldn't work," Bolton recalls. "All the neighborhood people were like, 'What are you doing? You need at least three television screens in here.'"

Pan-Roasted Squab with Pickled Sunchokes, Eggplant Caviar, and Freekeh / SAUL

SERVES 4

For the pickled sunchokes

1½ cups seasoned rice wine vinegar

1 teaspoon coriander seeds

1 bay leaf

Pinch of crushed red pepper flakes

Pinch of coarse salt

½ pound sunchokes (Jerusalem artichokes), peeled and diced

*For the eggplant caviar
(makes about 2 cups)*

1 large eggplant

Extra-virgin olive oil for coating the eggplant, plus ½ cup

½ tablespoon whole cumin seeds

1 garlic clove, minced

2 tablespoons tahini (sesame paste)

1 teaspoon seasoned rice wine vinegar

1 teaspoon spicy *pimentón de la vera* (smoked paprika)

Coarse salt and freshly ground black pepper

Boerum Hill has always had a Middle Eastern flavor, even more so when Saul Bolton opened his restaurant back in 1999. This dish is a nod to that region's cuisine and to the neighborhood's influence on Bolton's cooking. Freekeh (sometimes spelled *farik*, *frikeh*, or just *frik*), is a roasted wheat grain that's similar to farro and is common throughout the Arab word; the eggplant "caviar," so named because the eggplant seeds resemble tiny fish eggs, is essentially a smooth and smoky baba ghanoush. True, there's nothing especially Middle Eastern about the squab, but the dark silky meat melds perfectly with everything else on the plate. Be careful not to overcook it; there should be plenty of pink at the center when you cut into it.

1. **To make the pickled sunchokes,** combine the rice wine vinegar, coriander seeds, bay leaf, red pepper flakes, and salt in a small nonreactive saucepan and bring to a boil. Add the sunchokes, remove from the heat, and pour into a nonreactive container. Set aside to cool, then refrigerate until completely chilled.

2. **To make the eggplant,** preheat the oven to 425°F. Generously rub the whole eggplant with olive oil, place on a baking sheet, and roast, turning occasionally, until collapsed and charred, about 50 minutes. (You can also cook the eggplant on a grill over high heat for 25 to 30 minutes, or until soft. This will give the caviar a smokier flavor.)

3. Place the cumin seeds in a small, dry skillet over low heat. Cook just until fragrant, 2 or 3 minutes, shaking the pan often to prevent burning. Allow the cumin to cool, then transfer to a spice grinder and grind to a powder.

4. Slice the eggplant in half and scrape out the flesh, discarding the skin. Transfer the eggplant flesh to the work bowl of a food processor. Add the cumin seeds and garlic and puree until smooth. With the

1 tablespoon extra-virgin olive oil

1 medium Spanish onion, chopped

1½ cups freekeh, rinsed and drained, or farro*

Coarse salt and freshly ground black pepper

For the vinaigrette

2 tablespoons sherry vinegar

2 tablespoons minced shallots

Coarse salt and freshly ground black pepper

3 tablespoons extra-virgin olive oil

For the squab

4 whole squab, breasts and legs separated, trimmed of excess fat

Coarse salt and freshly ground black pepper

2 tablespoons extra-virgin olive oil

2 tablespoons unsalted butter

4 fresh thyme sprigs

2 small bunches arugula, cleaned, dried, and stems trimmed

* When Saul serves this dish at the restaurant, he often uses farro verde, a young farro available only to professional chefs, from Anson Mills in South Carolina. We suggest freekeh as the closest substitute; it can be found in most Middle Eastern groceries. (If you live in Brooklyn, it's available at Oriental Pastry and Grocery on Atlantic Avenue.) But you can also use regular farro.

motor running, add the ½ cup olive oil, the tahini, rice wine vinegar, *pimentón,* and salt and pepper to taste. Set aside until ready to use.

5. To make the freekeh, heat the olive oil in a medium saucepan over medium heat. Add the onion and cook until soft and translucent. Add the freekeh and stir to coat. Add 2 cups water, season with salt, and bring to a boil. Cook for 10 to 12 minutes, or until the water is absorbed. Season with salt and pepper.

(If using farro instead of freekeh, sauté the onions and set aside. Add the farro to the pan with enough water to cover it by ½ inch. Season with salt and bring to a boil over medium heat. Cover tightly and simmer for 25 to 30 minutes. Drain off the water and mix the farro with the sautéed onion.)

6. To make the vinaigrette, in a small bowl, combine the sherry vinegar and shallots and let the shallots macerate for about 5 minutes. Season the shallots with salt and pepper. Add the olive oil in a slow stream, whisking until emulsified. Set aside.

7. To cook the squab, pat the squab dry with paper towels and season with salt and pepper. In a large sauté pan that can comfortably fit the squab, heat the olive oil over medium-high heat. Add the squab, skin side down, and cook until the skin is golden brown, 2 or 3 minutes. Add the butter and thyme sprigs to the pan. Turn the squab and continue cooking, flesh side down, for 4 to 6 minutes, or until the internal temperature of the breast registers 120°F on a meat thermometer. (The squab will continue to cook while it rests and should be served medium-rare.) Remove the pan from the heat and tent with foil.

8. To serve, spread ¼ cup of eggplant caviar on each of 4 plates. Divide the freekeh among 4 plates, mounding it in the center. Top with two squab breasts and two squab legs on each plate. Toss the arugula with the sherry vinaigrette. Scatter the arugula and pickled sunchokes around the squab. Garnish with freshly ground black pepper.

Diver Scallops with White Bean Puree, Chorizo, and Pine Nuts / SAUL

"It's just so freakin' logical," says chef Saul Bolton of this dish. "You have the spicy chorizo in there, which is fatty and bright red and just as tasty as can be (and it's nice having it on the line so I can eat it all night long). You have the kale, which is incredibly minerally. (I grew up having kale stuffed down my throat by my mom, so I appreciate kale in a big way; that's why I grew so tall.) You have the lemon in the pine nut condiment, which is like a reset button for the whole dish. And then you have the earth with the beans. You swish your fork through all that, take a sip of your wine . . . and hopefully you'll be able to work your way through this dish without getting incredibly bored." Be aware that you'll need to soak the beans overnight.

1. To make the white bean puree, place the white beans in a large bowl and cover with room-temperature water by 2 inches. Soak at room temperature overnight.

2. Drain and place the white beans in a medium saucepan with the olive oil, garlic, celery, onion, and bay leaf and cover with water by 3 inches. Cook until the beans are tender, about 1 hour. Remove the bay leaf and drain the beans, reserving the cooking liquid. Transfer the beans to a food processor and add ¾ cup of the bean liquid. Puree until smooth, adding more bean liquid and olive oil if needed; the puree should be the consistency of a thick milk shake. Season to taste with salt and pepper and reserve. Do not discard the remaining bean liquid; you may need it to thin the puree when ready to serve.

3. To make the pine nut condiment, soak the currants in hot water for 20 minutes, or until soft. Drain and reserve. In a small saucepan, heat the olive oil over medium-low heat. Add the shallots and cook until soft, 2 or 3 minutes. Reduce the heat to low, add the currants, pine nuts, lemon zest, sherry vinegar, red pepper flakes, and thyme, and mix well to combine. Season to taste with salt, pepper, and more sherry vinegar. Remove from the heat and allow to cool at room temperature.

SERVES 6

For the white bean puree

1 cup dried white beans

½ cup extra-virgin olive oil

8 garlic cloves, crushed

1 celery stalk, sliced

1 medium Spanish onion, diced

1 bay leaf

Coarse salt and freshly ground black pepper

For the pine nut condiment

¼ cup currants

6 tablespoons extra-virgin olive oil

¼ cup chopped shallots

½ cup toasted pine nuts

1 tablespoon finely grated lemon zest

2 tablespoons sherry vinegar, plus more if needed

½ teaspoon crushed red pepper flakes

½ teaspoon fresh thyme leaves

Coarse salt and freshly ground black pepper

For the kale

1 bunch Tuscan kale, about ¾ pound, cleaned, ribs removed, leaves roughly chopped

2 tablespoons extra-virgin olive oil

¼ cup chopped shallots

Coarse salt and freshly ground black pepper

For the scallops

24 large diver scallops

Coarse salt and freshly ground black pepper

2 tablespoons extra-virgin olive oil

½ pound chorizo, cut on the bias into ⅛-inch-thick slices

4. To cook the kale, prepare an ice bath and bring a medium saucepan of generously salted water to a boil. Add the kale to the boiling water and blanch for 2 minutes. Transfer the kale to the ice bath, drain, and squeeze out the excess water. Heat the olive oil in a small saucepan over medium heat. Add the shallots and cook until soft, 2 or 3 minutes. Add the kale, season with salt and pepper, and cook until heated through, about 2 minutes. Remove from the heat and set aside.

5. In a small saucepan, warm the white bean puree over low heat. Taste for seasoning and thin out with the reserved bean liquid, if necessary.

6. To cook the scallops, season the scallops with salt and pepper. In a large sauté pan, heat the olive oil over medium-high heat. When the oil is hot but not smoking, add the scallops and cook for 2 minutes, or until golden brown. Turn them over and cook for 2 minutes more. Transfer to a paper-towel-lined plate. Add the chorizo to the pan and cook until warmed through, about 2 minutes.

7. To serve, spread ¼ cup of the white bean puree on each plate. Place 4 scallops on top, arrange the kale between the scallops, and top the scallops with the pine nut condiment and warm chorizo slices.

GORILLA COFFEE / PARK SLOPE

DARLEEN SCHERER AND CAROL McLAUGHLIN

Gorilla Coffee has been around for a while now. So long, in fact, that when it opened, it was one of very few serious coffee shops in a borough that now rivals Seattle and Portland for its obsession with the bean. Partners Darleen Scherer (below left) and Carol McLaughlin roast their coffee in Sunset Park, a couple miles south of their Park Slope shop, in a twelve-kilo drum roaster. They roast more or less constantly, in batches of twenty-four to twenty-five pounds, and their name and logo tell you all you need to know about their strength preference. This is some brawny full-flavored joe.

When you first developed your positioning as a roaster of strong, bold coffees, what was behind that? Personal taste? Marketing strategy? Both?

DARLEEN: It started out as my personal preference. At home, I brew coffee really strong. And we do that here. Our espresso shots are pulled triple *ristretto*, so they're denser and sweeter than a typical double. But we've definitely evolved, and overall we've gotten a little bit lighter.

CAROL: We don't carry our Nicaragua anymore, which I loved. But that was darker. We have Peru now, and we don't roast that as dark. It just depends on the bean itself.

DARLEEN: Now we're much more open to just quality coffees. Except Costa Rica. I can't get into Costa Rica. It's almost tealike no matter how you roast it.

What were you doing before you started Gorilla?

DARLEEN: I was an Internet person, and I was *so* over not doing anything tangible. My life was e-mail and phone. I'd call my clients and be like, "Your site is done, it's live, who cares." I want to *make* something.

CAROL: This is tangible, that's for sure. There's a lot of labor involved in roasting coffee. It is *not* an easy job. You're working in a warehouse, basically. You're lifting these heavy bags. No one who is a delicate flower can work in coffee roasting.

How steep was the learning curve?

DARLEEN: When we got into this, I was amazed at how open other coffee roasters are. I always feel like chocolate is much more closed-door, like Willy Wonka: *Don't steal my recipe!* Coffee people won't talk that much about how they roast, because that's kind of a personal thing. But sourcing beans, helping you out if you're having trouble with your machinery—

CAROL: There's a real camaraderie among roasters.

DARLEEN: There's a real spirit of— what's that saying? "A rising tide lifts all boats."

CAROL: The community is definitely the part that drives me. I came from

social work, so I love the community aspect when we're at origin. I like the farmers, I like the pickers. And I like the customers. That's what gives me a charge.

What are some of the local cafés and restaurants that buy your coffee?

DARLEEN: Joyce Bakeshop, Union Hall, 1 Dominick, Palo Santo— those are a few. Grab and Marlow & Sons sell our coffee by the pound, and we do a lot with Whole Foods; they're big volume for us. And we also sell to Google. They use our espresso in their New York offices.

CAROL: And they're some of the best baristas you'll find. We've done training, and these Google engineers, they're on it. They were making latte art.

We won't name any names, but there are certain local roasters who take a top-down, our-way-or-the-highway approach to their customers, whether it's making sure they've absorbed every fetishistic detail about the grower or discouraging to-go cups or a million other little things. Has the coffee culture in Brooklyn gone a bit overboard?

CAROL: I think there are a lot of different types of consumers out there, and I don't feel okay judging someone for the way they drink coffee. Listen, I'm not going to do it in a way I can't live with, but what they do at that end of the counter, I'm not going to stop them. I want to make a product that appeals to the coffee snob, and I want to welcome everyone else. I even *more* appreciate the mom coming in with the stroller, struggling in, holding the baby, pushing the baby, got a dog on her arm, just getting a cup of coffee.

DARLEEN: But if you lose the snob, you're lost. You do always have to speak to that person who knows.

ROSE WATER

PARK SLOPE

In terms of food philosophy, few restaurateurs have traveled a greater distance than John Tucker. Back in the late eighties he was working as a sales supervisor for Wonder Bread in Carlstadt, New Jersey, in the shadow of Giants Stadium, and living on a diet of baked ziti and General Tso's chicken. A decade later he opened Rose Water, whose mission statement reads: "We're proud to offer a menu consisting of as much local, regional, organic and sustainably raised ingredients as the seasons will allow."

So what the hell happened in between? Peter Hoffman happened to John Tucker. The former Wonder boy talked himself into an entry-level managerial job at Hoffman's SoHo restaurant, Savoy, which helped introduce New Yorkers to the concept of farm-to-table dining, and he stayed for six years. "I treated it like my university," he says. "I learned about things I'd never heard of, like choux, roux, rouille, and pistou. And, most important, I adopted the principles around sustainability with an almost evangelical fervor." Hoffman's restaurant is also where he met Neil O'Malley, a Savoy sous chef who had worked at Oznot's Dish, the trail-blazing (but now closed) African-Moroccan place in Williamsburg. O'Malley became Tucker's business partner and Rose Water's first chef. The restaurant opened in August 2000, back when Park Slope offered little more than diners, pizzerias, and ethnic joints. "Because Neil was involved, we wanted it to have kind of an underpinning of North African and pan-Mediterranean influences," Tucker says. "It certainly wasn't going to be a North African or Moroccan restaurant, but because it was going to have that flavor in it, some of that crept into the design, and it even crept into the name."

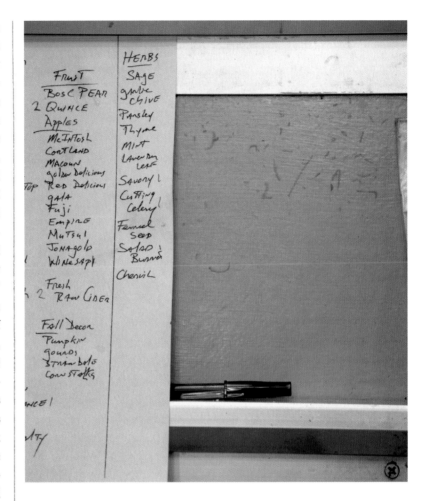

O'Malley left in 2003, taking his esoteric spice rack—his corn bread was flavored with fenugreek, and he liked to dust pita with paprika and powdered cherry pits—with him. But his adventurous spirit remains. Rose Water's current chef is Bret Macris, a Californian who arrived in spring 2009 and embarked on a crash course in Northeastern seasonal cooking. Kohlrabi, spigarello, and an ever-changing variety of mushrooms (maitakes, honshemejis, and shiitakes) are among the ingredients he uses to enhance crowd-pleasing entrées like smoked duck breast, grilled polenta, and our favorite, the perfectly seared swordfish that follows.

Seared Swordfish with Sautéed Grape Tomatoes, Fresh Corn and Kohlrabi Salad, and Avocado Aioli / ROSE WATER

SERVES 4

For the tomatoes

¼ cup extra-virgin olive oil

2 cups grape tomatoes, washed and dried

1 tablespoon minced shallots

Coarse salt and freshly ground black pepper

For the avocado aioli

1 Hass avocado, pitted and peeled

2 large egg yolks

3 garlic cloves, halved

½ jalapeño, seeded and finely diced

2 tablespoons minced fresh cilantro

2 limes, 1 finely zested and both juiced

¾ cup extra-virgin olive oil

½ cup canola oil

Coarse salt

½ teaspoon freshly squeezed lemon juice, or more to taste

Coarse sea salt, for garnish

A SoCal native (before Rose Water he worked at Campanile, the highly regarded Mediterranean restaurant in Los Angeles), chef Bret Macris initially had some trouble adjusting to the extreme seasonality of the Northeast. "I didn't even know what kohlrabi was," he admits. But he's a quick study, as this dish shows. Still, what pulls it all together is the avocado aioli. Dollop generously.

1. To make the tomatoes, heat the olive oil in a large sauté pan over medium-high heat and add the grape tomatoes, tossing once to coat, then allowing the tomatoes to sit until they start to pop and char, about 5 minutes. Reduce the heat to low. When the skins start to crack and the tomatoes begin to break down, add the shallots, season to taste with salt and pepper, and remove from the heat. Set the tomatoes and shallots aside. The tomatoes will continue to cook and release juices as they cool. This will create a sauce with the shallots and olive oil.

2. To make the avocado aioli, in a blender, puree the avocado, egg yolks, garlic, jalapeño, cilantro, and lime zest and lime juice. Blend well. With the motor running, slowly add the olive oil and canola oil. If the aioli is too thick, add a little water. The aioli should be the consistency of homemade mayonnaise. Transfer the aioli to a bowl and add salt and lemon juice to taste.

3. To make the salad, combine the corn and kohlrabi in a mixing bowl. Add the olive oil, lemon juice, tarragon, parsley, chives, and chervil. Mix well and season to taste with salt and pepper.

4. To make the swordfish, heat the canola oil in a medium sauté pan over medium-high heat. Season the swordfish with salt and pepper. When the oil is hot but not smoking, add the swordfish. Cook until golden, about 3 minutes. Lower the heat to medium, add the butter, and baste the swordfish by spooning the melted butter over the fish for 1 minute.

Carefully turn the fish and cook, basting, 3 to 4 more minutes. Transfer the fish to a cutting board.

5. To serve, divide the tomatoes with their juice among 4 plates. Place the corn and kohlrabi salad in the middle. Cut the swordfish in half on the bias and place it on top of the salad. Drizzle the fish with avocado aioli and sprinkle with a pinch of coarse sea salt.

For the corn and kohlrabi salad
(makes about 1½ cups per person)

2 cups fresh corn kernels, from about 4 ears corn

2 cups peeled, thinly sliced, and julienned kohlrabi (about 8 ounces)*

¼ cup extra-virgin olive oil

2 teaspoons freshly squeezed lemon juice

1 tablespoon minced fresh tarragon

1 tablespoon minced fresh flat-leaf parsley

1 tablespoon minced fresh chives

1 tablespoon minced fresh chervil

Coarse salt and freshly ground black pepper

For the swordfish

2 to 3 tablespoons canola oil

Four 6-ounce center-cut swordfish steaks, about 1 inch thick, skin and blood line removed

Coarse salt and freshly ground black pepper

2 tablespoon unsalted butter

* To slice the kohlrabi, use a mandoline or the slicing disk on a food processor.

Fried Goat Cheese with Prosciutto, Figs, and Honey / ROSE WATER

SERVES 4 AS A FIRST COURSE

One 11-ounce log fresh goat cheese

Canola oil

2 large eggs, lightly beaten

½ cup all-purpose flour

6 fresh Mission figs, cut in half lengthwise

4 thin slices prosciutto

Honey

Balsamic vinegar

Extra-virgin olive oil

¼ teaspoon crushed red pepper flakes

Maldon sea salt

This recipe is inspired by Spanish tapas. (Chef Bret Macris and his wife hope to open their own tapas bar someday.) And the dish starts Spanish, with the fried goat cheese balls (which, by the way, are also fantastic for salads). But then it takes an Italian turn, using prosciutto instead of Serrano ham, and figs. Taste the figs before adding honey. The sweetness should enhance the savory core of the dish, not overwhelm it.

1. Roll the goat cheese into 12 half-dollar-size balls, about ¾ ounce each, and place on a parchment-lined baking sheet. Freeze until firm, at least 1 hour.

2. Heat 4 inches of canola oil in a deep fryer or large, deep pot until hot but not smoking, until the oil registers 350°F on a deep fry thermometer.

3. Place the eggs and flour in 2 separate shallow bowls. Dip the goat cheese balls in the egg, then dredge in the flour, then dip back into the egg, then into the flour again. Working in batches, carefully add the goat cheese balls to the hot oil and cook until golden brown and crispy, 2 to 3 minutes. Using a slotted spoon, gently remove the goat cheese balls from the oil and transfer to a large plate lined with paper towels.

4. Arrange the goat cheese balls, figs, and prosciutto on 4 plates, then drizzle with honey, balsamic vinegar, and extra-virgin olive oil. Sprinkle the goat cheese with the red pepper flakes and sea salt.

CONVIVIUM OSTERIA

PARK SLOPE

Convivium is a Southern-European mutt: part Italian, part Spanish, part Portuguese. But those parts aren't equal, at least when it comes to the food. "I'd say the menu's sixty percent Italian, twenty percent each of the other two," says the chef-owner, Carlo Pulixi, who was born in Sardinia and raised in Rome. "But you can find things in Italy that relate in some way to just about everything in Spain and Portugal." True, Pulixi's braised artichoke appetizer with olive oil, mint, and garlic has a pan-Mediterranean quality, as does the pan-roasted snapper fillet with olives, tomatoes, and thyme. The gnocchi, though, is pure Italy (see page 36), and the forty-eight-ounce rib eye for two prompts couples to speak the international language of pleasure: plenty of sighing, interrupted by the occasional moan.

If Spanish and Portuguese food are relegated to supporting roles in the kitchen, the countries dominate the sound track. A fifty-fifty split of flamenco (Spain) and *fado* (Portugal) filters through the diners' chatter, bouncing gently off the copper cookware that hangs on the walls and seeping into the worn old wood of the farmhouse furniture. Pulixi's half-Portuguese wife, Michelle, is a former dancer, and at one point the couple experimented with live music during service. But Convivium's great atmospheric virtue, its coziness, made that difficult. There are a pair of intimate, votive-lit dining rooms upstairs and a bottle-lined cellar that's ideal for large groups. "We really wanted it to be a place where, when you walk in, you feel like you're getting away from the craziness of the city," says Michelle. Mission accomplished—and then some. Spend an evening at Convivium and you feel as if you've gotten away from the craziness of the entire country.

Carlo was a part-owner of Il Buco, the antique-shop-turned-*enoteca* on Bond Street in Manhattan, and Michelle was a waitress there when they met. Il Buco's influence is all over Convivium. "We ended up doing what we know," Carlo admits. The result: a real *osteria* in Park Slope, with all the rustic informality that implies. "We didn't even have stem glasses at first," recalls Carlo, who had worked the front of the house at Il Buco and had never cooked professionally until he took over Convivium's kitchen about six months after the restaurant opened in November 2000. But soon customers requested "proper" wineglasses, so they bought a few dozen— for those regulars only.

Spinach and Sheep's-Milk Ricotta Gnocchi with Asiago / CONVIVIUM OSTERIA

MAKES 32 GNOCCHI;
SERVES 4 OR 5

For the gnocchi

1½ pounds organic spinach, stems removed, coarsely chopped

1 cup (½ pound) sheep's-milk ricotta or well-drained whole-milk ricotta*

2 large eggs, lightly beaten

¼ cup unseasoned fresh bread crumbs

¾ cup all-purpose flour, divided

⅓ cup grated Parmigiano-Reggiano cheese

1 teaspoon coarse salt

For the sauce

3 tablespoons grated Asiago cheese, plus more for garnish

1½ cups whole milk

1½ cups heavy cream

* If using whole milk ricotta, wrap the ricotta in cheesecloth, gather into a ball, tie, and drain over a bowl in the refrigerator overnight.

As addictive as these gnocchi are, not even the man who makes them wants to eat more than six or seven at a time. "Sometimes customers complain that there's not enough gnocchi on the plate," says co-owner Carlo Pulixi with a sigh, who, being a traditional and highly principled Italian chef, has strong feelings about portioning and other such non-negotiable rules of his country's cuisine. "We just feel that with this richness, it's not something you want to fill your stomach with. If someone says something, we make another plate, free of charge. But I don't want to give them more than we give. I don't feel it's right."

1. To prepare the gnocchi, bring a large pot of salted water to a boil. Add the spinach and cook for 5 or 6 minutes, or until tender but not mushy. Drain in a colander and use the back of a wooden spoon to force out any excess water. Wrap the spinach in a clean dish towel and wring out any remaining water. Spread the spinach on a dry surface. When it is no longer steaming, transfer it to a large bowl. Add the ricotta and mix with a fork until well combined. Add the eggs, bread crumbs, ¼ cup flour, Parmigiano-Reggiano, and salt. Mix until smooth.

2. Place ½ cup flour in a shallow dish, line a rimmed baking sheet with parchment, and lightly flour the parchment. Using two tablespoons, shape the mixture into ovals. Dredge the gnocchi in flour to coat, then tap off any excess. Place the gnocchi on the baking sheet and refrigerate for 1 hour.

3. When you are ready to cook the gnocchi, bring a large pot of salted water to a boil. While the water is coming to a boil, prepare the sauce. Combine the Asiago, milk, and heavy cream in a medium saucepan over medium heat. Whisk until the sauce thickens and coats the back of a spoon, about 10 minutes.

4. Add the gnocchi to the boiling water and cook for about 3 minutes. Using a slotted spoon, transfer the gnocchi to the saucepan with the sauce. Gently toss to coat, cooking for 30 seconds. Divide the gnocchi and sauce among bowls and garnish with additional Asiago.

Frustingolo / CONVIVIUM OSTERIA

SERVES 12–14

1 cup dried Turkish figs,
sliced in half

Frangelico hazelnut liqueur

¼ cup whole hazelnuts

½ cup whole almonds

1½ cups walnuts halves

10 ounces dark chocolate
(60% cacao), chopped

4 tablespoons (½ stick) unsalted
butter, diced

⅓ cup honey

¼ cup sugar

1½ teaspoons ground cinnamon

½ teaspoon freshly ground nutmeg

¼ teaspoon ground cloves

2 large eggs

¼ cup all-purpose flour

5 ounces (½ cup plus 2 tablespoons)
extra-virgin olive oil, plus more for
the pan

Co-owner Michelle Pulixi came up with the recipe for this cool-weather cake when she was "looking for something *antico.*" She'd been studying formulae for old desserts—*really* old, as in ancient Rome—and was finding dishes that used *garum* (fermented fish juice) and plenty of honey-based sweets as well. Nothing seemed approachable enough until she happened upon a recipe for *frustingolo,* or chocolate fig cake. "The original recipe doesn't even call for chocolate—just a little cocoa powder—and it was dry, dry, dry," she says. "So I modified it to be a little bit lighter and softer. I also soak the figs instead of boiling them. But with the spices and honey, I think it still has an old-world feel." Pulixi's *frustingolo* should be served at room temperature and is just as good the day after you've baked it.

1. Place the figs in a small saucepan with enough water to cover them by ½ inch, about 1½ cups. Bring to a boil over medium heat and cook until plump, about 5 minutes. Transfer to a bowl with half of the poaching liquid. Add enough Frangelico to cover and let stand for 1 hour. Drain and reserve the figs and liquid separately.

2. While the figs are macerating, position a rack in the center of the oven and preheat the oven to 400°F. Place the hazelnuts on a small cookie sheet. Toast the hazelnuts in the oven until they are brown and fragrant, stirring occasionally, about 14 minutes. Cool slightly, then gather the hazelnuts in a clean dish towel and rub to remove the husks. Transfer the hazelnuts to a small food processor and pulse until finely chopped;* set aside. Repeat with the almonds, then the walnut halves. Divide the chopped walnuts, reserving ½ cup for dusting the pan. Reduce the oven temperature to 375°F.

3. Melt the chocolate and butter in a double boiler or a metal bowl set over a saucepan of simmering water, stirring occasionally, until smooth and incorporated.

* Nuts contain a lot of oil, so it's easy to overprocess them and end up with nut butter. Work in small batches and stop pulsing while the nuts still have some texture.

4. Remove the stems from the figs and finely chop the figs in the food processor. Transfer the figs to a large bowl with ¼ cup soaking liquid. Add the honey, sugar, and melted chocolate, and stir to combine. Add the cinnamon, nutmeg, cloves, hazelnuts, almonds, and 1 cup of the walnuts. Add the eggs, one at a time, fully incorporating the first before adding the next. Stir in the flour and olive oil.

5. Grease a 10-inch round cake pan with olive oil and dust with the reserved ½ cup walnuts to evenly coat the pan. Pour the batter into the pan and spread evenly. Bake for 30 minutes, or until the center of the cake is set. Allow the cake to cool for 10 minutes, then turn it out onto a rack and cool completely.

LOCANDA VINI E OLII

CLINTON HILL

Locanda Vini e Olii just wanted to be a neighborhood restaurant—actually, *the* neighborhood restaurant—in a restaurant-starved neighborhood. That happened almost immediately after it opened in January 2001. Then word spread. Soon people were making special trips to this restaurant whose name they weren't sure how to pronounce in this neighborhood they'd never visited.

The first time you pull up at 129 Gates Avenue, confusion. *Is this it?* The address is right, but this appears to be a drugstore—the Lewis Drug Store, as the big sign says. Don't worry, this is it. The pharmacy was here for 103 years—the entire twentieth century—so the restauranteurs elected to honor that longevity by restoring and retaining the sign. It was a charming, slightly confusing decision—and one of many such choices that define Locanda as (still) a cult restaurant. There's the novel method for measuring wine consumption: holding a painted wooden stick up to the bottle and charging by the inch. There's the flamboyant fashion sense of co-owner François Louy, who favors purple pants. And of course there's the cooking, which somehow manages to be at once authentic, modern, and idiosyncratic without ever losing its fundamental Italian-ness.

François's wife, Catherine de Zagon-Louy, is the on-again, off-again chef and permanent overseer of the kitchen. She was born in New York and raised in Florence by a Hungarian father and a Belgian mother. So she's respectful of Italy's culinary heritage, but she's not stifled by it. She likes to "play" with it. She'll marry traditional flavors like olives, orange zest, and wild boar, but maybe the olives will go in the

pasta dough, not the sauce. (Every pasta dish on the menu has a different flavor of pasta.) Or she'll do an *arrabbiata,* but instead of slow-cooking the tomatoes into a sauce, she'll just chop fresh tomatoes and finish them in the pan. "*Arrabbiata* means upset, because it's hot and it's spicy," she says. "This is *sfuriata.* It's still spicy, it's still upset, but it's a quicker upset."

About the name. Even an Italian-menu-literate New Yorker might have trouble with that last word. *Olii* is the plural of "oil," and it's pronounced "OH-lee." In Italy, a *vini e olii* is a neighborhood shop that sells wine and olive oil. It's a

specific retail license, like the "T" logo that indicates a tobacco shop. The first time Catherine walked into the Lewis Drug Store (back when it was still a dusty pharmacy that never seemed to have anything you needed), it reminded her of an old *vini e olii.* The problem? "Nobody remembers Locanda Vini e Olii," de Zagon-Louy concedes, citing yet another reason the restaurant remains under the radar after all these years. If the name slips your mind, just Google "Lewis Drug Store." Locanda Vini e Olii appears on the first page of results, after several listings for a Lewis Drug Store in Sioux Falls, South Dakota.

Handmade Ravioli with Fresh Ricotta and Pecorino / LOCANDA VINI E OLII

**SERVES 4 TO 6
(MAKES 25 RAVIOLI)**

For the pasta dough

Heaping 1½ cups (300 grams) durum wheat semolina flour

3 large eggs

1 tablespoon extra-virgin olive oil

Pinch of coarse salt

All-purpose flour, for dusting

For the filling

1¾ cups fresh ricotta

1 cup aged Tuscan Pecorino (¾ cup if using Pecorino Romano), finely grated

Fresh thyme leaves from 4 sprigs

1 tablespoon extra-virgin olive oil

Pinch of coarse salt*

For the tomato sauce

3 tablespoons pure or light olive oil (not extra-virgin)

½ large Spanish onion, minced

1 small carrot, finely chopped

1 celery stalk, finely chopped

One 28-ounce can San Marzano peeled tomatoes, with their liquid

4 fresh plum tomatoes, cored and halved

10 to 15 fresh basil leaves, plus more, chiffonade-cut, for garnish

* Taste the mixture before salting; Pecorino can be very salty.

This is chef Catherine de Zagon-Louy's interpretation of a classic ravioli from the Abruzzo region of Italy, where she and her husband own a home. "It should be made with sheep's-milk ricotta," she says, "but you can't buy that here easily, so we use cow's-milk instead." The Pecorino, more common in and around Rome than in Abruzzo, adds to the regional mix. But the real key to this dish is the sauce. It should be bright in color and not too thick, so be careful not to overcook it.

1. To make the pasta dough, on a very smooth, clean surface, make a mountain with the flour and use your hand to make a well in the center. Add the eggs, olive oil, and salt to the well. With a fork, whisk the eggs and slowly incorporate the flour. When it is too hard to continue whisking with the fork, use your hands and start kneading with your palms until enough flour is incorporated and the dough is no longer sticky. Continue kneading until you have a smooth elastic ball of dough, about 10 minutes. Cover with plastic wrap and let the dough rest for at least 30 minutes.

2. To make the filling, while the pasta is resting, mix the ricotta, grated Pecorino, thyme, olive oil, and salt in the bowl of a standing mixer until well combined and very smooth. Transfer to a pastry bag without a tip and refrigerate for 30 minutes. (If you don't have a pastry bag, use a resealable plastic bag instead. Refrigerate, then cut a large ¾-inch opening in one corner.)

3. To make the tomato sauce, in a large saucepan, heat the olive oil over medium-low heat. Add the onion, carrot, and celery and cook until the onion is translucent, about 8 minutes. Add the canned tomatoes with their liquid, increase the heat to medium, cover the pan, and cook for 20 minutes. Add the fresh tomatoes, cover, and cook for 35 minutes more. Add the basil and cook for another 5 minutes. Remove the pan from the heat and allow the sauce to cool slightly. Pass the sauce through a food mill to remove the seeds and skins, making a smooth sauce. Return the sauce to the saucepan and reheat before serving.

4. To make the ravioli, cut the chilled dough into 5 slices. Working with one slice at a time and dusting with flour as necessary, roll the dough into an oblong piece thin enough to pass through the widest setting on a pasta rolling machine. Pass the dough through the machine, turning the dial down each time to make the dough thinner, until it is about ⅙ inch thick, 5½ inches wide (the standard width of roller attachments), and about 20 inches long. Lay the dough flat on a clean surface. Pipe the chilled ricotta mixture onto half of each sheet of pasta lengthwise, making 5 quarter-size mounds of filling about 3 inches apart. Fold the pasta lengthwise over the filling and press gently all around to get rid of any air. Cut the ravioli in half-moons with a pastry rolling cutter. Transfer the ravioli to a floured baking sheet and refrigerate until ready to cook. (Save trimmed bits of pasta. Cover with plastic wrap, refrigerate, and re-knead to make other pasta shapes.) If you're not going to use the ravioli right away, place the ravioli on a floured baking sheet in the freezer. Once they are frozen, transfer the ravioli to a flour-dusted container and freeze for up to 6 weeks.

5. To serve, bring a large pot of generously salted water to a boil. Gently add the ravioli to the boiling water and cook for about 6 minutes. Spoon about 3 tablespoons of sauce into the center of the plate. Drain the ravioli and place 5 to 6 on each plate around the sauce. Sprinkle with basil and serve.

Spicy Seafood Guazzetto with Sicilian Cherry Tomatoes / LOCANDA VINI E OLII

In Italy, the word *guazzetto* refers more to a preparation than a specific recipe. "When birds are in a bird feeder and they're splashing around, that's called making a *guazza*," says chef Catherine de Zagon-Louy. "And so *guazzetto* comes from that. It's a wet dish, a traditional coastal dish that changes depending on where you are in Italy." This version, with its tomatoes and spiciness, is from the south. You'll definitely need a crusty loaf of bread for sopping.

1. Fill a large bowl with salted water. Add the cockles and soak for 10 minutes. Drain, then scrub the clams with a brush to remove any remaining grit.

2. In a 10- to 12-quart stockpot, heat the olive oil over low heat. Add the garlic, parsley, and red pepper flakes and cook for 2 minutes. Discard any mussels or cockles that have broken or cracked, or have open shells that do not close when tapped firmly. Increase the heat to high and add the mussels and cockles, shaking the pan until the shells begin to open. Add the wine and cook until it evaporates, about 3 minutes. Add the cherry tomatoes with their liquid and the fish stock; reduce the heat to medium. Simmer until all the shells have opened (discard any that remain closed). Add the shrimp and calamari and cook for another 2 minutes. Transfer the fish to a large serving bowl or divide among individual dishes, sprinkle with chopped parsley, and serve.

SERVES 6

60 New Zealand cockles* (about 2½ pounds)

60 mussels (about 2 pounds), debearded and scrubbed

Coarse salt

2 tablespoons extra-virgin olive oil

3 whole garlic cloves, peeled

1 small bunch fresh flat-leaf parsley, stems removed and discarded, leaves chopped

1 tablespoon crushed red pepper flakes

1 cup dry white wine

One 28-ounce can Sicilian cherry tomatoes

1 cup homemade fish stock or salted water

24 large shrimp, peeled, deveined, tail on

2 calamari, cleaned, halved lengthwise, and thinly sliced

You can also use Littleneck clams.

SIXPOINT
CRAFT ALES / RED HOOK

SHANE WELCH

In his ever-expanding brewery in Red Hook, Wisconsin native Shane Welch makes six beers on a regular basis, a handful more as semi-regular seasonals, and a steady flow of one-off experiments that he sells in minuscule quantities to his best customers and closest allies, including Prime Meats (page 210) in Carroll Gardens and Bierkraft, the specialty beer shop in Park Slope. But you can't buy a six-pack of any of them; with the occasional hand-bottled exception, Sixpoint is draft only.

When did you start brewing?

In college, at the University of Wisconsin at Madison, I built a small brewery in my basement, and I made a *lot* of beer. We used to throw these huge parties . . . there'd be several hundred college students, and all we would serve was my home brew.

You were able to produce enough for hundreds of college kids?

Barely enough, but yeah. We had this enormous house with a big basement, with high ceilings. It was a very nice space to make beer.

How much time did that take?

Basically all of my time. I was a total nerd. I totally absorbed myself in the brewing process. Eventually I dropped out of school so I could make more beer.

And you weren't yet twenty-one at the time, I assume?

You know, it's funny you mention that. I dropped out when I was twenty. Looking back, it was one of the best decisions I ever made in my life, although very hard at the time. My parents were very upset. They were worried that I was going to be a bum. But I can't do something if my heart's not in it. I started out studying chemistry and physics. *What if I do med school?*

What if I do law school? What if I do computers? And you get in these groups, and you look around, and you think, *I'm not so sure that everyone who's doing this is doing it because they really want to do it.* But in the beer community, everyone is one hundred percent: *This is what I've always wanted to do.* There aren't a whole lot of opportunities unless you really hit it out of the park. Meaning, it's not a very lucrative industry. But you go to these beer festivals and you can tell that the people are super-happy with what they do.

Did you ever commercialize any of that beer you made in college?

Not at the time, but every single beer at Sixpoint is based on one of those original home brews.

Including the Northern Lights, which is made with wormwood?

Yep, that's based on an old recipe. It's got a little sting on the aftertaste.

Sixpoint doesn't bottle—it's draft only. What's up with that?

There are so many studies that have been done over the last twenty or thirty years that have shown that a person's perception of the quality and the taste of a product is largely, if not dominantly, influenced by the packaging. But when you have a product that's completely void of printed material, there's no six-pack carrier, there's no case—none of those things that serve as a miniature billboard inside your refrigerator every time you open it. All you have is the name in chalk. So what you've done is put almost the entire focus of that brand onto the product. It forces you to have a superior product, and to have a sense of genuineness.

In the beginning, there must have been some skeptics.

Oh yeah. When we first started, my distributors had nothing but criticism. *You need bottles, the logo sucks, there's no printed material,*

Sixpoint Hoppy American Brown Ale— Home Brew Version

Our first thought when Shane sent us the following recipe? Whoa, don't try this at home. Our second thought: Oh, right, trying it at home is the *point*. Obviously, some brewing experience is required.

MAKES 7.5 GALLONS

10.5 pounds Marris Otter Malt

3.75 pounds Durzt Munich Malt

27 ounces Crystal, 50-60 L

18 ounces Weyermann Carafoam

12 ounces Crystal, 120 L

3 ounces chocolate malt

3 ounces roasted barley

18 pounds, 3 ounces total grains
Mashed with 19.5 quarts water at 171°F
Mash in: 10:00
Mash temp: 155°F
Sparge: 11:00
Boil: 12:00
1st hop: 12:00
2nd hop: 12:40
Irish moss: 12:45
3rd hop: 12:50
Knockout: 1:00
Total Brew Time: 4:15

Bittering hop: 3.2 ounces Cascade @ 5.1 AA
Flavor hop 1: 1.1 ounce Centennial @ 9.2 AA
Flavor hop 2: 0.9 ounce Centennial @ 9.2 AA

Aroma hops: add 1 ounce Cascade, 1 ounce Centennial during whirlpool

Total IBU: 46

FERMENTER

28 BBL

Rack the cooled wort into a clean, sanitary fermenter. Pitch ½ pint active Sixpoint house yeast or your favorite yeast strain. Ferment until the activity stops, then rack to the secondary for 1 or 2 weeks conditioning at 50 to 55°F. Bottle with the priming sugar and allow to condition at room temperature for 2 weeks. Move to the cellar for storage, and enjoy.

the names of the beers are dumb, your beers are too aggressively flavored. Why is it Sixpoint Craft Ales? It should be called Sixpoint Brewing Company or Sixpoint Brewery. And how are people gonna know that it's from Brooklyn? Every single possible criticism you could imagine.

Now, though, part of Sixpoint's following—its brand—stems from the fact that you *can't* buy a six-pack. Was that an unexpected by-product of not bottling, that sense that it's kind of cool? Or was that part of the strategy all along?

We've never tried to position ourselves as a company that says: *We're unique in the sense that we don't bottle and that's why you should support us.* But we've found that people do find it kind of unique. Since they can't get it in bottles, that entices them to go out to bars. And as a result, bars like to carry our beer because they know that their customers can only get it there. So it's turned out to be a pretty potent business model.

So will you *ever* bottle?

I think one day we will, yes. But for now it seems like everyone's cool with what we do.

DUMONT
WILLIAMSBURG

DuMont owner Colin Devlin is a *proprietor.* Old-school. Irish, of course, and handsome. Easy smile. He likes to serve. He likes to make people happy. He's the kind of guy who invites you out to his twenty-acre spread in the Delaware Water Gap within an hour of meeting you. You both know it won't happen, but that's not the point. It's the connection that such an offer creates— *that's* the point.

A bartender by trade, Devlin has been making those kinds of connections since long before he opened DuMont in a 120-year-old Union Avenue tenement house in May 2001. In some ways it's an odd mix: Colin Devlin's earnest hospitality in the heart of Williamsburg, the least earnest place on the planet. Devlin's aware of this. "I always felt like we were a sobering force in an über-hip situation," he says with pride. He's right. The neon sign out front sets the tone right away. Devlin saw it one day hanging over an old appliance store that used to sell DuMont televisions. He just liked the look of the neon and the sound of the word. He asked the owner if he could buy the sign. The guy said if Devlin could find a licensed contractor to take it down, he could have it. And that was that. His restaurant had a name.

Now, almost a decade later, that sign is what people think of when they think of DuMont. They think of chef Polo Dobkin's food, too, of course, especially the decadent Du-mac and Cheese (page 53) and the DuMont burger, a massive sandwich on a brioche bun. (That burger is so beloved that Devlin had to open a second restaurant, DuMont Burger, in 2005 just to handle the overflow.) They think about the garden, an oasis in the concrete desert, and those awesome red-and-black leather seats in the front room. And they think about the extensive nightly specials board, which reaches a little higher and which itself was spun off into yet another restaurant, Dressler (page 114), in 2006.

It's an impressive little empire for a guy who not all that long ago was a bartender living in the dusty shell that would become his flagship restaurant. "The last month before opening, I was sleeping on the banquette," he recalls wistfully, knowing he'll never get that ragtag feeling back. "I think it was table one, if anyone's keeping score at home."

Dumac and Cheese / DUMONT

Hungry? You'd better be. "The mac and cheese!" exults chef Polo Dobkin. "It's a gut-buster, man. Even when I was like twenty-one or twenty-two, at the height of my eating prowess, I don't think I could have put down a burger, fries, and a mac. But people do that here—routinely." This is a deeply satisfying, devil-may-care preparation, made with love and a classic mornay sauce. "That's the secret," Dobkin says, though there really isn't one. "No truffle oil, no weird stuff. Make a good sauce, buy good cheese. That's it."

1. Preheat the oven to 400°F.

2. Bring a large pot of salted water to a boil and cook the pasta al dente, according to the package directions. Drain, toss with the olive oil in a large bowl, and set aside to cool.

3. Meanwhile, combine the milk and cream in a medium saucepan over medium-low heat; bring to a gentle simmer.

4. Melt the butter in a large, heavy-bottomed pot over medium heat. Add the flour and whisk until the flour is fully incorporated and the mixture is smooth. Continue mixing with a wooden spoon until the mixture is a pale golden color, about 4 minutes. Slowly add the hot milk and cream mixture to the flour mixture, whisking constantly to incorporate. Bring to a simmer, whisking occasionally to keep the mixture from burning. Add half the Gruyère and half the cheddar and whisk until the cheese has melted and the sauce is smooth. Season to taste with salt and pepper.

5. Add the cooked pasta and toss well to combine. Pour the pasta into a buttered 9 x 13-inch baking dish or 3-quart gratin dish. Top with the remaining Gruyère and cheddar and sprinkle with the bread crumbs. Bake for 20 to 25 minutes, or until golden and bubbly. Allow the mac and cheese to rest for 5 minutes before serving.

SERVES 6

1 pound radiatore, elbow macaroni, or fusilli

2 tablespoons extra-virgin olive oil

2 cups whole milk

2½ cups heavy cream

8 tablespoons (1 stick) unsalted butter

½ cup all-purpose flour

½ pound Gruyère, grated, divided

½ pound sharp white cheddar, grated, divided

Coarse salt and freshly ground black pepper

¼ cup unseasoned bread crumbs

Blueberry Crumble / DUMONT

SERVES 6

For the crumbs

2 cups all-purpose flour

1 cup sugar

½ teaspoon salt

½ teaspoon ground cinnamon

10 tablespoons (1¼ sticks) unsalted butter, melted

For the blueberries

5 cups fresh blueberries

⅔ cup sugar

1 tablespoon freshly squeezed lemon juice

1 tablespoon cornstarch

Vanilla ice cream, for serving

The cobbler is the anchor of DuMont's dessert menu, says chef Polo Dobkin. "Because we have a younger clientele, I think it's really important to serve food that people can connect to, that they have a history with." When you scoop the filling into the ramekins, leave plenty of room for the crumbs—there should be a thick, crunchy layer—but be sure to let some berries poke through for color.

1. **To make the crumbs,** combine the flour, sugar, salt, and cinnamon in a large bowl. Mix well to combine. Drizzle the mixture with the melted butter and, using your hands, mix until all ingredients are evenly incorporated and you have loose crumbs. Set aside.

2. **To make the filling,** place the blueberries, sugar, and lemon juice in a nonreactive saucepan over medium heat. Simmer, stirring occasionally, until the blueberries have broken down, 10 to 15 minutes. In a small bowl, combine the cornstarch with 2 tablespoons cold water; mix until no lumps remain. Slowly stir the cornstarch into the simmering blueberries. Cook for 30 seconds, or until slightly thickened.

3. Preheat the oven to 350°F. Spoon the blueberries into six 6-ounce ramekins, leaving about ¾ inch at the top. Crumble a generous amount of the crumb topping over the blueberries to cover.

4. Place the ramekins on a rimmed baking sheet and bake until the crumbs are golden to dark brown, 20 to 25 minutes.

5. Cool for at least 30 minutes before serving. Serve with vanilla ice cream.

ALISEO OSTERIA DEL BORGO

PROSPECT HEIGHTS

Aliseo is probably the least known restaurant in this book. The owner, an eccentric former photographer named Albano Ballerini, seems to want it that way. He has no Web site. He feels guilty for "ruining" the neighborhood after a *New York Times* article about his restaurant's opening in 2003 led to a spike in interest in the area. And he admits that he barely even thinks of Aliseo, which serves ambitious Italian cuisine from Ballerini's native Marche region, as a business. His pizza place across the street, Amorina—*that's* a business. But Aliseo? "This is my living room," he says.

That's almost literally true: He lives upstairs with his wife and daughter. (The family owns the building, which takes the pressure off in terms of revenue.) The narrow room certainly feels homey. A pair of lamps on the bar look like they were just unplugged from a wall socket upstairs and carried down here. Everything has that ubiquitous distressed look—the brick wall, the tin ceiling, and on some nights, the staff—and votive sconces bathe it all in just the right light.

An evening at Aliseo is an unpredictable experience, gastronomically and otherwise. One night, two naked people rapped on the door. They were waiters from Amorina, doing the traditional "naked run," which happens every time they break a sales record. "I have a couple people over there that are looking for any excuse to get naked," says Ballerini, who wears chunky eyeglasses and a kufi-style hat. The naked waiters weren't unappetizing, though, which was good because we hadn't eaten dessert yet. By then we'd worked our way through a starter of beet flan with *agrodolce* (sweet-and-sour) and Parmesan sauce, striped bass tartare that was shaped into a slender cylinder and topped with a little pile of microgreens, chanterelle lasagna with squash and a béchamel drizzle, and crispy striped-bass fillets atop a fried leaf of black Tuscan cabbage (a type of kale) and a medley of mushrooms. This was an informal tasting menu, and it was tasty, but you kind of need to roll with it at Aliseo. For example, did you notice that the menu doubled up on both striped bass and mushrooms?

That's Aliseo. Ballerini doesn't apologize. He just shrugs and jokes. Hey, it's what's for dinner in his living room. You don't like it? There's pizza across the street.

Crispy Octopus with Agrodolce and Roasted Potatoes / ALISEO OSTERIA DEL BORGO

SERVES 4 AS A FIRST COURSE

For the agrodolce

4 cups balsamic vinegar

2 cinnamon sticks

5 whole cloves

Pinch of freshly grated nutmeg

For the octopus

One 2½- to 3-pound octopus, thawed

⅓ cup coarse salt

½ cup apple cider vinegar or white wine vinegar

2 cups dry white wine

5 large garlic cloves, peeled

7 bay leaves

1 tablespoon whole black peppercorns

1 sprig fresh rosemary

20 juniper berries (optional)

6 parsley stems (optional)

2 tablespoons extra-virgin olive oil

For the potatoes

6 fingerling or baby red bliss potatoes, skin on, fingerling cut in half lengthwise, red bliss quartered

2 tablespoons extra-virgin olive oil

Coarse salt and freshly ground black pepper

"I'm a freak for octopus," says owner Albano Ballerini, who loves the word *freak*. (He's a freak for rosemary, too.) We know this dish may sound (and look) intimidating, but it's really not that difficult. The most important step is after the octopus is boiled, when it's covered off the heat, but still cooking. That's when the tentacles become tender. And they'll stay that way when you sauté them, giving the outside a crispy texture while preserving the supple (but not at all chewy) meat within.

1. **To make the agrodolce,** combine the balsamic vinegar, cinnamon sticks, cloves, and nutmeg in a small nonreactive saucepan. Cook over low heat until the mixture is syrupy and reduced by one third, about 1½ hours.

2. **Meanwhile, cook the octopus.** In an 8-quart pot, combine 6 quarts water with the salt, vinegar, wine, garlic, bay leaves, peppercorns, rosemary, juniper berries, and parsley stems, if using. Add the octopus. Insert a stainless-steel colander into the pot to weigh down the octopus. Bring to a boil over high heat. Reduce the heat to medium and cook at a gentle boil for 30 minutes.

3. Take the pot off the heat and remove the colander. Cover the pot with a lid and let the octopus sit in the cooking liquid for 45 minutes. The octopus should yield to the point of a small, sharp knife with little resistance.

4. While the octopus is sitting, preheat the oven to 400°F. Toss the potatoes with the olive oil and season with salt and pepper. Spread the potatoes cut side down in a single layer on a parchment-lined baking sheet and roast until tender and golden, about 35 minutes.

5. When the octopus is cool enough to handle, cut the tentacles from the head. (Discard the head or save it for another recipe.) Heat the olive oil in a large sauté pan over medium-high heat and cook the tentacles, turning, until crisp on all sides, 2 to 3 minutes total.

6. **To serve,** divide the potatoes among 4 plates. Place 2 tentacles on each plate. Drizzle with the agrodolce and serve.

MARLOW & SONS

WILLIAMSBURG

Andrew Tarlow and Mark Firth seem to really know what they're doing. And what they do best is experiment. Every business they start morphs into something else.

Diner, their first restaurant, was envisioned as a modest neighborhood lunch spot when it opened on the last day of 1998. (Who's gonna come to Williamsburg for *dinner*?) Under the direction of chef Caroline Fidanza, it became a pillar of the market-menu movement, and while Fidanza has since left, it remains hugely popular from late morning till late at night. Bonita, a Mexican cantina that opened down the street a few years later, is now closed, as is a second outpost in Fort Greene, which has reopened as Roman's, an Italian restaurant with a small menu that changes daily.

And then there's Marlow & Sons. First it was going to be a grocery store. "But we didn't really have the guts to open a full store," Tarlow says. "And we kind of didn't have the guts to open a full restaurant, either." So in February 2004, in a snug space around the corner from Diner, they opened a specialty grocery shop up front and a wine bar in the back. The front would showcase the ingredients they serve in the restaurants; the back would serve oysters and Champagne to people waiting for their tables at Diner (and at prime time, that can be a long wait). But then something

unexpected happened. (By then, this must have been expected.) Marlow & Sons began to morph. The chef, Sean Rembold, added entrées like the brick chicken (page 65), the restaurant's signature dish. Soon people started getting so full at Marlow & Sons that they no longer needed their tables at Diner. And a few years after *that*, the retail shop migrated to Marlow & Daughters, a butcher-grocer just down the block. These days, all you can buy up front at Marlow & Sons is chocolate, honey, and "trashy candy from your childhood," says Tarlow.

That's about all you'll have room for after gorging on Rembold's assertive cooking. Marlow & Sons is a flexible restaurant, built for any dining scenario. Not all that hungry? The cauliflower puree with croutons, chives, and a swirl of olive oil would be ample. Famished? Start with a half-dozen Shibumi oysters from Washington, snack on some crostini with wilted radicchio, goat cheese, and sweet plum raisins (to name one of approximately seven bazillion crostini combinations Rembold's dreamed up over the years), and finish with an entrée-size clam chowder, thick and creamy with chunks of smoky bacon, big meaty clams, and buttered anchovy toasts on the side. Except that the menu changes constantly, so you'll probably never be able to follow this exact advice. The point is Marlow & Sons is a complete restaurant where you can have one course or eight, depending on the size of your party and stomach.

Or at least that's what it was when this book went to the printer.

Brick Chicken with Mustard Greens / MARLOW & SONS

Chef Sean Rembold put this now-famous dish on Marlow's menu years ago, and it's the only one he's never taken off. Feel free to substitute Tuscan kale or spinach for the mustard greens, and anything heavy and heatproof for the bricks.

1. Heat 2 tablespoons of the olive oil and the canola oil in a 10-inch cast-iron skillet over high heat. Season the chicken generously with salt and pepper. When the oil begins to smoke, add the chicken halves to the skillet, skin side down. Place another 10-inch skillet, right side up, on top of the chicken and gently place two bricks or several soup cans in the top skillet to weigh it down.

2. Reduce the heat to medium high and cook the chicken until the skin is golden brown and crisp, about 18 minutes. Remove the top skillet and weights, turn the chicken with tongs, and pour off any excess fat from the skillet.

3. Add the chicken stock and lemon juice and cook the chicken until an instant-read thermometer inserted into the thickest part of the thigh registers 160°F, about 3 minutes.

4. While the chicken finishes cooking, prepare the mustard greens. In a large bowl, combine the remaining 2 tablespoons olive oil and the sherry vinegar. Add the greens and toss to coat. Season to taste with salt and pepper.

5. Serve the chicken and mustard greens with the pan juices.

SERVES 2 OR 3

4 tablespoons extra-virgin olive oil, divided

1 tablespoon canola oil

One 3- to 4-pound organic chicken, halved, with the backbone, rib cage, and thigh bones removed (the butcher will do this for you)

Coarse salt and freshly ground black pepper

⅓ cup homemade chicken stock or prepared low-sodium chicken broth

1 tablespoon freshly squeezed lemon juice

1 bunch mustard greens (about 1 pound), washed, stems removed, and leaves cut into 1-inch pieces

2 tablespoons sherry vinegar

WHEELHOUSE PICKLES / PARK SLOPE

JON ORREN

A former cook who's worked at Rose Water and Franny's, among other restaurants, Jon Orren now counts eight types of pickles—cukes, beets, okra, wax beans, pears, peppers, turnips, and sliced bread-and-butters—in his "permanent collection." He likes to make one-off batches of whatever's in season (ramps, for example) under his Wheelhouse Whims label. He has a habanero pepper sauce called Minor Threat. And finally, he sporadically produces a quirky condiment called Ploughman's Pickle, which is his take on Branston Pickle Relish, an old-timey British sandwich spread. In a Brooklyn collaboration, Orren's recipe is flavored with wort (a sweet liquid drained from mash and used in brewing) from Sixpoint Craft Ales; see page 46.

Every self-respecting briner has his learning-to-pickle story. What's yours?

Well, my mother used to buy pickles for the house, and I loved them so much that I would devour them all the minute she got home, then immediately demand more. I don't know if she was trying to teach me a lesson in moderation, or moderate my sodium intake or something, but she said, "I'm not going to buy

you a replacement jar just yet, but why don't you take this empty jar of brine and make your own?" So at six years old I was slicing up cucumbers and putting them back in the brine. Much later, when I was working in restaurants, I got exposed to the creative side of pickling and eventually started making my own.

Your sour-barrel cucumbers are the closest thing you make to what most people would recognize as a straight-up pickle. What's in the brine for those?

Water, horseradish, onion, garlic, chile, salt, mustard seed, coriander, dill, and fresh *ajwain* leaves (an Indian herb). Those are my bestsellers—a classic full sour. They're lacto-fermented, which basically means they're packed in salt water with spices and allowed to sit at room temperature for a period of time before being refrigerated. As the pickles ferment they produce

lactic acid, which is what gives them their distinctive tang. That's the old-world style of pickling.

Like the barrels on the Lower East Side.

Exactly.

Do you have a favorite of your pickles?

Right now it's my pickled beets. We roast our beets rather than boil them. A lot of pickled beets are boiled because it makes the peeling incredibly easy; something about the boiling process allows you to just wipe the skin off. When you roast them, since it's a dry process, the peeling becomes a lot more time consuming. But I think it adds a real depth of flavor.

We love your okra.

Okra can make a really terrible pickle if you're not using extremely fresh, just-picked okra. Even if it's a couple days removed from being picked, the sliminess really comes through. But if you pickle it fresh, it still retains that crunch. So I just do a simple white-wine-vinegar brine, with a little bit of heat.

Anything you've tried to pickle that just hasn't worked?

Cauliflower. It *can* work, but I just haven't gotten it to where I like it. I think I got seduced by the baby cauliflowers and was trying to do them whole. That was getting too complicated.

You started a couple years after Rick's Picks [another pickle brand], and have mentioned that consumers often confuse your product for his. That must be frustrating.

Yeah. In certain senses it's hard to get out from underneath his shadow, but I like to think we benefit from each other's presence. The notion of artisanal pickles is still new, it's a hard sell, but he sort of broke through that ceiling. It's not that different from the early years of the microbrew revolution. In the mid-eighties, it would have been preposterous to ask someone to pay five dollars for a pint of beer. And now . . .

Why "Wheelhouse"?

It's from baseball parlance. When a pitcher throws the ball right over the heart of the plate, they'll say he threw the ball in the hitter's wheelhouse. For most hitters, their wheelhouse is this very narrow space—not too high, not too low, not too inside, not too outside. Pickles are a delicate combination of vinegar and water and spices and sugar. And only when everything is in proper proportion do you have the perfect pickle.

FRANNY'S
PROSPECT HEIGHTS

Can there be a better example of the new Brooklyn cuisine than the clam pizza at Franny's? For starters, it's a pizza. Very Brooklyn. But everything else about it—the briny chewiness of the clams, the fiery zing of the chiles, and the olive-oily crunch of the wafer-thin crust—adds up to something entirely original.

So where's the recipe? Good question. We had every intention of requesting it, but then we realized we don't have a 900-degree brick oven made by a third-generation Neapolitan brick-oven maker, as Franny's does. Which is kind of a shame because if we did have that oven, maybe we could pull off the clam pizza. After all, Andrew Feinberg, the chef and the husband of co-owner Francine Stephens, had practically no pizza-making experience until just before the restaurant opened in April 2004.

Years earlier, Feinberg and Stephens had met at Savoy in SoHo, where Feinberg worked in the kitchen and Stephens tended bar. In a previous life Stephens had worked in the nonprofit sector, advocating for sustainable agriculture, but she gave that up when she and her husband decided they wanted to open a restaurant. Still, her activist background manifests at Franny's

in a prominent emphasis on locally sourced seasonal ingredients; the restaurant's vendors are all listed on the back of the menu. "That was our way of letting people know what we're doing without hitting them over the head with it, without our servers going into a diatribe about how great we are and all the good things we're doing for the earth," Stephens says. "It was there if you wanted to read it. Some people never turned their menu around and some people did."

The restaurant's environmental focus has certainly never stopped it from delivering pure hedonism on the plate. Franny's added pasta to the menu in earnest a couple years after opening, and these days a perfect meal for two consists of a pasta (the spaghetti with Meyer lemon is sublime), a clam pizza (though they're all fantastic), and a couple starters (the crostino on page 71, for example, and whatever salad Feinberg is serving that night).

Franny's menu is designed to encourage lots of sampling and, yes, the check can add up. Looking to save a few bucks? Skip dessert and make the vanilla panna cotta with strawberries (page 74) at home.

Chicken Liver Crostini / FRANNY'S

In the trattorias of Tuscany, it's common to begin a meal with a crostino of pancetta and crushed chicken liver. Marsala is the traditional alcohol, but this recipe calls for vermouth, which gives a less sweet, more earthy flavor. It's a decadent snack—and a Franny's staff favorite.

1. Heat 2 tablespoons of the olive oil in a large sauté pan over medium-high heat. When the oil is hot, but not smoking, season the livers with salt and pepper and cook until brown on all sides, about 5 minutes. Set the livers aside in a bowl and add ¼ cup of the vermouth to the pan, scraping the bottom to release any browned bits. Reduce the vermouth over medium-high heat until it is slightly syrupy, about 3 minutes, and pour it over the chicken livers. Cool completely.

2. Wipe the sauté pan clean and heat the remaining 2 tablespoons olive oil over medium-low heat. Add the onions and cook until they are soft and begin to caramelize, about 6 minutes. Add the garlic and cook for 1 minute. Add the anchovies and herbs and cook, mashing the anchovies until they melt into the mixture. Remove from the heat, add the capers, and stir to combine. Transfer the mixture to a separate bowl. Add the remaining ¼ cup vermouth to the pan, scraping the bottom to release any browned bits. Cook for 2 minutes and pour over the onion mixture. Cool completely.

3. Transfer the chicken livers and onion mixture to a food processor and pulse until the mixture is a rough puree. There should be visible bits of caper, onion, and garlic. (Chicken liver can be refrigerated up to 4 days. Bring to room temperature before spreading on the toasted bread.)

4. Preheat the oven to 400°F. Arrange the bread slices on a baking sheet and toast for 8 minutes, or until the bread starts to crisp but not brown. Set aside.

5. While the bread is toasting, cook the pancetta. Working in batches, lay the slices in a single layer in a sauté pan and cook, 1 minute each side, until golden and crispy.

6. To assemble, spread about 1 teaspoon mayonnaise on each slice of bread. Top with 2 tablespoons chicken liver and 2 slices pancetta.

MAKES ABOUT 1 CUP CHICKEN LIVERS FOR ABOUT 8 LARGE CROSTINI (EASILY CUT IN HALF FOR SHARING)

4 tablespoons extra-virgin olive oil, divided

½ pound chicken livers, cleaned and patted dry

Coarse salt and freshly ground black pepper

½ cup dry vermouth

1 medium onion, cut into medium dice (about 1 cup)

1 garlic clove, thinly sliced

3 anchovy fillets

1 tablespoon chopped fresh sage

½ teaspoon chopped fresh rosemary

1½ tablespoons capers, drained

1 loaf Brooklyn Scratch South Slope Boule or Sullivan Street Bakery *finole* or other rustic bread, sliced ¾ inch thick

16 slices pancetta, about 1/16 inch thick*

3 tablespoons prepared mayonnaise

* Most stores carry round pancetta, but the housemade pancetta at Bklyn Larder is flat and looks like bacon (see page 70).

M'hamsa Couscous with
Almonds and Spicy Raisins / BKLYN LARDER

In June 2009, Francine Stephens and Andrew Feinberg opened the Bklyn Larder, which is the grocery store you'd shop from if your grocery list contained nothing but artisanal cheeses, sliced meats, flavor-packed prepared food, spectacular sandwiches, and a variety of oils, jellies, condiments, and other specialty items from around the world. So, okay, you need the regular old grocery store, too. But the Larder, as its customers call it, is a supplementary shopping experience that's become an essential treat for food lovers in Park Slope, Prospect Heights, and beyond. Here's one of their staple dishes.

SERVES 6

For the spicy raisins

⅔ cup golden raisins

1 teaspoon crushed red pepper flakes

½ cup sherry vinegar

For the couscous

⅔ cup whole raw almonds

2 cups M'hamsa hand-rolled couscous, available at Bklyn Larder and Marlow & Daughters or online at www.zingermans.com

1 teaspoon coarse salt

3 tablespoons extra-virgin olive oil

½ cup roughly chopped fresh flat-leaf parsley

1. To make the spicy raisins, place the raisins and red pepper flakes in a small glass or stainless-steel bowl. Bring ½ cup water and the vinegar to a boil in a small saucepan. Pour the water and vinegar over the raisins; the liquid should cover the raisins by ½ inch. Allow the raisins to cool to room temperature. Drain, reserving the liquid, and set aside.

2. To make the couscous, preheat the oven to 350°F. Spread the almonds on a rimmed baking sheet in a single layer. Toast for 15 minutes, or until browned and fragrant. When the almonds are cool, chop them coarsely and set aside.

3. Meanwhile, bring 3 cups water to a boil. Stir in the couscous and salt and return to a full boil. Remove the couscous from the heat, add the olive oil, and cover. Allow to stand for 10 minutes, or until all the water is absorbed. Fluff the couscous with a fork, then spread it in a single layer on a rimmed baking sheet to cool to room temperature.

4. When the couscous is cool, stir in the spicy raisins and 2 to 3 tablespoons of their liquid, the almonds, and the parsley. Taste and adjust the seasonings with a splash more olive oil, salt, and red pepper flakes to taste.

Vanilla Panna Cotta
with Strawberries / FRANNY'S

SERVES 8

For the strawberries

Zest of 2 lemons*

2 tablespoons aniseed or 3 whole star anise

2 tablespoons whole black peppercorns

4 sprigs fresh edible lavender or ¾ teaspoon dried lavender buds

2 pints strawberries, rinsed, hulled, and halved

2 tablespoons almond grappa or amaretto (if using amaretto, eliminate the sugar)

2 tablespoons sugar (if using grappa)

For the panna cotta

1 quart organic cream

½ cup sugar

1 vanilla bean, split lengthwise and seeds scraped

¼ teaspoon coarse salt

3½ teaspoons unflavored powdered gelatin

½ cup cold water

½ cup boiling water

* Use an old-fashioned lemon zester, vegetable peeler, or paring knife, not a Microplane.

This is a quintessential Franny's dish. (And yes, that's possible for a non-pizza.) It's a classic Italian preparation, it's extraordinarily simple, and it relies on exceptional ingredients. Make sure to take the cream off the stove as soon it comes to a simmer; reducing it will change not only the flavor but also the ratio of cream to gelatin. For best results use Tristar berries. Fresh lavender is available at greenmarkets and some specialty grocers.

1. To make the strawberries, prepare a sachet by wrapping and tying the lemon zest, aniseed, peppercorns, and lavender in a cheesecloth.

2. Combine the strawberries, grappa or amaretto, and sugar (if using) in a container with a lid and toss gently. Add the sachet and carefully stir. Cover and refrigerate for at least 2 hours or overnight.

3. To make the panna cotta, combine the cream, sugar, vanilla bean with scraped seeds, and salt in a medium saucepan over medium heat. Bring to a simmer over low heat, whisking occasionally to dissolve the sugar. Remove from the heat and set aside to steep for 15 minutes. Strain the mixture into a bowl through a fine-mesh strainer.

4. Place cold water in a small bowl, sprinkle the gelatin over the water. Let stand for 1 minute. Add the boiling water, stirring constantly until the granules are completely dissolved.

5. Whisk the gelatin into the cream mixture. Cool the mixture slightly.

6. Ladle the cream mixture into eight 4-ounce ramekins. Cool to room temperature, then cover and refrigerate until set, at least 4 hours or overnight.

7. When ready to serve, remove the sachet from the strawberries and squeeze all the liquid from the sachet into a small saucepan. Strain the liquid from the berries through a fine-mesh strainer into the same saucepan and return the berries to the bowl. Bring the liquid to a simmer over medium-high heat and reduce to a thick syrup, about 5 minutes. Taste the syrup and add more grappa or amaretto, as desired. Pour the syrup over the berries and gently toss to coat. Cool and set aside.

8. To serve, run a thin, sharp knife around the edges of the ramekins to loosen the panna cottas. Carefully turn each panna cotta out onto a small dessert plate. (If necessary, dip the bottom of each ramekin in a shallow bowl of hot water to loosen.) Garnish with the macerated strawberries.

ICI

FORT GREENE

Ever since it opened in the summer of 2004, iCi has had to dispel misconceptions about itself. Misconception number one: Since it was opened by a French couple, it must be yet another French bistro in a neighborhood that already had a few. Wrong. "Obviously I couldn't be more French," concedes Catherine Saillard, the statuesque woman from northern Provence who now runs the spare, elegant restaurant alone, after she and her husband, Laurent, split a couple years ago. "The idea of iCi is to just serve good food. You will never find steak frites or pâté. We have grits on the menu because grits are fantastic. Fried green tomatoes, you would *never* see that in France. So the idea is, like, whatever is good, in season, and local could get on the menu."

Misconception number two: With the restaurant's interest in "natural" wines, its close relationship with the Red Hook Community Farm, and its emphasis on sustainability, it must lean in a vegetarian direction, yes? Nope. iCi's tightly edited menu has plenty of meatless options—including the two perfect salads that follow—but also a crispy "sweet-and-sour" pork belly; a duck cassoulet with white beans, root veggies, and escarole; and a robust entrée of Spanish mackerel (the opposite end of the fish spectrum from mild white fishes like cod and halibut) with a ginger rosemary beurre blanc. Chef Emily Sims is from South Carolina, so she's more than comfortable with hedonistic food. "We're natural," says Saillard, "but we're far from vegan."

Misconception number three: Since Laurent had been the primary face of the restaurant—and before that, the villainous manager of Rocco's on the reality show *The Restaurant*—iCi couldn't possibly survive after the couple divorced and he returned to France . . . right? Wrong again. "When I split with Laurent, all of a sudden people think I'm going to be dead," she says. "Most of the industry thought the restaurant would die within a few months. *The mother with two kids? What does she know about restaurants?*" She pauses, a look of defiance on her face. It's not like she didn't have any experience in the restaurant world. Before taking a break to raise her two boys, she'd worked for Alain Ducasse, Keith McNally, and Jean-Georges Vongerichten. "But guess what? I'm doing *great*."

Fried Green Tomatoes with Corn and Fava Bean Succotash / ICI

SERVES 4 AS A FIRST COURSE

3 large eggs

¼ cup whole milk

1 cup all-purpose flour

2 cups panko (Japanese bread crumbs)

3 green tomatoes, sliced ½ inch thick

¼ cup packed fresh basil leaves, plus 1 tablespoon finely chopped fresh basil

1 tablespoon extra-virgin olive oil

1 cup canola oil, for frying

Coarse salt and freshly ground black pepper

2 tablespoons unsalted butter

Kernels from 3 ears fresh corn

1 pound fresh fava beans (also called broad beans), shucked, blanched, and hulled, or 1 cup frozen fava beans, blanched and hulled

½ large red onion, cut into ¼-inch dice

½ red bell pepper, cut into ¼-inch dice

1 tablespoon minced fresh chives

4 tablespoons goat fromage blanc*

Available in cheese shops and at specialty grocers.

Here's a fun summer dish that'll lift you right out of Brooklyn and set you down in the South Carolina of chef Emily Sims's youth. Sims started out with a vague notion to combine fried green tomatoes with succotash; owner Catherine Saillard later suggested the pesto underneath "to give it a little kick." If you can't find the goat fromage blanc, substitute soft spreadable goat cheese or regular fromage blanc.

1. Beat the eggs and milk in a medium bowl. Place the flour and panko in two separate bowls. Place each tomato slice in the flour bowl and coat thoroughly. Transfer the tomato slice to the egg bowl and coat it in egg, letting any excess egg drip off. Lay the tomato slice in the panko, coating both sides thoroughly. Remove to a large plate.

2. In a small food processor or blender, combine the ¼ cup basil leaves with the olive oil and puree. (If this is too small a quantity for your machine, you can finely chop with a knife. Just add the oil a little at a time and drag the blade across the chopped leaves to create a paste.) Set the basil puree aside.

3. Heat the canola oil in a shallow pan until a deep-fat thermometer registers 300°F. (If you don't have a thermometer, test the oil temperature by adding one battered tomato to the pan. If it bubbles vigorously, the oil is ready for frying.) Fry the tomatoes in batches until golden brown, about 2 minutes per side. Remove from the oil and drain on a rack or paper towels. Season with salt and pepper immediately.

4. In another pan, heat the butter until bubbly. Add the corn, fava beans, onion, and bell pepper and sauté until the corn is cooked through, about 4 minutes. Stir in the chopped basil, the chives, and salt and pepper to taste.

5. Spread the goat cheese on the tomato slices. Smear 1 tablespoon basil puree on each of 4 serving plates. Spoon the succotash on top, then lay on the fried green tomatoes, overlapping them like shingles.

Summer Vegetable Salad
with Buttermilk Dressing / ICI

"We could call this the Added Value Salad, basically," says owner Catherine Saillard. Added Value is a nonprofit organization that runs the Red Hook Community Farm, where local high school kids grow greens, vegetables, and herbs—and learn the principles of sustainable agriculture—on a formerly vacant lot in one of Brooklyn's grittier neighborhoods. "We love Added Value and what they do," Saillard says. So do her regulars. Sometimes the greens are still warm from the sun when she serves the salad to customers who know exactly when Added Value delivers—and time their lunch dates accordingly.

1. To make the dressing, combine the buttermilk, mustard, and herbs in a bowl. Add the olive oil in a thin stream, whisking constantly to emulsify it. Season to taste with salt and pepper and set aside.

2. To make the salad, in a large bowl, mix the lettuce, arugula, carrots, radishes, snow peas, onions, and fennel. Season with salt and pepper. Drizzle the salad mixture with dressing and toss to coat. Serve immediately.

SERVES 4

For the dressing

¼ cup buttermilk

1 teaspoon Dijon mustard

2 tablespoons chopped mixed fresh herbs: sage, chives, parsley, thyme

⅓ cup extra-virgin olive oil

Coarse salt and freshly ground black pepper

For the salad

1 large head loose leaf lettuce, such as red leaf or green leaf

2 cups arugula

8 to 10 greenmarket baby carrots, white or orange, peeled

1 or 2 radishes, thinly sliced

¼ cup snow peas, cut into ¼-inch pieces

¼ cup thinly sliced sweet onion

2 heaping tablespoons chopped baby fennel or regular fennel

Coarse salt and freshly ground black pepper

APPLEWOOD
PARK SLOPE

How committed is Laura Shea to her restaurant? She has the applewood logo—rendered as her daughters' names, Tatum and Sophie—tattooed on her back. If that seems a tad over the top . . . well, okay. But it's entirely consistent with the way she and her chef husband, David, have always approached the restaurant. Tatum and Sophie are their children. But no matter how old it gets, applewood—the middle child—will always be their baby.

The restaurant opened in September 2004, when Laura was pregnant with Tatum, their younger daughter. After Tatum was born, Laura didn't take much of a maternity leave—she *is* the front of the house at applewood—and in fact used to wear the sleeping Tatum in a sling while seating and attending to diners. (We can recall one dinner when Laura picked up our own cranky infant son and whisked him around the dining room, then disappered with him into the kitchen.)

It's hard to find an upscale Brooklyn restaurant that *doesn't* stress its seasonal menu, its sustainability, and its locally sourced ingredients. This PC chatter can become white noise or, worse, opportunistic marketing speak. But the Sheas walk their talk. Their restaurant holds monthly Meet the Farmer dinners, prix-fixe meals where one of the restaurant's vendors comes in and talks about his products. And the origin of the Sheas' philosophy goes way back—before Michael Pollan, before Blue Hill or Savoy, all

the way back to 1986, when David (right) worked at the Old Chatham Sheepherding Company in Chatham, New York. "That was where I experienced for the first time working in a garden at the beginning of my shift, picking product and bringing it into the kitchen and then working with it," David recalls. "And realizing the difference. And really just making that connection of, Wow, this is a whole new thing. *This* is what food is really all about."

Now the Sheas are moving to apply that philosophy on a much grander and more ambitious scale: by becoming farmers themselves. They're looking for protected land in Massachusetts or New York where they can grow produce and raise animals. Initially the food would be exclusively for use at applewood, but eventually the farm would evolve

into a "learning center," Laura says, that would offer lodging for city folk who want to harvest some kale or maybe birth a lamb before driving their Zipcars back to Park Slope.

That's the vision, anyway. If it happens, will there be more tattoos? Maybe one for David this time? "Ha!" says Laura. "He already has a very, very embarrassing tattoo that he got when he was eighteen, when he was drunk and in the Navy. That's a good story in a different way altogether."

Coriander-Cured Wild Salmon with Pickled Sweet Corn and Pea Shoot Salad / APPLEWOOD

SERVES 8 AS A FIRST COURSE

For the salmon

¾ cup whole coriander seed

¼ cup whole black peppercorns

3 cups coarse salt

1 cup sugar

6 garlic cloves, smashed

6 bay leaves, crushed

1 teaspoon crushed red pepper flakes

4 ounces spicy bush basil or Italian basil

Grated zest of 1 large lemon

One sockeye or coho salmon fillet, about 2 pounds, skin on, pin bones removed

Coarse sea salt

For a restaurant so focused on local ingredients, it's ironic that applewood's sole source for salmon is more than three thousand miles away. "But Christopher just does things the right way," chef David Shea says of Christopher Nicholson, who runs Iliamna Fish Company in Alaska. "He nets the fish in small skiffs, does all the processing by hand. He's totally passionate, he loves his fish, and he's so conscious of the environment." If you can't find sockeye—and if you're on the East Coast, you probably can't—use coho salmon. It won't have sockeye's deep red color, but it'll still be delicious. This recipe nets more salmon than you'll need for the salad—yes, even after sixty-four slices—leaving you plenty of leftover fish for bagels in the morning. Ideally, the corn should be pickled and the salmon cured at least one day before you serve the dish.

1. To prepare the salmon, combine the coriander seed and peppercorns in a large skillet over low heat. Toast until fragrant, about 3 minutes. Allow to cool slightly, then, working in batches, grind them to a powder in a spice grinder.

2. In a medium bowl, make a curing mixture by combining the ground spices, salt, sugar, garlic, bay leaves, red pepper flakes, and basil. Lay the salmon fillet skin side down on a rimmed baking sheet lined with parchment paper. Coat the fish generously with the curing mixture, cover with plastic wrap, and refrigerate at least 4 hours or overnight.

3. Rinse the fish well, pat dry, wrap in plastic wrap, and store, refrigerated, for up to 1 week.

half, about 10 minutes. Reduce the heat to the lowest setting, cover, and keep warm.

5. Using tongs or two forks, shred the pork and remove any excess fat.

6. To make the ricotta dumplings, bring a large pot of salted water to a simmer. Beat the egg yolk in a medium bowl. Fold the ricotta cheese into the egg, then add the Parmigiano-Reggiano cheese, nutmeg, and salt. Slowly incorporate the flour, about ½ cup at a time, mixing gently with a rubber spatula. Check the batter; it should hold together with 1 cup flour, but still be moist. Add more flour if the batter is too loose.

7. To form the dumplings, shape rounded tablespoons of the mixture into ovals. Working in batches, add the dumplings to the water. Simmer for 10 minutes, or until the dumplings are cooked through. (To check for doneness, cut a dumpling in half. It's ready when the color is consistent throughout.) Remove the dumplings with a slotted spoon and transfer to a large plate lined with paper towel.

8. Heat the remaining 2 tablespoons olive oil over medium-high heat in a Dutch oven or a large skillet. Add the shredded pork and cook, without stirring, until it caramelizes, about 5 minutes. Season with coarse salt, then add the reduced cooking liquid and bring to a simmer. Adjust the seasonings to taste. Add the dumplings and simmer until heated through.

9. To serve, place ½ cup of the braised pork in the center of each of 4 bowls. Place three dumplings around the meat.

10. Whisk the butter into the reduced braising liquid. Spoon the sauce over the pork and dumplings. Garnish with coarse salt and fresh thyme leaves.

---

applewood's House-Made Ricotta

Here's a recipe for homemade ricotta adapted from chef David Shea. But whether you've made your own or are using store-bought, drain the ricotta before using. Line a fine-mesh strainer with cheesecloth and add the cheese. Refrigerate and drain for at least eight hours or overnight. You can also wrap it up like a ball in cheesecloth and squeeze to help it along.

MAKES ABOUT 1 POUND

1 quart organic whole milk

1 quart organic heavy cream

2 cups organic buttermilk

1 tablespoon coarse salt

1½ tablespoons champagne vinegar

Combine the milk, heavy cream, buttermilk, and salt in a heavy-bottomed stainless-steel pot. Heat over medium heat, stirring gently, until the mixture registers 185 to 190°F on a candy thermometer. Reduce the heat to low. Add the vinegar and gently stir once to combine. Curds should form immediately. Remove the pan from the heat and allow the mixture to sit for 15 minutes, without stirring, to allow the whey to drain away from the curds. Gently scoop the curds into a cheesecloth-lined sieve. Allow the cheese to drain in the refrigerator overnight. Ricotta cheese can be refrigerated up to 3 days.

SALVATORE BKLYN / BOERUM HILL

BETSY DEVINE AND RACHEL MARK

Salvatore Bklyn is one of two small food businesses hatched in the kitchen of Lunetta (see page 142) in Boerum Hill. (The other is Pizza Moto, a mobile brick-oven pizzeria.) Devine, a former chef de cuisine at Lunetta, makes the cheese—ricotta and smoked ricotta, made with whole milk curdled in lemon juice—while Mark, her wife and business partner, handles sales and marketing. Mark's day job at a wine importer keeps her in close contact with chefs, and in fact that's where she was when we interviewed Devine (far right) at Lunetta.

So, how'd you wind up becoming a cheesemaker?

Rachel was in Italy for a couple months a few years ago, learning to speak Italian, and at the tail end of the trip I joined her. We rented a car, drove around, and basically gorged ourselves. At one point we were in San Gimignano. Rachel had been there about a month earlier, and she'd met this guy Salvatore, who owned a place called Enoteca Gustavo. So we went to eat there,

and he served us this ricotta on tomato toasts. He had this technique where he would put the tomato on grilled bread and cut it *on* the bread, so the tomato would just seep into the cheese and bread. *Sooo* good. And we were like, That's the *bomb*.

But there wasn't this eureka moment: *Oh, let's start a business and do that*. In fact, after we left Italy we went to South America for five months, where there was quite the opposite of a culinary culture, in a lot of ways. But when we came back home, I started cooking at Lunetta, and at one point we said, Remember Salvatore and that amazing ricotta? How can we make that?

Did his ricotta make such an impression because it was just delicious or because it was delicious *and* stylistically different—thicker and creamier—than typical ricotta we have here?

Both. Like many things over there, it was just: *This is how it's supposed to be.*

Did he show you how to make it?

He didn't *really* tell us how to make it. It wasn't like we sat and he taught us his ways. We ended up calling the company after him because he was just an inspirational person; he awakened us to something. And we thought he was just the bee's knees.

You started serving it at Lunetta before you officially founded Salvatore Bklyn. What was the dish when you first put it on the menu?

A grilled piece of bread, rubbed with garlic, spread with cheese, and topped with a little salt, pepper, olive oil, and lemon zest.

How much cheese will you make this month?

We average 300 pounds a week, so about 1,200 pounds. About 40 percent of that goes to retail, 60 percent wholesale.

Has Salvatore had your cheese?

No, he hasn't! But we're in contact. We're planning to go over there soon, to hang out with him, and maybe see some mozzarella production facilities for giggles.

Is that in the long-term plan—expanding into mozzarella production?

[*big inhale*] I don't know. We'll see how it goes. I mean, it's definitely another huge project. . . . I'm torn. I kinda love the simplicity of just doing one item, and doing it well.

EGG

WILLIAMSBURG

You can practically hear the screen doors slamming at Egg, a plain white box of a restaurant that opens at seven A.M., when many of its neighbors are just getting home from last night's party, and keeps on serving eggs until closing time fifteen hours later. (Also biscuits, stone-ground grits, Kentucky ham, candied bacon, and scrapple.) In an earlier incarnation, the restaurant closed in the afternoon before opening up again at six with semi-fancy dinner service, breakfast not included. "*Big* mistake," says George Weld, the owner and original chef. Weld (right) learned the hard way that at Egg, the most important meal of the day is the most important meal *all* day. All night, too.

Weld grew up in both Carolinas, so he's fully steeped—like his sweet tea—in the proud dogma of Southern cooking. But he's not hostage to it. The high points of Egg's menu seem about, oh, 85-percent familiar. There's always a curveball in there, though, an unexpected ingredient or cooking method that modernizes the dish. Kentucky ham on a biscuit, for instance, comes with Grafton cheddar and fig jam. Biscuits and gravy are served with a side of pan-seared mushrooms. A chorizo, egg, and cheese sandwich is sloppy and glorious, an unwieldy mess slathered with jalapeños, pickled onions, and salsa verde. You'll need a fork.

Writing in the *New York Times*, Peter Meehan described the menu at Egg as "guileless." That might even be a better word for Weld. After abandoning a Ph.D. program in literature at the University of Virginia, he moved to New York and worked for a dot-com while struggling to finish a novel. In April 2005, for reasons he still has trouble articulating, he opened Egg. The restaurant served breakfast only and closed at noon, when the space converted to an all-natural hot-dog joint. "I can't emphasize how clueless I was about doing this," Weld says, with what appears to be genuine amazement that he's still in business more than five years later. "I mean, I knew how to cook on a small scale, and I had

some sense of how to cook under pressure for a larger room because I'd worked in short-order restaurants." But he freely admits that he had no business running a business. Years of self-education, and self-doubt, ensued.

Things looked dire as recently as early 2009. Battered by the recession, Weld decided to bail on the upscale dinner menu, which confused customers, and serve breakfast all day. (He took over the space from the hot-dog restaurant in 2007.) Finally, everything felt right. Egg still offers lunch and dinner options, but "people overwhelmingly order breakfast, no matter what time," Weld says. "And fried chicken."

Duck Legs and Dirty Rice / EGG

SERVES 6

For the braised duck legs

1 teaspoon fennel seed

1 teaspoon coriander seed

1 teaspoon whole cloves

1 teaspoon whole black peppercorns

6 duck legs and thighs, about
2½ pounds total, trimmed of excess fat

Coarse salt and freshly ground black
pepper

2 tablespoons extra-virgin olive oil

1 large yellow onion, peeled and cut
into ½-inch dice

1 large garlic clove, minced

2 large carrots, peeled, cut into
½-inch dice

1 celery stalk, cut into ½-inch dice

1 fennel bulb, trimmed, cut into
½-inch dice

1 cup dry red wine

6 cups homemade duck or chicken
stock or prepared low-sodium chicken
broth

1 tablespoon cold unsalted butter

Thinly sliced scallions, minced fresh
chives, or minced fresh flat-leaf
parsley (optional)

Egg's menu is anchored by pure Southern comfort: fried chicken with biscuits and lima-bean salad; kale and grilled corn bread; a pulled pork sandwich with vinegar-pepper sauce and coleslaw. And then there's owner George Weld's duck obsession, which has more to do with the sporting tradition of the Carolinas (he grew up in both) than with their culinary heritage. "Duck in general isn't eaten all that much in the South, it's just shot at a lot," says Weld, who never got much into hunting himself. "So I had this relationship with duck, but it wasn't a relationship that had much to do with food." While we have neither the space nor the qualifications to speculate on the psychology behind the man's passion for waterfowl, we'll just say we're grateful it's there. We especially love this rich and soulful invention, an Egg special in heavy rotation. It's a time-consuming dish, but well worth the effort. And you can do steps one through seven the night before you plan to serve it.

1. To make the duck, preheat the oven to 300°F.

2. Combine the fennel seed, coriander seed, cloves, and peppercorns in a skillet over medium-low heat and cook until fragrant, about 3 minutes. Transfer to a spice grinder and grind to a powder.

3. Season the duck generously with salt and pepper, then coat with the spice mixture.

4. In a Dutch oven, heat the olive oil over medium-high heat until hot but not smoking. Working in batches, carefully add the duck legs, skin side down, and cook until the skin is golden brown, 6 to 8 minutes. Turn and cook for 2 minutes more. Transfer to a paper-towel-lined plate and set aside.

5. Pour off all but 2 to 3 tablespoons of fat from the pot and reduce the heat to medium. Add the onion, garlic, carrots, celery, and fennel and season with salt. Cook, stirring occasionally, until the vegetables are tender and beginning to caramelize, 10 to 15 minutes. Add the wine, scrape the bottom of pan to release the brown bits, and cook for 2 minutes more. Return the duck legs and add the stock. Bring the liquid to a simmer.

6 duck gizzards and 6 duck hearts or 10 chicken gizzards and 10 chicken hearts*

6 cups homemade duck or chicken stock or prepared low-sodium chicken broth

9 slices bacon

1 cup diced yellow onion

1½ celery stalks, thinly sliced

3 garlic cloves, thinly sliced

2¼ cups Anson Mills Carolina Gold Rice or Carolina Gold Rice Grits† or short-grain rice

½ cup dry white wine

Coarse salt and freshly ground black pepper

2 scallions, white and green parts, thinly sliced

3 tablespoons minced fresh flat-leaf parsley

* If your butcher hasn't done so already, clean the gizzards by removing the thick inner lining and most of the tough cartilage between the gizzard halves, then slice them across the striated muscle into chunks. Wash the hearts to remove any congealed blood.

† Available online at www.ansonmills.com or at specialty grocers.

6. Cover the pot and place it in the oven. Cook for 1½ hours, or until the duck legs are very tender but not falling from the bone. Remove the duck from the pot and set aside.

7. Strain the cooking liquid through a fine-mesh strainer. Freeze until the fat rises to the top, about 2 hours, then skim off the fat and discard. This braising liquid will form the base for your sauce.

8. To make the rice, in a pot of salted water, boil the gizzards and hearts for 1 hour, or until tender. Drain, coarsely chop, and reserve.

9. Meanwhile, in a medium saucepan over medium heat, bring the stock to a simmer. Reduce the heat to low, cover, and keep warm.

10. In a Dutch oven or large deep pot, cook the bacon over medium heat until crispy. Drain the bacon on a paper-towel-lined plate. Pour off all but ¼ cup of fat from the pot. Crumble the bacon and reserve.

11. Sauté the onion in the bacon fat until golden brown, about 5 minutes. Add the celery, garlic, gizzards, and hearts and sauté until the gizzards and hearts are brown, 3 to 4 minutes. Add the rice and mix well to coat; cook for 2 minutes. Add the wine and cook over medium-low heat until the wine is evaporated and the alcohol burns off, about 2 minutes. Add 2 cups of the stock and cook, stirring frequently, until the stock is absorbed. Continue adding the stock, 1 cup at a time, until the rice is cooked through, about 20 minutes. Season to taste with salt and pepper.

12. To finish the duck, preheat the oven to 400°F. Lay the duck legs in a roasting pan large enough to accommodate them in a single layer and put them in the oven until heated through, 15 to 20 minutes.

13. Meanwhile, heat ½ cup of the reserved braising liquid in a small saucepan over medium-high heat and reduce by half. Add the cold butter, whisking, until the sauce thickens. If you like, finish the sauce with scallions, chives, or parsley.

14. To serve, divide the rice among 4 plates. Sprinkle with the crumbled bacon, sliced scallions, and parsley. Top with 1 duck leg and finish with the sauce.

Sweet Tea / EGG

Yep, that's a glass of iced tea. The thing is, it's *sweet* tea, and not because we stirred in half a pack of Splenda or a drizzle of agave nectar. "I've had some battles in the kitchen with people who wanted to steep mint in the tea or add lemon to the tea or use fancier teas, and it's just— the tea is what it is," says owner George Weld, his voice thick with the pride of tradition. "It's just Lipton. Don't screw with it." And don't even think about cutting back on the sugar. That would just be rude.

In a heat-proof container, combine the tea bags and sugar. Boil 1 quart of water and pour it into the container. Stir briefly, then steep for 15 minutes. Add enough ice to bring the volume up to 2 quarts.

MAKES 2 QUARTS

8 bags Lipton or other black tea

¾ cup granulated sugar

Ice

NORTHEAST KINGDOM

BUSHWICK

A whole bunch of restaurants in this book can call themselves pioneers, and justifiably so. Al Di Là (page 4) opened during the Clinton administration on a then-sketchy Fifth Avenue in Park Slope. The Good Fork (page 106) is located in the remote waterfront village, to paraphrase the real-estate brokers, of Red Hook. The Farm on Adderley (page 122) was the first of several fine establishments now serving the former restaurant wasteland of Ditmas Park. But nobody rolled the dice quite as recklessly as Paris Smeraldo and Meg Lipke, the owners of Northeast Kingdom. More than three years *before* Roberta's (page 200) was heralded as a quixotic effort to plant a flower in the barren culinary desert of Bushwick, Smeraldo and Lipke opened in December 2005, directly across the street from a twenty-foot gray brick wall that suggests a maximum-security prison.

The winter opening was fitting: There's no better place in all of Brooklyn to spend a frigid evening than perched on a cushioned bar stool at Northeast Kingdom, working your way through the half-dozen draft beers scrawled on the chalkboard. The place feels like the only tavern in some rural New England town: exposed brick, faux deer heads mounted on the wall, and woodland oil paintings that look like they were brushstroked by the PBS master himself, Bob Ross.

Northeast Kingdom's food has evolved along the way. When the restaurant opened, it was straight-

up comfort that mirrored the décor: burgers, potpies, and so on. Then it got a bit more sophisticated. Maybe too sophisticated. This is a true neighborhood restaurant in the sense that it relies almost entirely on its neighbors for business. (Adventurers from other parts of Brooklyn and even Manhattan aren't unheard-of, but you can't rely on them.) And while the neighborhood is changing, the neighbors remain price-sensitive. Extremely so, according to chef Gil Calderon, a veteran of Diner and Marlow & Sons, who took over the kitchen of Northeast Kingdom in mid-2009. "I'm definitely thinking as a musician on a budget here," says Calderon, a tall, soft-spoken guy from Astoria, Queens. "I'm thinking like that guy, and I'm thinking about what it is that I want from my neighborhood restaurant."

So what do these artists and writers who've been priced out of Williamsburg and Greenpoint want to eat? Burgers and potpies remain, of course, though the burger is made from grass-fed Vermont beef and the chicken potpie is "all natural." But Calderon's also trying nightly specials that are a bit more daring. "A watermelon, red onion, and pork cracklings salad—that's a dish I feel like I could do right now," he says. And while the two recipes on these pages are carryovers from before his time, he feels like he can sell them, too. Gil, we're sold.

Branzini with Mussels, Cockles, and Spring Vegetables / NORTHEAST KINGDOM

SERVES 4

For the fish stock

2 branzini, 1 to 1½ pounds each (ask your fishmonger to fillet the fish and give you the bones)

1 large onion, cut into ½-inch dice

1 small carrot, peeled and cut into ½-inch dice

½ large celery stalk, cut into ½-inch dice

2 garlic cloves, smashed

2 whole cloves

2 whole star anise

Kosher salt

⅔ pound New Zealand cockles, scrubbed

For the vegetables

6 cups mixed spring vegetables:

New potatoes, quartered

Greenmarket baby carrots, peeled

Pattypan squash, halved or quartered depending on size

Small zucchini, cut into ¼-inch-thick rounds

English peas, shelled

If the short ribs on page 103 are the edible equivalent of the atmosphere at Northeast Kingdom, then this colorful, multitextured dish represents the range of the restaurant. This is a (comparatively) light preparation, but that doesn't mean it lacks flavor. It packs plenty, and from a variety of sources, from the béchamel to the vegetables to the fish itself (including the crispy skin). And the cool thing about this recipe is, while you serve only the fillets, you use the whole fish to make the stock, so nothing's wasted. If your fishmonger doesn't have branzino, any white-fleshed, nonoily fish will work.

To save time, make the stock, cook the potatoes, and blanch the vegetables 1 day ahead.

1. To make the fish stock, using scissors, snip out the gills from the fish bones and discard. Run the bones under cold water until no traces of blood remain. Place the bones in a pot with 4 cups water, the onion, carrot, celery, 2 of the garlic cloves, 2 of the cloves, and the star anise. Simmer over low heat for 45 minutes; strain and set aside.

2. Fill a large bowl with salted water. Add the cockles and soak for 10 minutes. Drain, then scrub them to remove any remaining grit.

3. Place the new potatoes in a medium saucepan and add cold water to cover by 2 inches. Salt the water. Bring to a boil over high heat, then reduce the heat and simmer for 15 to 20 minutes, or until the potatoes are tender.

4. Prepare an ice bath and bring a large pot of salted water to a boil. Add the baby carrots and pattypan squash and cook for 3 minutes. Add the zucchini and peas and cook for 2 more minutes. Remove the vegetables with a slotted spoon and immediately transfer to the ice bath to stop the cooking. Drain and pat dry.

5. To cook the shellfish, melt 2 tablespoons of the butter in a large pot with a tight-fitting lid. Add the shallots and the 2 remaining garlic cloves and sauté until the shallots are soft and translucent, about

2 tablespoons (¼ stick) unsalted butter

4 shallots, peeled and thinly sliced, about 1½ cups

2 garlic cloves, smashed

⅔ pound Prince Edward Island mussels, scrubbed and debearded

1 cup dry white wine

For the béchamel

4 tablespoons unsalted butter

¼ cup all-purpose flour

4 cups whole milk

½ cup baby spinach

Canola oil

Sea salt

Freshly squeezed juice of ½ to 1 whole lemon

3 minutes. Add the mussels, cockles, and wine. Cover the pot and cook over medium heat until the shellfish open, about 4 minutes. Discard any mussels and cockles that do not open. Strain and reserve the shellfish and the broth separately.

6. To make the béchamel, melt the remaining 4 tablespoons butter in a medium saucepan over medium-low heat. Add the flour and stir until smooth. Cook over medium heat until the mixture turns golden in color, 6 to 7 minutes. Meanwhile, heat the milk in a separate pan until it is just about to boil. Add the hot milk to the butter and flour mixture 1 cup at a time, whisking continuously until it is very smooth. Bring to a boil. Cook for 10 minutes, stirring constantly. Season to taste with coarse salt.

7. Add the fish stock and shellfish broth to the béchamel and simmer, whisking to incorporate. Add the vegetables and spinach and return to a simmer over medium heat until the vegetables are heated through. Add the mussels and clams, reduce heat to low, and keep everything warm.

8. To cook the branzini, heat a cast-iron grill pan or sauté pan over medium heat. (If using a sauté pan, add canola oil to coat the bottom of the pan.) Season the fish on both sides with salt and pepper. Cook the fish skin side down and press as you go with the back of your spatula so the fillets do not buckle. Then cook the fish undisturbed for 3 minutes, or until the skin is crisp. Flip the fish, turn off the heat, and let the fish cook through with the remaining heat in the pan, 3 to 4 minutes.

9. To serve, divide the vegetables and shellfish among 4 bowls. Spoon the béchamel over the vegetables and place a fillet on top of each serving. Sprinkle with sea salt and lemon juice.

Braised Short Ribs with Winter Vegetables and Beer Mustard / NORTHEAST KINGDOM

This is a typical Northeast Kingdom recipe—rustic, masculine, and perfect for a cold winter's night. Rustic because chef Gil Calderon urges you to not overthink how the vegetables are chopped. Masculine because you're cooking meat on the bone (with beer!). And perfect for a cold night because your oven will be on for hours, warming the house and filling it with mouthwatering aromas. The meat's done when it's tender but not falling apart; the ribs should remain intact. And a note on the vegetables: these are the ones Calderon likes to use if he has them, but they're just suggestions. Use whatever veggies you have on hand.

1. Place the potatoes in a medium saucepan and add cold water to cover by 2 inches. Salt the water. Bring to a boil over high heat, reduce the heat, and simmer for 15 to 20 minutes, or until the potatoes are tender. Drain and reserve.

2. To blanch the vegetables, prepare an ice bath. Bring a large pot of salted water to a boil. Add the carrots to the boiling water. After 2 minutes, add the celery. Cook for 2 more minutes, then add the onions. Cook for 1 minute, then use a slotted spoon to transfer the vegetables to the ice bath to stop the cooking. Drain and pat dry. (The vegetables can be blanched 1 day ahead. Cool to room temperature and refrigerate in an airtight container until ready to use.)

3. To cook the squash, preheat the oven to 425°F. Peel and seed the butternut squash and cut it into ¼- to ½-inch slices. Place the squash on a rimmed baking sheet, brush both sides with olive oil, and season with salt and pepper. Roast for 25 minutes, or until the squash is tender and begins to caramelize. Remove from the oven and reserve.

4. Reduce the oven temperature to 375°F.

SERVES 4

For the vegetables

6 baby new potatoes, peeled and cut in half

8 greenmarket baby carrots, peeled, or 2 medium carrots, peeled and cut into 2-inch pieces

2 celery stalks, cut on the bias into ¼-inch-thick slices

8 small (half-dollar size) cipollini onions, peeled

1 medium butternut squash

2 to 3 tablespoons olive oil

Coarse salt and freshly ground black pepper

5. To make the bouquet garni, tie the thyme, rosemary, and dill into a bundle with kitchen string. Set aside.

6. To make the short ribs, season the short ribs with salt and pepper. Heat the olive oil in a heavy 6-quart ovenproof pot or Dutch oven over medium-high heat until it is hot but not smoking, and brown the meat on all sides, about 3 minutes per side. Transfer the meat to a plate. Add the onion, carrot, and celery to the pot and cook until the vegetables begin to soften, about 5 minutes. Add ¼ cup ale and scrape up any brown bits from the bottom of the pot. Cook for 2 minutes. Stir in the tomato paste and cook for 2 minutes. Return the short ribs to the pot. Add the remaining 30 ounces of ale, the bouquet garni, Worcestershire sauce, caraway seed, bay leaf, and peppercorns to the short ribs. Add enough water to cover the meat, about 6 cups.

7. Cut a circle out of parchment paper that's slightly larger than the pot's lid. Place it in the pot, pushing it down so it is touching the top of the liquid. This will allow some of the stock to reduce, but will keep the liquid from boiling vigorously and reducing too much. Cover the pot, place it in the oven, and cook for 2½ hours, or until the meat is tender but not falling apart.

8. Transfer the short ribs to a plate and tent with foil to keep warm. When the short ribs are warm enough to handle, remove the bones and discard. Strain the braising liquid through a fine-mesh strainer into a medium saucepan. Skim off the excess fat from the surface of the sauce. Keep the sauce warm over low heat.

9. To finish the vegetables, melt the butter in a large sauté pan over medium heat. Add the reserved blanched vegetables to the pan with the melted butter, tossing to coat. When the butter begins to brown, add the *mirin* and vinegar. Toss and cook the vegetables until they are glazed, about 2 minutes. Add the meat to the pan just long enough to reheat. Sprinkle all with minced parsley.

10. To make the beer mustard, in a small bowl, mix the Dijon mustard and ale until well combined.

11. To serve, divide the vegetables among 4 bowls. Top with the short ribs and reduced braising liquid. Serve with the beer mustard (or store-bought Ipswich Ale Mustard).

For the bouquet garni

2 fresh thyme sprigs

1 fresh rosemary sprig

1 fresh dill sprig

For the short ribs

2 pounds beef short ribs, cut into 4-inch pieces

Coarse salt and freshly ground black pepper

2 tablespoons extra-virgin olive oil

1 large yellow onion, chopped

2 medium carrots, chopped

2 celery stalks, chopped

32 ounces Boddingtons Pub Ale or other ale, divided

2 tablespoons tomato paste

¼ cup Worcestershire sauce

1 tablespoon caraway seed

1 bay leaf

1 teaspoon black peppercorns

1 tablespoon unsalted butter

½ teaspoon *mirin* (rice wine, available in most supermarkets and Asian markets)

1 tablespoon red wine vinegar

2 to 3 tablespoons finely minced fresh flat-leaf parsley

For the beer mustard

¼ cup plus 2 tablespoons Dijon mustard

2 tablespoons Boddingtons Pub Ale or other ale

THE GOOD FORK

RED HOOK

What do Al Di Là, the Grocery, Convivium, Locanda Vini e Olii, Franny's, applewood, Beer Table, James, Five Leaves, Vinegar Hill House, and the Good Fork have in common? They're all run by couples. Not just owned by couples. *Run* by couples, night in, night out.

"We wash our own napkins," says Sohui Kim, who oversees the Good Fork's kitchen while her husband, a carpenter-builder named Ben Schneider who pretty much built the restaurant himself, mans the front of the house. "It's very hands-on, very mom-and-pop oriented. A throwback. And the feedback we got from our customers, initially"—the Good Fork opened in March 2006—"and still today, especially from the older generation, is, 'Wow, we used to have a restaurant like this in, say, Bay Ridge, like fifty years ago.' That mom-and-pop thing is something that sort of died for a little while, and now it's coming back to Brooklyn."

A few of the couples that own the aforementioned restaurants take it all the way, European-style, and live in apartments directly upstairs. Not Kim and Schneider: They commute two whole blocks. They've lived in Red Hook since 2001 and adore

the isolation of the neighborhood. (There's no subway service.) That's a challenge, sure, but it's also the source of the small-town vibe that prevails here. "We found a sense of community in Red Hook that I personally have never experienced in the city," says Kim, who grew up in the Bronx. "So I wanted to create a funky, comfortable environment for the neighborhood folks, but also showcase the food. And I was hoping that the food would attract more than the neighborhood folks."

That worked almost immediately. Barely a month after the Good Fork opened, the *New York Times* published a review that "changed everything," Kim says. Soon a steady parade of diners marched in from all over the city. Many, if not most, ordered the Korean-style steak and eggs (see page 108), probably the best example of Kim's signature move: lifting a dish from America's culinary vernacular and giving it a pronounced Asian accent. That dish has never come off the menu (nor have Kim's pork-and-chive dumplings), but the rest of it changes constantly. Kim loves Italian food, especially hearty ragùs over homemade pasta.

And many of her dishes are built around whatever produce she just received from Added Value, the farm down the street.

All this crowd-pleasing cuisine is served in an intimate dining room that feels a bit like someone's DIY basement apartment: exposed brick walls, stoop-sale artwork, a string of amber Christmas lights. "We wanted it to be an extension of our house, never thinking it would take off as well as it did," Kim says. "Our business plan was written on a piece of napkin."

Steak and Eggs Korean Style / THE GOOD FORK

SERVES 4

For the steak marinade

¼ cup *mirin* (rice wine, available in the Asian section of supermarkets)

2 tablespoons finely grated Granny Smith apple

2 tablespoons soy sauce

2 tablespoons light corn syrup

1½ tablespoons finely chopped scallion (white and light green parts)

1 scant tablespoon Korean hot pepper paste*

1 scant tablespoon peeled and minced fresh ginger

2 garlic cloves, minced

1½ teaspoons toasted sesame oil

1½ teaspoons unseasoned rice wine vinegar

Four 5-ounce pieces skirt steak

* Korean hot pepper paste (gochujang or kochujang) can be found at Korean markets and online at koamart.com.

This is probably chef Sohui Kim's most famous creation. It uses a small, inexpensive cut of meat that Kim completely transforms by marinating it in "an extreme amount of Asian flavors." The marinade is a tweaked version of her mother's *kalbi* recipe, with lots of soy, Korean pepper paste, and *mirin*, and the fried egg is borrowed from *bibimbop*, another cornerstone of Korean cuisine.

1. To marinate the steaks, whisk the marinade ingredients in a large bowl. Add the steaks. Cover and chill overnight.

2. To make the rice, bring 2 cups water to a boil in a small saucepan. Add the rice and 1 teaspoon salt and return to a boil. Reduce the heat to low, cover, and cook until the water is absorbed, about 20 minutes.

3. Meanwhile, prepare the grill for cooking or heat a ridged grill pan over medium-high heat until hot. Grill the steaks until they are slightly charred but still pink in the center, about 3 minutes per side. Transfer to a plate and let stand for about 5 minutes.

4. Heat 2 tablespoons of the canola oil in a large skillet over medium heat. Add the kimchi and *mirin* and stir until heated. Fold in the rice. Season to taste with salt and pepper and keep warm.

5. Heat the remaining teaspoon of canola oil in a large nonstick skillet over medium heat. Crack the eggs into the skillet, being careful not to break the yolks. Sprinkle with salt and pepper. Cook until the whites are set, about 3 minutes.

6. In a small bowl, toss the baby arugula with the olive oil and season with salt and pepper.

7. To serve, divide the kimchi rice among 4 plates. Slice the steaks thin across the grain and arrange over the rice. Top each plate with an egg, sprinkle with chopped scallions, and serve with arugula.

1 cup sushi rice or other short-grain rice

Coarse salt

2 tablespoons plus 1 teaspoon canola oil, divided

1½ cups napa cabbage kimchi,* coarsely chopped

2 tablespoons unseasoned rice wine vinegar

Freshly ground black pepper

4 large eggs

Chopped scallions, for garnish

1 cup baby arugula (Kim buys from Added Value; see page 81)

1 tablespoon extra-virgin olive oil

* Napa cabbage kimchi can be found at Korean markets and online at koamart. com.

Mussels with Lemongrass, Kaffir Lime Leaves, and Coconut Milk

/ THE GOOD FORK

Here's chef Sohui Kim's take on a classic Southeast Asian dish, but with none of that cloying, swimming-in-coconut-milk quality that's typical of takeout Thai. It's very easy to make and works great as a starter or an entree.

1. In a large, heavy pot, heat the canola oil over medium heat. Add the lemongrass, shallots, chiles, kaffir lime leaves, and garlic. Cook until translucent and fragrant, about 10 minutes.

2. Add the wine and coconut milk. Increase the heat to medium high, bring to a boil, then reduce to a simmer and cook for 10 minutes, until the mixture is reduced by half. Season to taste with salt and pepper.

3. Discard any mussels that are cracked or open. Add the remaining mussels to the pot, cover, and cook until the mussels open, 3 or 4 minutes. Discard any mussels that don't open.

4. Divide the mussels and broth among 4 plates, garnish with cilantro, and serve.

SERVES 4 AS A FIRST COURSE OR 2 AS A MAIN COURSE

2 tablespoons canola oil

1 lemongrass stalk, tough outer leaves discarded, tender white center minced

2 large shallots, thinly sliced

3 small Thai bird's-eye chiles, seeded and minced

3 kaffir lime leaves, stems removed, leaves thinly sliced

2 garlic cloves, minced

2 cups dry white wine

One 13.5-ounce can unsweetened coconut milk

Coarse salt and freshly ground black pepper

2 pounds Prince Edward Island mussels, scrubbed and debearded

Fresh cilantro, for garnish

HOT BREAD KITCHEN / GOWANUS

JESSAMYN WALDMAN

Hot Bread Kitchen is, in Jessamyn Waldman's words, "an international immigrant-led women's baking collective." The nonprofit bakery hires immigrant women to make the breads of their homelands and helps them transition into their new lives in America. That's the long-term vision, at least. Waldman (far right), a former immigration-policy expert who made her bones as a baker during a two-and-a-half year stint at Restaurant Daniel in Manhattan, feels as if she's just getting started.

Let's start with the big picture.

Sure. The long-term model would be a six-month training program for eighty women a year. So forty women at a time will come in, get on-the-job training, intensive English classes, and math classes, and then we'll help them either launch a micro-enterprise or get another job somewhere in the culinary field. Until we get there, it's sort of a one-on-one conversation.

How much diversity have you had so far, nationality-wise?

We've had bakers from Mexico, Ecuador, Mali, Chad, Afghanistan, Palestine, and Tibet. On our administrative staff, we have a woman who was born in the Philippines, and I was born in Canada. So we're getting close to having representation on every continent.

What is it about bread, specifically, that makes this concept work?

There's just something symbolically powerful about it. It's totally ubiqui-

tous. Every culture has bread. And when I say bread, we cast a wide net. I don't really want to get into sweets and pastries, but spinach pies, pork buns, flatbreads, dumplings—I think all those things fall into the mission of what we're trying to do.

You do one product line for stores and different breads for farmers' markets, correct?

Right. There are two lines of bread, one that we wholesale and another that we take to CSAs and farmers' markets. Now we're wholesaling three products: the lavash, which is a Central Asian bread, the corn tortillas, and my mother's hippie granola. For the farmers' markets and CSAs, we do a more complete line of fresh breads.

Restaurant Daniel—not a bad place to learn to bake at a high level.

I was the first woman ever hired in the bakery at Daniel. I got a master's degree from Columbia, I worked at the United Nations, I had all these accomplishments in my life, but getting hired by Daniel to bake, to me, was, like, *I could die now.* It felt like the biggest accomplishment.

Your first employee, a Mexican woman named Elidia Ramos, is still with you.

Yes, and I hope she takes this whole thing over some day. I could not be here without her, and I credit a lot of our success to her perseverance. I knew that the first product that I wanted to bring to market was a handmade corn tortilla, because there are very few places in the city

that are marketing them. Ninety percent of the tortilla factories in the city are using *maseca*, which is a ground flour product that's made in Idaho. If you come from the West Coast, or you've spent any time in Central America, you understand the difference between a real corn-made tortilla and one made with *maseca*; they taste completely different. So I saw a hole in the market.

Elidia knows a lot about Mexican food, and she makes great tortillas. Which is kind of the profile of the women we try to hire. We don't require our bakers to have any professional experience, but we want them to speak about the foods from the countries they come from. And hopefully know how to make a few of them.

DRESSLER

WILLIAMSBURG

There are only four Michelin-starred restaurants in Brooklyn, and two of them are directly across the street from each other. They couldn't be much more different, though. One is Peter Luger, the cash-only steak house where the testosterone is as thick as the porterhouse and the place seems lighted for an interrogation scene on *24*. The other is Dressler, which rivals Vinegar Hill House (page 204) for the unofficial title of Most Atmospheric Restaurant in the Borough.

That's partly because Dressler's owner, Colin Devlin, did a two-and-a-half-year stint as a bartender at Balthazar, the most artfully lighted restaurant in New York, where Keith McNally taught him plenty about flattering his guests. Everyone's gorgeous at Dressler. But it's not just lighting. The seventy-seat restaurant's high ceilings, towering flowers, and multiple mirrors make it feel a lot bigger and grander than it is. Unlike, say, Vinegar Hill House (and many other restaurants in this book), there's nothing homemade about Dressler. This space is designed to within an inch of its life. There's a metal-filigree motif that runs throughout: the backs of the bar stools, circling the mirrors, behind the bar, along the booths. Dressler is a sexy and festive restaurant, the kind of place that can make an ordinary Tuesday feel like New Year's Eve.

The restaurant opened in April 2006, five years after Devlin's flagship restaurant, DuMont (page 50). Like DuMont, Dressler was conceived as a neighborhood place, but one with more culinary ambition. Chef Polo Dobkin, who oversees all three of Devlin's kitchens (the third is DuMont Burger), is a traditionalist who excels at striking a balance between comfort and creativity. The artichoke salad (see page 119) is a signature dish, a deceptively hearty creation with an addictive dressing that's as good sopped up with a roll as it is on the salad. One night we were blown away by a crispy duck cooked medium-rare and served with a Swiss chard tamale, braised celery, and cipollini onions. Another evening we capped our meal with an impossibly moist gingerbread that came with Seckel pear, a very rummy butter rum sauce, and crème fraîche; the gingerbread itself had a crunchy, porous crust that gave way to a soft center. This is high-end restaurant cooking, but without the pyrotechnics. "Everything's very straightforward," says Dobkin. "No foams, no smears."

About that Michelin star. As soon as Dobkin got word that they'd earned it (this was back in the fall of 2007), he sent Devlin a text with the news: "Dude, we got a Michelin star!" Devlin's response: "Is that good?" He knew about the Michelin guide, of course, but since this was the first time the company had published a New York edition, he wasn't really up to speed on the ranking system.

Well, only one other Brooklyn restaurant has earned one since. So yeah, Colin, that's pretty good.

Grilled Hanger Steak with Horseradish Whipped Potatoes, Creamed Spinach, and Sauce Bordelaise / DRESSLER

For the sauce bordelaise

2 tablespoons canola oil

1 small carrot, peeled and cut into ¼-inch dice (about ¼ cup)

4 celery stalks, cut into ¼-inch dice (about 1½ cups)

1 Spanish onion, peeled and cut into ¼-inch dice (about 2 cups)

6 garlic cloves, thinly sliced

2 cups dry red wine

4 cups homemade or prepared veal stock, such as D'Artagnan Veal Demi-Glace

1 fresh thyme sprig

1 bay leaf

6 whole black peppercorns

Coarse salt

For the whipped potatoes

1½ pounds russet or Idaho potatoes, peeled and cut into 1-inch pieces

2 tablespoons unsalted butter, diced

½ cup heavy cream

½ cup milk

1 tablespoon crème fraîche

2 tablespoons prepared horseradish

Coarse salt and freshly ground black pepper

"I like classically prepared food, classic technique," says chef Polo Dobkin. "I'm a big believer in classic reduction sauces." And it doesn't get much more classic than bordelaise, a concentrated sauce that rewards the patient cook. This is a crowd-pleasing plate of straightforward, satisfying food—and what's not to love about that?

1. **To make the sauce bordelaise,** heat the canola oil in a medium saucepan over medium heat. Add the carrot, celery, onion, and garlic and sauté until the vegetables are caramelized, about 15 minutes. Add the wine and reduce until almost all the liquid is evaporated, about 20 minutes. Add the stock, thyme, bay leaf, and peppercorns. Bring to a boil, then reduce to a simmer and cook until the sauce is lightly syrupy and coats the back of a spoon, about 1 hour. Strain through a fine-mesh strainer into a clean pan, season to taste with salt, and set aside.

2. **To make the potatoes,** place them in a large pot and cover with cold salted water. Bring to a boil and cook until tender, 12 to 15 minutes.

3. Combine the butter, cream, and milk in a small saucepan over medium-low heat. Bring to a simmer, then reduce heat to low, cover, and keep warm.

4. Drain the potatoes in a colander, then immediately pass them through a potato ricer into a large bowl. Slowly add the warm milk mixture to the potatoes and stir to combine. Fold in the crème fraîche and horseradish and season with salt and pepper. Keep warm.

For the creamed spinach

2 tablespoons unsalted butter, divided

1 shallot, peeled and finely diced

1 pound spinach, coarse stems discarded, leaves washed and drained

½ cup milk

⅓ cup heavy cream

1 tablespoon all-purpose flour

Kosher salt

Pinch of cayenne

Pinch of freshly grated nutmeg

Six 10- to 12-ounce hanger steaks, trimmed of fat, sinew, and center connective tissue

5. Meanwhile, make the spinach. Melt 1 tablespoon of the butter in a large sauté pan over medium heat. Add the shallot and sauté until translucent, about 2 minutes. Raise the heat to high, add the spinach, and sauté, stirring, until wilted, about 3 minutes. Set the spinach in a colander to drain for 10 minutes.

6. Combine the milk and heavy cream in a small saucepan. Bring to a simmer. Cover and keep warm.

7. Melt the remaining 1 tablespoon butter in a heavy-bottomed pot. Add the flour and cook over medium heat, whisking constantly, about 4 minutes. Slowly add the warm milk mixture, whisking constantly, until it thickens, about 1 minute. Season to taste with salt, cayenne, and nutmeg. Turn the heat to low and add the thoroughly drained spinach to the pot. Stir to combine well and cook until just heated through.

8. Prepare the grill for cooking or heat a ridged grill pan over medium-high heat until hot. Grill the hanger steaks on both sides, about 10 minutes total for medium-rare. Allow the steaks to rest for 5 minutes. Slice the meat against the grain into ½-inch-thick slices.

9. Reheat the sauce bordelaise over low heat in a small, covered saucepan.

10. To serve, divide the potatoes among 4 plates. Top with creamed spinach and sliced steak. Drizzle with the sauce bordelaise.

Warm Artichoke Heart Salad with White Beans, Arugula, and Salsa Verde / DRESSLER

Between the whole beans, the bean puree, the "turned" artichoke, and the creamy dressing, this dish takes some effort—but it absolutely pays off. This is a stunning salad with cascading flavors that synthesize into a rich, tangy freshness that'll just blow you away. And the dish aptly captures the spirit of Dressler. "You eat with your eyes first," says chef Polo Dobkin. "And I thought it would be a really nice visual presentation to have a beautifully turned artichoke to showcase the skill and the effort that went into the dish."

1. To prepare the beans, drain and rinse the beans. In a large saucepan, combine the beans with the carrot, celery, onion, and garlic and add enough cold water to cover. Bring to a boil over medium-high heat, then reduce the heat to low and simmer, covered, until the beans are tender, about 45 minutes. Remove and discard the vegetables. Allow the beans to cool in the braising liquid. Drain the beans and reserve both the beans and the braising liquid.

2. To make the salsa verde, combine the parsley, capers, and garlic in a blender or small food processor and puree until smooth. With the motor running, add the olive oil in a slow stream and process until emulsified. Transfer to a bowl and reserve.

3. To make the white bean puree, combine ½ cup of the beans and 4 teaspoons of the reserved braising liquid in a food processor and puree until smooth. Season with salt and pepper and set aside. (Reserve the rest of the beans and braising liquid.)

4. To prepare the artichoke hearts, place the stock in a large saucepan. Squeeze the lemon into the stock and drop the lemon into the pot. Set aside.

SERVES 6

For the beans

½ cup dried Great Northern beans, rinsed and soaked overnight in room-temperature water to cover

1 carrot, halved

1 celery stalk, halved

½ yellow onion, peeled

1 small garlic clove, peeled

Coarse salt and freshly ground black pepper

For the salsa verde

1 cup fresh flat-leaf parsley leaves, coarse chopped

1 tablespoon drained capers

1 small garlic clove, minced

½ cup extra-virgin olive oil

For the artichokes

4 to 6 cups homemade chicken stock or prepared low-sodium chicken broth

1 lemon, cut in half

6 large globe artichokes, each 4 to 4½ inches in diameter

3 fresh thyme sprigs

1 carrot, cut in half

1 celery stalk, cut in half

½ medium onion, cut in half

1 garlic clove, peeled

For the creamy garlic dressing

1 large egg yolk

1 garlic clove, shaved on a Microplane or sliced as thin as possible

2 tablespoons freshly squeezed lemon juice

2 tablespoons red wine vinegar

1¼ cups canola oil

¼ cup heavy cream

1 teaspoon freshly ground black pepper

2 tablespoons finely grated Parmigiano-Reggiano

Coarse salt

For the arugula salad

2 cups loosely packed baby arugula

½ cup shaved Parmigiano-Reggiano

5. To clean the artichokes, cut off the stems and remove the outer leaves either one at a time or by cutting the leaves only at the base of the leaf with a paring knife, taking care not to cut into the hard heart while exposing the yellow and light green interior leaves. Locate the top of the heart and with a paring knife cut off and discard the top of the choke. Scrape out and discard the fuzzy choke from the heart and immediately place the artichoke hearts in the pot of stock.

6. Add the thyme, carrot, celery, onion, and garlic to the pot with the artichoke hearts. There should be enough stock in the pan to cover the vegetables by 2 inches; add a little more stock or water if necessary. Bring to a boil over medium heat. Reduce the heat to low and simmer gently until the artichoke hearts are tender, 10 to 15 minutes.

7. Allow the artichoke hearts to cool in the braising liquid. Remove the artichoke hearts, set aside, and reserve the liquid.

8. To make the dressing, place the egg yolk, garlic, lemon juice, and red wine vinegar in a blender and blend well. With the blender on medium speed, slowly drizzle in the oil. It should look like loose mayonnaise. Pour the dressing into a bowl and whisk in the cream, pepper, and Parmigiano-Reggiano. Season with salt.

9. Place the artichoke hearts in a medium saucepan with 2 cups of the artichoke braising liquid over medium-low heat. Cook until heated through.

10. Meanwhile, place the remaining whole white beans in a small saucepan with 1 cup of the bean braising liquid over medium-low heat and cook until heated through.

11. Just before plating the dish, dress the arugula with the creamy garlic dressing. Set aside.

12. Place a dollop of white bean puree in the center of each plate. Top with an artichoke heart. Fill each heart with a spoonful of white beans topped with arugula salad and shaved Parmigiano-Reggiano. Drizzle the salsa verde on the plate around the artichoke heart and serve.

THE FARM
ON ADDERLEY

DITMAS PARK

If there were a Michael Pollan Seal of Approval for restaurants, we'd bet you a bottle of bio-dynamic pinot noir that the Farm on Adderley would claim the first stamp in Brooklyn. A visitor to its website quickly learns that the restaurant composts all its food waste and recycles its cooking oil into renewable fuel. That all of its meat "comes from animals that were humanely cared for." That it buys birds from Freebird in Pennsylvania Amish country, coffee from Jim's Organic Coffee in West Wareham, Massachusetts, and soy from Vermont Soy in Hardwick, Vermont. And that it recently started selling beef-liver dog treats made from cattle butchered specifically for the restaurant.

And yet chef Tom Kearney, who operates the restaurant for owners Gary Jonas and Allison McDowell, has a surprising take on the food philosophy he so fully subscribes to. "Every time I try to characterize what we do, it always comes around to the same buzzwords, and I really hate that," he says. "I like the movement itself, but I hear the word *locavore* and I cringe. What's next, a 'locavore pizza' from Pizza Hut?"

"We're not in the business of indoctrinating customers," he says. "Sometimes you just want to come in and have a burger."

Back in the mid-2000s, Gary Jonas noticed how badly his Ditmas Park neighborhood needed a quality restaurant. He borrowed the name from a South African expression—Jonas grew up in South Africa—that means long shot, as in, "If you manage to make a go of that restaurant, I'll buy you a farm on Adderley." (Adderley is a Cape Town thoroughfare.) In this case, the long shot paid off. The restaurant was an overnight smash hit and has paved the way for a flurry of other new dining options—Mimi's Hummus, Purple Yam, Picket Fence—on or near Cortelyou Road.

Key to the Farm's success was a conviction that while dishes like short rib ravioli and acorn squash tart should be in the mix, the menu needed to be anchored by familiarity. "We'll probably always have a chicken, a burger, and vanilla ice cream," says Kearney. "We have customers who come in four times a week."

Our theory on the main reason those customers can't stay away? The crispy thick-cut fries with curry mayo. We could eat those 365 days a year.

Lamb Meatballs with Escarole, Cipollini Onions, and Cranberry Beans

/ THE FARM ON ADDERLEY

SERVES 6 TO 8 (MAKES TWENTY-FOUR 2-OUNCE MEATBALLS)

For the beans

¾ cup dried cranberry beans, borlotti beans, or Roman beans, or 1½ cups shelled fresh cranberry beans

2 teaspoons salt

1 bay leaf

¼-pound piece smoky slab bacon (optional)

For the meatballs

2 pounds ground lamb

3 tablespoons dried marjoram

1 tablespoon dried rosemary

1 medium yellow onion, minced (about 1 cup)

1 medium garlic clove, minced

4 large eggs, lightly beaten

1½ cups fresh bread crumbs or finely ground panko bread crumbs

2 teaspoons coarse salt

½ teaspoon freshly ground black pepper

2 teaspoons plus 2 tablespoons extra-virgin olive oil, divided

2 quarts homemade beef stock or prepared beef broth, or lamb stock, if you have it

Chef Tom Kearney is always trying to deliver something fresh and unexpected in a familiar package. "I love the homespun aspect of it, the familiarity of the meatballs—but they deliver the flavor of lamb," he says. This recipe makes excellent use of all those dried herbs in your spice rack; the flavors really hold their own during the cooking process and shine through in every bite.

1. If using dried beans, soak the beans overnight in room-temperature water to cover. (If using fresh beans, shell the beans and skip to step 3.)

2. To cook the beans, drain the beans and place in a medium sauce pot with 5 cups water, the salt, bay leaf, and bacon (if using). Simmer over low heat for 1 to 1½ hours, or until the center of the beans reaches a creamy texture.

3. If using fresh beans, bring a large pot of water to a boil. Add the shelled beans, bay leaf, and bacon (if using). Cook for 20 to 25 minutes until the beans are tender, stirring occasionally and adding the salt just before the beans are done.

4. Meanwhile, to prepare the meatballs, combine the lamb, marjoram, rosemary, onion, garlic, eggs, bread crumbs, salt, and pepper in a large bowl. Mix with clean hands until well combined. Heat 2 teaspoons of the olive oil in a 7- to 8-quart Dutch oven or sauce pot over medium heat. Form one small meatball and sauté until the meat is no longer pink, 4 to 5 minutes. Taste the meatball and adjust the seasoning of the meat mixture as needed.

5. Use a 2-ounce ice cream scoop to form 24 meatballs and lay them on a rimmed baking sheet. (Or, divide the mixture into 4 parts and make 6 meatballs per part.) Add the remaining 2 tablespoons olive oil to the pot and heat over medium-high heat until hot but not smoking. Working in batches, brown the meatballs on all sides, 5 to 6 minutes per batch. Drain the fat from the pot, then return the meatballs to the pot. Add enough beef or lamb stock to cover. Bring to a simmer over medium heat, then reduce the heat to low and allow the meatballs to simmer gently until they are cooked through, about 1 hour.

6. Remove the meatballs from the braising liquid with a slotted spoon and transfer to a large platter or baking sheet. Tent the platter with foil to keep the meatballs warm. Strain the braising liquid and reserve.

7. To make the vegetables, heat a large sauté pan over medium heat and add the olive oil. Add the cipollini onions, season with salt and pepper, and cook, stirring occasionally, until golden, about 10 minutes. Add the escarole, season with salt and pepper, and cook until just wilted, 2 or 3 minutes. Add the beans and ¼ cup of the reserved meatball cooking liquid, stirring to combine.

8. To serve, spoon the onions, escarole, and beans with the pan juices into bowls. Top with 3 or 4 meatballs per serving and garnish with Parmigiano-Reggiano and the parsley and celery leaves.

For the vegetables

¼ cup extra-virgin olive oil

15 cipollini onions, peeled and quartered

Coarse salt and freshly ground black pepper

1 head escarole, about 1¼ pounds, trimmed, leaves cut into 2-inch pieces and rinsed well

For serving

Freshly grated Parmigiano-Reggiano cheese

¼ cup fresh flat-leaf parsley leaves

¼ cup celery leaves

Chilled Pea Soup with Fresh Lump Crabmeat / THE FARM ON ADDERLEY

This is a clean, beautiful soup that works year-round; use fresh peas when they're in season or frozen any other time. Unlike so many vegetable soups that are thickened with butter or cream, this one uses neither, showcasing the featured ingredient's natural flavor (with an assist from the sautéed onions). "We cook in the restaurant with water a lot," says chef Tom Kearney. "A lot of the vegetables are just heated up in water, which lets them speak for themselves. And the crab here has a kind of natural butteriness, its own richness."

MAKES 4 SERVINGS (ABOUT 6 CUPS)

6 tablespoons canola oil, divided

1 small yellow onion, cut into ¼-inch dice

Coarse salt and freshly ground black pepper

3 cups shelled fresh English peas or frozen peas, thawed (if using fresh peas, add 1 teaspoon sugar or ¾ teaspoon agave nectar)

½ pound lump crabmeat, about 1½ cups loosely packed, picked over

Grated zest of ½ lemon, plus ½ tablespoon freshly squeezed lemon juice

Grated zest of ½ lime, plus ½ tablespoon freshly squeezed lime juice

1 medium garlic clove, minced

1 or 2 teaspoons extra-virgin olive oil, plus more for drizzling

1. Heat 3 tablespoons of the canola oil in a large sauté pan over medium-low heat. Add the onion, season with salt and pepper, and cook until translucent but not brown, about 5 minutes. Transfer to a bowl and reserve.

2. Prepare an ice bath. Bring a large pot of generously salted water to a boil. Add the peas to the boiling water. Blanch fresh peas for 2 or 3 minutes or frozen peas for 1 minute. Transfer the peas to the ice bath for 1 minute, then drain. Combine the peas, reserved onion, and 1 cup water in a blender and puree until smooth. With the motor running, slowly drizzle in the remaining 3 tablespoons canola oil. Season with salt and pepper. If using fresh peas, add sugar or agave nectar.

3. In a medium bowl, combine the crabmeat, lemon zest and juice, lime zest and juice, garlic, and olive oil. Toss until well combined. Season with salt and pepper.

4. To serve, divide the soup among 4 bowls. Place 2 heaping tablespoons of crabmeat in the center and finish with a drizzle of olive oil.

FLATBUSH FARM

PARK SLOPE

It's a witty sign: FARM in a modern sans-serif font, huge red block letters, juxtaposed against the meaning of the word, which itself is juxtaposed against Flatbush Avenue, one of the most clogged and charmless boulevards in Brooklyn. Sure, there may be some arable land down near the Atlantic Center, but it's about to be covered by a basketball arena.

You get the sense that the owner, Damon Gorton, thinks the sign is pretty funny, too. But you can't be sure, because the man doesn't laugh much. Doesn't talk much, either. Here's what he'll tell you: He's been in the restaurant business, more or less, since college. He had his own place in the city in the late 1990s, an organic café called Babylon. He was inspired by Williamsburg pioneers like Oznot's Dish and Diner. So he decided to open Flatbush Farm in August 2006. And that's it. His weird reticence is kind of refreshing. Gorton doesn't have a self-promotional bone in his body.

The restaurant doesn't call that much attention to itself, either, but it's a perfectly pleasant companion, especially at brunch. Try the Ranch Hand breakfast: two eggs sunny-side up over braised corn tortillas, flavored with salty crumbly cheese, wafer-thin slices of radish, herbs, and salsa. (And while they're cooking your food, order a boozy, well-made Bloody Mary.) At dinner, don't deny yourself the pork belly (see page 130), which may be the best of its kind in Brooklyn. A good bet on any given night is whatever grass-fed beef chef David Gulino is serving; the cut and preparation change on a regular basis.

As for that city-country thing Gorton is playing with on the sign out front, it continues inside, too, but more subtly. The décor is modern, but not aggressively so: high ceilings, exposed bulbs, a rectangular chandelier. This aesthetic harmonizes just fine with the rural motif, which is conveyed with a light touch. Antique farm tools—a rake, a shovel—are displayed behind the bar, near a little drawing of a pig. Meanwhile, the sound system plays Radiohead. Just another day on the FARM.

Braised Pork Belly with Fennel-Apple-Chile Salad and Mustard Verde / FLATBUSH FARM

SERVES 8 AS A FIRST COURSE

One 2- to 2½-pound pork belly, skin on and scored

For the pork-belly cure

½ cup brown sugar

¼ cup coarse salt

½ tablespoon crushed coriander seed

½ tablespoon ground fennel seed

1 ground star anise

1 teaspoon freshly ground black pepper

1 tablespoon fresh thyme leaves

½ tablespoon cayenne pepper

Canola oil to cover, about 48 ounces

For the mustard verde

1 tablespoon Dijon mustard

½ Spanish onion, coarsely chopped

¼ cup sherry vinegar

2 tablespoons honey

1 cup canola oil

¼ cup chopped mixed fresh herbs: cilantro, tarragon, flat-leaf parsley

4 tablespoons whole-grain mustard

Coarse salt and freshly ground black pepper

Pork! Brooklyn chefs are obsessed with it, and David Gulino at Flatbush Farm is no exception. And nothing's porkier than pork belly. This is full-contact eating—rich, salty, swiney—but Gulino's dish is nicely balanced with heat from the serrano and the cool, sweet crunch of the apple and fennel. (The tangy sauce doesn't hurt, either.) Small doses, though. This is an excellent first course—as long as the main course is something lighter.

1. To prepare the pork belly, combine all the curing mixture ingredients except the oil in a medium bowl. Sprinkle the bottom of a 9 x 13-inch roasting pan with half of the curing mixture. Lay the pork belly on top, skin side up. Rub the skin side with the remaining cure mixture. Cover with plastic wrap and refrigerate for 24 to 36 hours.

2. Preheat the oven to 250°F.

3. Use a paper towel to wipe the curing mixture from the pork belly, then rinse and pat dry. Place the belly in a large Dutch oven with a tight-fitting lid. Add the canola oil (the belly should be covered) and heat over medium heat until the oil registers 275°F on a thermometer. Cover the pan and roast for 3 to 4 hours, or until the belly is tender. Remove the belly from the oil, blot with a paper towel, and allow to cool completely.

4. To make the mustard verde, while the pork belly is warming, combine the Dijon mustard, onion, sherry vinegar, and honey in a blender and puree until incorporated. Add the canola oil in a slow, steady stream, until the mixture is emulsified. Fold in the herbs and whole-grain mustard and season with salt and pepper.

5. When ready to serve, preheat the oven 400°F. Slice the pork into 24 pieces and lay them on a rimmed baking sheet. Roast until the belly is warmed, crispy, and tender, turning once halfway through, about 15 minutes.

6. To make the salad, in a large bowl, toss the fennel, apples, serrano chile, lemon juice, and basil until well combined. Season with salt and pepper.

7. To serve, divide the salad among 8 plates. Spread 2 tablespoons of the mustard verde on each plate, alongside 3 pieces of the pork belly. Garnish with gooseberries.

For the fennel-apple-chile salad

1½ fennel bulbs, trimmed and thinly sliced

2 Granny Smith apples, peeled, cored, and julienned

1 serrano chile, thinly sliced (seeded if you want a less spicy salad)

Juice of ½ lemon

Thai basil or regular basil, chiffonade-cut

Coarse salt and freshly ground black pepper

Ripe gooseberries (available May through August), husked, rinsed, trimmed, and halved, for garnish (optional)

Molten Chocolate Cake with Chocolate Sauce / FLATBUSH FARM

SERVES 6

For the molten chocolate cake

10 ounces dark chocolate (70% cacao, preferably Valrhona)

14 tablespoons (1¾ sticks) unsalted butter, cut into ½-inch cubes

1 cup granulated sugar

5 large eggs

Confectioners' sugar, for dusting

Vanilla ice cream, for serving

Blackberries, for garnish (optional)

Fresh mint sprigs, for garnish (optional)

For the chocolate sauce

5 ounces dark chocolate (70% cacao, preferably Valrhona)

9 ounces heavy cream

1 tablespoon (½ ounce) dark rum

There's not a whole lot to say about this recipe. It's incredibly easy to make and includes the word *molten,* possibly the sexiest adjective in the English language.

1. Preheat the oven to 350°F.

2. **To make the cake,** combine the chocolate and butter in a metal bowl over simmering water or in a double boiler, mixing frequently until melted.

3. In a separate bowl, mix the granulated sugar and eggs, whisking until well combined. Temper the sugar-egg mixture by adding a small amount of the melted chocolate, whisking constantly. Add the remaining chocolate, whisking until incorporated.

4. Spray six 4-ounce ramekins with nonstick cooking spray. Divide the batter among the prepared molds, filling about three-quarters full. Bake for 15 to 18 minutes, until the outside edges of the cakes are set and the middle still looks a little wet.

5. **Meanwhile, to make the chocolate sauce,** combine the chocolate and cream in a double boiler, stirring occasionally until melted and smooth. Remove from the heat and whisk in the rum. Set aside.

6. **To serve,** unmold each cake and place it on a plate. Dust with the confectioners' sugar and drizzle the cake and plate with the chocolate sauce. Serve with vanilla ice cream, and if using, garnish with blackberries and a mint sprig.

MAST BROTHERS
CHOCOLATE / WILLIAMSBURG

RICK AND MICHAEL MAST

Mast Brothers Chocolate is one of only a handful of "bean to bar" chocolate makers in America and the only one in New York City. This means they buy their beans from the source and roast them themselves. Rick, the chief chocolate maker, is a former cook who's worked at Gramercy Tavern and Soho House as well as at Jacques Torres's chocolate factory in Manhattan. Michael, who comes from the financial side of film and TV production, focuses more on business matters. The brothers grew up in Iowa City, Iowa, and have been known to wear beard nets in the kitchen.

What's the main reason you decided to become chocolate makers?

RICK: In restaurants, you have to deal with annoying customers. But with chocolate, anytime people talk about it, they start smiling. When they taste it, even if it's bad chocolate, they're like, "Oh, this is great!" Also the idea that this kind of chocolate making is brand-new. The way the microbrewery scene was about twenty years ago, that's where chocolate is now. There's just this untrodden path.

So it's sometime in 2007 and you say to yourselves . . .

RICK: I had finished at Jacques Torres, and I talked to my brother—I'm an idea guy, right? And I love food. I'm a *food* idea guy. My brother is much more business-minded. So I've always given him ideas, saying, *Here's something we could do.* My whole life, he's always been like, "Rick, shut up." But when I told him about this bean-to-bar chocolate idea, he said,

"You might be onto something here." I was like, "What?! All right!" We were roommates at the time, and we decided we were gonna live apart for the summer, and just get away from the idea and see if we were still eager to do it. And if we were, on September 4, 2007, we were gonna do it. We were, and so we did.

How much chocolate can you make in your factory?

MICHAEL: We're doing about 2,000 to 2,500 bars a week now. We could probably double that before outgrowing this space. We joke lately that we started out reading about and being passionate about and loving making chocolate. Next thing you know, we're reading books on management.

Your beans come from farmers in Madagascar, Venezuela, the Dominican Republic, and Ecuador. Do you blend the beans or keep them separate?

RICK: Pretty separate right now. We really want to work with the origins for a while and develop those relationships, then we'll start blending.

What kind of sugar do you use?

RICK: We're actually in the middle of doing sugar experiments. There are two general schools of thought in chocolate making. Do you choose your sugar like you would choose a cocoa bean? From the best region, the best flavor, and all that stuff? Or does that just detract from the cacao flavor you're going for, and so you should use a general sugar instead. We've tended to use the fancy raw cane sugars from exotic regions, but we just bought a bunch of Domino's sugar just to see what would happen.

MICHAEL: It just depends on what bean we're working on. The beauty of being small is being able to switch things up a little bit more. Not every batch tastes exactly the same, but that's kind of the fun of what we do.

You've talked about doing a "chocolate board" dessert at Frankies 457 and Prime Meats—like a cheese board, except with chocolate. Will we see that on those menus soon?

MICHAEL: We're getting some new beans in from different regions, and I think we're going to wait until we have those. Because I think part of the fun is having variety—different regions so people can really tell the difference, and really get the true flavors of the beans.

When you were first getting started, you bartered chocolate to the Marlow & Sons guys in exchange for your convection oven. Many words have been spilled about Brooklyn's we're-all-in-this-togetherness. What's your take on that?

RICK: Well, I think it's more common here. Most people who come to New York arrive with ambitions and stars in their eyes—they want to *do* something. Same for the people who end up in Brooklyn, which historically is such a tight community, but Brooklyn combines those two things. So you've got these ambitious creators who are drawn to Brooklyn because of the community vibe. When I get off the subway here from Manhattan, I breathe a big sigh of relief.

PALO SANTO

PARK SLOPE

The first time we met Jacques Gautier, he was right where he loves to be: standing in the open kitchen of Palo Santo, serving his nine-course tasting menu (with wine pairings) to a pair of appreciative and increasingly intoxicated customers. (Us.)

He was just a few feet away, and though he was busy keeping track of all the other dishes coming off the line, we got more than our share of his attention. (The tasting menu's available at the bar only, so Gautier can pace, plate, and serve the meal himself.) Over an exuberant three-hour feast—highlights include ceviche of lobster, clams, and shrimp; pan-roasted bluefish with corn, coconut, and collard greens; and braised rabbit with raisins, olives, fingerling potatoes, and summer squash—we heard the full story of Gautier and Palo Santo. How he'd worked at Vong in Manhattan and Azie in San Francisco before becom-

ing chef at a Williamsburg restaurant called La Brunette, now closed. How he'd spent a year traveling in Latin America before opening Palo Santo, working at restaurants (and an Argentinian winery) along the way. How that journey, along with childhood visits to relatives in Cuba, Puerto Rico, and the Dominican Republic (and the influence of his Haitian father, who helped him open Palo Santo), informed his self-described "Latin Market" cooking. How he'd found this brownstone after a long search back in 2005 and proceeded to gut the ground-level space, formerly an Italian market and then a storefront church, for the restaurant. How he'd planned to do an architecturally correct restoration, but then decided it would be a lot more fun (and a lot more affordable) to mix new with the old, repurposing not just the original floorboards but also materials scavenged from the neighborhood and beyond. ("Four or five years ago, every single block in Park Slope and Carroll Gardens had three or four brownstones that were being

renovated," he says. "People were throwing away doors, wood, bricks. We took all that stuff.") How the resulting décor—candlelight, exposed brick, bursts of colorful mosaics, and giant burlap sacks that once held oats, cumin, and cinnamon—is instantly transporting, even in the cold drab middle of a Brooklyn February. And how he buys local ingredients whenever possible—those pickled chile peppers he uses in March were sourced from a New Jersey farmer in late August—but doesn't let food politics stop him from serving pumpkin chowder in a coconut.

Besides, his credentials on that front are pretty impeccable. On the roof of the brownstone that houses the restaurant, as well as Gautier's apartment, is an urban farm that provides the kitchen with tomatillos, squash, tomatoes, and enough herbs to make chimichurri sauce all summer long. How much more local can you get?

Bluefish with Plantain, Hot Slaw, and Salsa Verde / PALO SANTO

SERVES 6

For the hot slaw

½ small head red cabbage, cored and shredded (about 7 cups)

1 scotch bonnet pepper, seeded and minced

1 garlic clove, minced

1 tablespoon white wine vinegar

2 tablespoons extra-virgin olive oil

Coarse salt and freshly ground black pepper

For the salsa verde

10 ounces small green tomatoes or tomatillos, husked and rinsed, or a combination of both

⅓ cup minced fresh chives

2 cups minced fresh cilantro leaves

1 jalapeño, seeded and minced

Juice of 1 lime

1 tablespoon extra-virgin olive oil

Coarse salt

For the plantains

3 very ripe large plantains

1 tablespoon melted butter

For the fish

Six 8-ounce bluefish fillets

Coarse salt and freshly ground black pepper

¼ cup canola oil

Poor bluefish. Fishermen consider them too easy to catch (but do give credit for how hard they fight), and diners tend to dismiss their flesh as "too oily," preferring it smoked. But the truth is, super-fresh bluefish can be fantastic. It just needs to be paired with flavors that don't back down. And that's exactly what chef Jacques Gautier has done here. The heat in the slaw stands right up to the fish, as does the bracing citrus in the salsa verde. (Make extra slaw; it's a versatile condiment and will keep for at least a month in the fridge.) As for the plantain, the riper the better. Don't be afraid to use them after they've turned black.

1. Preheat the oven to 425°F.

2. **To make the hot slaw,** combine the cabbage, scotch bonnet, garlic, vinegar, and olive oil in a large mixing bowl. Season to taste with salt and pepper and set aside to marinate.

3. **To make the salsa verde,** using a paring knife, make a small x on the bottom of each tomato or tomatillo. Bring a pot of water to a boil and prepare an ice bath. Blanch the tomatoes or tomatillos in the boiling water until the skin starts to split, 10 to 20 seconds. Plunge them in the ice bath, then remove them with a slotted spoon. Peel them, discard the seeds, and chop them. Place the tomatoes or tomatillos in a small mixing bowl with the chives, cilantro, jalapeño, and lime juice. Stir in the olive oil and season to taste with salt. Set aside.

4. **To prepare the plantains,** roast them on a rimmed baking sheet until they puff up and burst, about 20 minutes. Remove from the oven and set them aside to cool slightly. When they are cool enough to handle, slice them in half lengthwise and brush the cut surfaces with melted butter. Place them cut side up on the baking sheet and return them to the oven until they are golden brown, 5 to 10 minutes.

5. **To prepare the fish,** heat a large ovenproof sauté pan over medium-high heat. Season the fish with salt and pepper. Add the canola oil to the sauté pan and carefully place the fish in the pan, skin side down.

Cook for 2 to 3 minutes, or until the skin turns golden brown, then place the pan in the oven to finish cooking, about 5 minutes, or until the fish is opaque in the center.

6. To serve, place an unpeeled plantain half on each plate and a small mound of the hot slaw next to the plantain. Place a piece of fish on top of the slaw and garnish it with 2 tablespoons of the salsa verde.

Chayote Salad with Grapefruit and Vanilla / PALO SANTO

Back in 2001, when he was working at a French Caribbean restaurant in Williamsburg, chef Jacques Gautier made a version of this salad for a reviewer from a local Haitian-American newspaper. When the dish arrived, the man took one look at it and said, "Where's the chayote?"

A member of the squash family, Chayote is a kind of comfort food in the Caribbean and in Central America, where it's typically boiled until soft and served in soups or with a little butter as a side dish. Slicing it thin and eating it raw, as this recipe calls for, is rare in many places where it's a staple of the cuisine. But it works beautifully, adding crunch and texture to a salad with no shortage of flavor. And it speaks to the central theme of Gautier's cooking: giving uncommon treatment to common ingredients, and producing unexpected dishes in the process.

1. Combine the grapefruit juice and the split vanilla bean in a small saucepan. Simmer over low heat until the juice is reduced by one third. (It is best to do this at the lowest flame possible so you don't scorch the reduction. This may take up to an hour.)

2. Remove the saucepan from the heat and let cool to room temperature. Strain through a fine-mesh strainer. Transfer the reduction to a large mixing bowl. Slowly add the olive oil, whisking until emulsified.

3. Thinly slice the chayote, preferably on a mandoline. Layer the watercress and chayote on 6 serving plates as follows: watercress, chayote, watercress, chayote, watercress. Top with the grapefruit segments, drizzle with the dressing, and season with salt and pepper.

SERVES 6 AS A FIRST COURSE

4 small grapefruits, 2 juiced (about 1 cup) and 2 cut into segments

1 fresh vanilla bean, split in half lengthwise

2 tablespoons extra-virgin olive oil

3 chayote (about 2¼ pounds), peeled,* halved, and seeded

1 bunch watercress, cleaned and picked (about 7 ounces)

Coarse salt and freshly ground black pepper

* If the chayote is young and the skin is light green and rather smooth, you don't need to peel it.

LUNETTA

BOERUM HILL

Don't get us wrong: Adam Shepard is proud of the food he serves at Lunetta, a contemporary-Italian restaurant with an emphasis on market ingredients, small plates, and big flavors. Here are a few phrases plucked randomly from a typical Lunetta dinner menu: spicy mayo, garlic-anchovy dressing, pork belly alla porchetta, spaghetti carbonara, smoked pancetta, and porcini-rubbed hanger steak. You get the gist. You've had it all before, yes, but you'll want it all again. And again after that.

But if you want to see Shepard (below left) *really* light up—and he's a fairly jaded restaurant lifer, so he doesn't light up easily—ask him about a pair of spin-off businesses started by his employees. You can read about one, a ricotta producer called Salvatore Bklyn, on page 90. The other, Pizza Moto, a staple of the Brooklyn Flea, is a mobile pizza truck. (Its motto: "Truckin' Good Pizza!") Shepard's like a proud daddy who can't stop gushing about his offspring. "Salvatore and Pizza Moto are incredible businesses, both of them," he says. "My utopia is to have this place be not only a restaurant but kind of a cauldron of talent where we're building and spitting out these great businesses that are great for the food scene in general, but the Brooklyn food scene especially."

Betsy Devine, the cofounder and cheesemaker at Salvatore, rarely

cooks these days at Lunetta, which she opened with Shepard after working for him at Union Pacific, Rocco DiSpirito's pre-infamy restaurant in Union Square. Dave Sclarow, the founder of Pizza Moto, has moved on as well, dedicating himself full-time to his own business. Working on stage in a kitchen that's easily visible from the five-seat bar, Shepard and his new cooks turn out a crowd-pleasing selection of bruschetta, antipasti, pastas, and meat and fish courses at notably reasonable prices; very few dishes cost more than twenty dollars.

Speaking of economics, Shepard offered an unusually candid answer to a question about the state of his business in the fall of 2009, at the height of the malaise: "It's dismal, and if anyone says otherwise they're liars." But he also saw some upside to the downturn. "I think it's one of the great silver linings in this horrible economy, what we're being forced to do to bring things back down to earth, where they belong, to focus on what makes more sense for the planet as well as our pocketbooks—to focus on what's *really* available now, what's *really* coming from within a hundred miles of the store, what *really* can be used and reused and recycled. I think the economy is showing that to everybody."

Fluke Crudo / LUNETTA

SERVES 4 AS A FIRST COURSE

¾ pound fresh fluke or other lean white fish, sliced paper thin

Grated zest of 1 lemon, juice of ½ lemon

Grated zest of 1 lime, juice of ½ lime

2 teaspoons coarse salt

1 tablespoon chardonnay vinegar* or more to taste

⅓ cup julienned radish

⅓ cup julienned red bell pepper

1 small jalapeño, seeded and thinly sliced

½ small beet, peeled and julienned

½ cup celery leaves

2 teaspoons pink peppercorns, crushed and chopped

¼ cup olive oil, plus more for the greens

¼ cup canola oil

2 bay leaves

2 fresh thyme sprigs

1 small garlic clove, thinly sliced

2 ounces arugula, dandelion greens, or other bitter green

Coarse salt and freshly ground black pepper

* If you can't find chardonnay vinegar, substitute a good quality white wine vinegar.

"People have a hard time with raw fish unless they're in a Japanese restaurant, which doesn't make a whole lot of sense to me," says chef Adam Shepard. In this Italian preparation, Shepard uses an aromatic hot oil to lightly sear Long Island fluke, then serves it with julienned radishes, beets, and peppers. But if different veggies are in season when you make this, by all means use them instead. And feel free to substitute any other local fish—striped bass, for example, or even Littleneck clams—for the fluke. The point is: raw fish, hot oil, fresh veggies.

1. Arrange the fish in a single layer on a large heat-proof plate or rimmed baking sheet. Season the fish with the lemon zest and juice, lime zest and juice, salt, and vinegar. Scatter the radish, bell pepper, jalapeño, beet, and celery leaves evenly over the fish. Top the fish with the peppercorns and let the fish marinate while the oil heats.

2. Heat the olive oil and canola oil in a sauté pan over high heat until very hot and shimmering. Remove the pan from the heat and carefully add the bay leaves, thyme sprigs, and garlic to the hot oil. The water in the herbs will cause some popping and splattering. Using a large spoon, pour the hot oil over the fish one spoonful at a time until all the fish is seared. This may or may not require using all the oil.

3. Allow the fish to cool enough to handle, about 2 minutes. Discard the bay leaves and thyme. Transfer the fish and vegetables to a large bowl and gently toss to evenly coat the fish. If necessary, adjust the seasoning with more salt and vinegar.

4. Season the greens lightly with salt, pepper, and olive oil. Divide the greens among 4 plates and arrange the fish and vegetables over the greens.

Pizzette with Tomatoes and Basil / LUNETTA

MAKES 4 INDIVIDUAL-SIZE
PIZZAS

For the dough

3 cups all-purpose flour, plus more for
dusting

¼ teaspoon rapid-rise yeast

¾ teaspoon coarse salt

1⅔ cup warm water

Olive oil, as needed

For the tomato and basil topping

3 large tomatoes, chopped, or 3 cups
grape or cherry tomatoes, halved

Coarse salt and freshly ground
black pepper

20 fresh basil leaves, washed, dried,
and torn

3 tablespoons extra-virgin olive oil,
plus more for drizzling

1 teaspoon red wine vinegar

1 teaspoon freshly squeezed
lemon juice

1 cup grated Parmigiano-Reggiano or
Grana Padano cheese, divided

We didn't include recipes from Brooklyn's astounding selection of great pizzerias (see the list on page 251) for one simple reason: We don't own a 900-degree oven to bake them in. (Do you?) But this pizza-like dish is a very respectable stand-in. Adam Shepard and his former chef de cuisine, Dave Sclarow, came up with their pizzette concept when they were experimenting with leftover dough from Sclarow's MacGyveresque side project, Pizza Moto, a mobile brick oven mounted on a boat trailer. But Shepard doesn't have a pizza oven at Lunetta, either. "The way we do it is exactly the way people should make pizzas at home: in a pan," he says. "Spending money on a fancy pizza stone, trying to get your oven hotter than it should be—for the most part, you're not going to do anything but set the smoke alarms off." Mix the dough the night before you plan to make the pizzette.

1. To make the dough, combine the flour, yeast, and salt in a medium glass or stainless-steel bowl. Add the water and mix with a wooden spoon or your hands; the dough should be slack and sticky. Cover the bowl with plastic wrap, pressing down so the wrap touches the dough. Place the dough in a warm place (75°F is ideal) for 12 to 18 hours.

2. Remove the plastic wrap and dust the top of the dough with flour. Turn the dough onto a clean, generously floured work surface. Fold the dough over on itself 5 or 6 times, incorporating more flour if it's too runny or sticky. Do not overwork the dough.

3. Moisten a paper towel with olive oil and lightly coat 4 bowls large enough to hold one quarter of the dough. (Chef Adam Shepard suggests saving pint-size takeout Chinese soup containers instead of bowls.)

4. Divide the dough into 4 equal-size balls, 6 to 7 ounces each, and place them in the bowls or containers. Cover and refrigerate until ready to use. They can be held in the refrigerator for up to 5 days, or in the freezer for up to 1 month.

5. Two hours before serving, bring the dough to room temperature.

6. Preheat the oven to 500°F at least 30 minutes before baking the pizzettes.

7. Moisten a paper towel with olive oil and lightly coat an 8-inch heavy, ovenproof stainless-steel or cast-iron pan. With floured hands, place 1 ball of dough in the pan and press the dough out to the edges of the pan.

8. To make the topping, combine the tomatoes, salt and pepper, basil, olive oil, vinegar, and lemon juice in a medium bowl.

9. Distribute one quarter of the tomato mixture evenly over the dough. Sprinkle with the grated cheese, drizzle with olive oil, and season with salt. Place the pizzette in the oven and cook for 13 minutes, or until the top starts to brown and the bottom is golden brown. Slice and serve. Repeat with the rest of the dough and topping.

BEER TABLE

PARK SLOPE

"It feels risky, it feels exhilarating, it feels like we might totally screw it up," says Justin Philips, a former beer importer who opened this beer-nerd's paradise with his wife, Tricia, in February 2008. You can understand his concern. He hired Julie Farias (who'd cooked at his wedding at iCi, page 76, and is now the chef at the General Greene, page 162) to help develop the menu, and then he took over the kitchen full-time in the summer of 2009. Guess how much professional cooking experience he had? Zilch. ("I wouldn't generally call myself the chef, but I do make the food.")

Fortunately he'd learned a ton from Farias. And Beer Table's menu lends itself to on-the-job training. The Philipses offer a homey-feeling prix fixe dinner—three courses for twenty-five dollars, plus fifteen for beer pairings, available a few nights a week—and a regular menu of about a dozen snacks and small plates, including marinated picholine olives with rosemary, bay leaf, orange, and chile; a spinach salad with pears and Parmigiano-Reggiano; and *posole*, a spicy pork and hominy stew.

country and evangelizing (in his quiet, low-key way) to retailers and restaurateurs about the rare (and pricey) beers that rival the world's great wines for depth and complexity. He originally conceived Beer Table as a boutique beer store, not a bar, an idea that was complicated by New York licensing laws. (A certain percentage of sales would have had to come from grocery items, and Philips didn't want to be in that business at the time, though he hasn't ruled it out as a future project.) But the plan was always to stress the relationship between beer and food, so that led naturally to the beer bar concept and eventually to the prix-fixe menu, which started as a way to boost business on Tuesday, the slowest night of the week. "We weren't really prepared to jump in full force and play restaurant," he says. "It was kind of an experiment, just to see if people would show up."

At Beer Table, though, the question isn't so much *What do I feel like eating?* It's more like *What would go well with this beer?* The Beer Table crew loves to answer that question. In addition to a daily lineup of three or four special drafts (usually including a cask beer), Philips maintains a rotation of about twenty-five bottles from around the world, the only near-permanent selection being J.W. Lees Harvest Ale from Manchester, England. Which is fitting, since that's the beer that changed Philips's life. The first time he tasted it, he was living in Boston and working at a wine and beer shop. (He knew next to nothing about either when he started there.) "It just blew me away," he says of the Harvest Ale, which is described as "hedonistic" on Beer Table's list. "It's very much an age-worthy beer, very sweet, not something you'd drink every day. I got kind of excited about it."

He moved to New York City and spent the next four years working for a beer importer, traveling the

Pickled Eggs with Jalapeño Powder

/ BEER TABLE

MAKES 1 DOZEN EGGS

1 dozen large eggs

6 cups malt vinegar or cider vinegar

4 tablespoons coarse salt

4 tablespoons sugar

2 tablespoons whole black peppercorns

4 bay leaves

Green jalapeño powder*

Gray sea salt or coarse sea salt

* If you have a dehydrator, prepare jalapeños according to the machine's directions, then grind to a fine powder in a spice grinder. Green jalapeño powder can also be purchased in some specialty stores, especially those that sell Mexican products. In Brooklyn, it can be found at Union Market. It can also be ordered online at www.888eatchile.com or www.myspicer.com.

When Justin Philips and his wife, Tricia, opened their beer bar–restaurant in Park Slope, they were determined to avoid traditional bar snacks—with this one exception. "There's this nostalgic idea of pickled eggs sitting in a jar on the bar," Philips says. "So many people have those memories. I didn't. I'd never eaten one—the first ones we ate were the first ones we made—but I thought it was interesting. And I love vinegary flavors with beer." There's nothing traditional about the jalapeño powder, though; that's a modern touch. It looks gorgeous against the egg, and it smells a lot spicier than it tastes. Making these requires some long-term planning. Ideally they should sit in the fridge for three weeks before you serve them, but then they'll keep for up to six months.

1. Place the eggs in a large saucepan with cold water to cover. Bring to a boil. Remove from the heat, cover the pan, and allow to sit for 15 minutes. Drain the eggs and rinse them under cold water. Peel the eggs and place them in a heat-proof pan or bowl.

2. Combine the vinegar, salt, sugar, peppercorns, and bay leaves in a large saucepan. Bring to a boil over medium heat. Pour the vinegar mixture over the eggs. Allow the eggs to cool completely, then transfer the eggs and the vinegar mixture to an airtight container, cover, and refrigerate for 3 weeks before serving.

3. To serve, slice the pickled eggs in half. Sprinkle each egg with gray sea salt and green jalapeño powder.

4. After 3 weeks, discard half of the brine and replace it with the same amount of water. This will help keep the eggs from becoming rubbery.

Pickled Watermelon Rind / BEER TABLE

This recipe was developed by Julie Farias, who did a part-time stint at Beer Table before taking over the kitchen at the General Greene. It's more of an Italian-style *mostarda di frutta* than a pickle, with lots of sugar and dried mustard seeds that blend into a sweet, tangy flavor. Give it at least three days in the brine and then serve it just like they do at Beer Table, with a Belgian blond ale.

1. Scrub the watermelon with a brush under running lukewarm water. Cut the watermelon in quarters and remove the flesh (use for another purpose). Slice the rind, then peel and cut into 1-inch cubes. Set aside.

2. In a large nonreactive saucepan, combine the vinegar, water, honey, sugar, mustard seeds, ginger, and Colman's Mustard and bring to a boil over medium heat.

3. Add the watermelon rind and return to a boil. Cook for 5 minutes, then remove from the heat and allow to cool completely. Transfer the watermelon and pickling liquid to an airtight container, cover, and refrigerate for 3 days before serving. The pickles will last in the refrigerator for up to 3 months.

MAKES ABOUT 8 CUPS

1 large watermelon, about 8 pounds, to yield about 2½ pounds firm watermelon rind

2 cups unseasoned rice wine vinegar

2 cups water

1 cup honey

1 cup sugar

½ cup whole mustard seeds

One 2-inch piece fresh ginger, peeled and crushed

2 tablespoons Colman's Mustard (dry powdered mustard)

CUT BROOKLYN / GOWANUS

JOEL BUKIEWICZ

Before he started making knives, Joel Bukiewicz wrote a novel. No publisher wanted to buy it. So he started another one. After about 150 pages, he gave up that one, too. "It was terrible," he says. "It was awful." He stopped writing, but he needed a creative outlet. So he started making knives. And he was good at it. Really good. So he started selling them. *Holy shit,* he thought. *People want to pay me for these?* They do—and they're willing to wait. As of this writing, if you order a knife from Bukiewicz—a knife that he makes entirely by hand in his cluttered workshop beneath the Smith-Ninth Street stop on the F train—you'll get it a year later.

You started out making hunting knives in Georgia. That's pretty far—physically as well as culturally—from making kitchen knives in Brooklyn.

Yeah. There's a whole subculture devoted to these knife shows. It's not a complete crossover with gun shows, but it's not *exactly* my people. Don't get me wrong: There are really great people in that world. I just felt like I was at the wrong college or something. So, knowing that I was coming back to Brooklyn, I thought, *Let's start designing a kitchen line.* How hard can it be? It turned out to be *really* hard. I probably went through forty prototypes before I got it right.

Who taught you how to do this?

Nobody. I've never actually visited another knife-maker's shop. I'm self-taught. I just read up as much as I could.

Never visited a single shop? That's amazing.

I know, it's a little weird. It could be I'm doing everything completely backward. But there are plenty of books out there that tell you the basics. I mean, there's only maybe five or six steps involved. Of course, there's a difference between knowing what they are and being able to do them well. But I was just good at

No, knock on wood, nothing too bad. But I've poked myself good a couple times. Last year I was getting knives ready for the Unfancy Food Show. The night before, I was hustling to get some stuff done. It was like four in the morning, and I had just finished one of these French-style knives, but the handle wasn't on it yet. I was going over here [points to a piece of equipment], and I felt like I brushed my arm. I looked down at it, and this rope of blood just went [makes a shooting sound and an arcing motion through the air]. I was like *Woaah-hhh*. I put a cotton ball and some duct tape around it, and it stopped. But it's only a matter of time before something bad happens.

it really fast. I take my time. What you give up is speed.

How long does it take you to make a knife?

Ten to twelve hours each, for the larger pieces.

What's been the hardest thing for you to master?

Grinding is a really weird thing, when you grind a blade freehand. On any given day, it never seems exactly the same. One day my one hand—like when I grind this way I'll be doing great, and then this way it'll be all weird. I can't get the lines that I want. If it just isn't working, I'll walk away for ten or fifteen minutes. That's one of the best things I've learned here in the shop. If things aren't going well, you gotta just back off.

Like writing.

It's exactly like that. It didn't take me long to recognize the *really* close parallels between busting my ass to turn out a thousand words a day and trying to turn out a knife. You work your butt off and at the end of the day you've done something beautiful and good. And that's all it is. It's just work, you know? Maybe it's a book or maybe it's a story or a photograph or a knife. There's a certain methodology to good work. The patience that's required. And I think that's part of the reason that people are doing so well in the borough now. None of these guys [making artisanal food in Brooklyn] is interested in being a millionaire tomorrow. They just want to do things right. I'm okay producing six knives a week for now. And if you can be patient like that, and love the work for what it is, then I think that shows in the results. And it improves your own quality of life.

JAMES

PROSPECT HEIGHTS

As soon as you walk in, you know you'll be back. A regular (you can just tell) is perched at the end of the bar, sipping something soothing and flipping through the *Times*. Each of the restaurant's ten tables glows with a single votive, supplementing the early-evening light that slants in from the windows facing Carlton Avenue. A plush, deep-brown leather bench runs the length of one long wall, wrapping around the corners and forming the best tables at either end. By the time you've tucked in with a James' Revenge (rye, Cointreau, sweet vermouth, bitters, blood orange) and a plate of grilled brioche and soft butter with chives and sea salt, you feel as comfortable as that guy at the bar. Which is exactly what chef Bryan Calvert and his wife, Deborah Williamson, were going for when they opened in August 2008. James is a neighborhood place that's serious about food, but not so serious that it loses its identity as a neighborhood place.

A dozen years earlier, Calvert had moved to Prospect Heights as a young cook with more ambition than rent money. Back then the space that now houses James was a bodega with bulletproof glass between the customer and the register. But as Calvert's career developed— he was Rocco DiSpirito's sous chef at Union Pacific in Manhattan and a partner at Café Atlas before opening a catering company, Williamson Calvert, with Deborah—so did the neighborhood. In 2005 the bodega morphed into a New American restaurant called Sorrel. But Sorrel,

maybe a couple years ahead of its time for the location, never quite clicked. When the owners decided to sell, Calvert and Williamson, who were living in the apartment directly upstairs (and still are), leaped at the chance to open their own place.

The menu reflects the chef's big-city training filtered through Williamson's more relaxed sensibility. "She kinda reins me in," says Calvert, whose food can feel familiar (burger with New York cheddar on brioche with herb fries), adventurous (cauliflower soup with smoked sturgeon, Marcona almonds, and lovage oil),

or somewhere in between (quail with duck sausage, Brussels sprouts, and hazelnuts). Sweetbreads are almost always on the menu, mainly because Bryan loves them but also because his mother went into labor while eating a plate of them in a West Village café. (Another family theme in the James story: The restaurant is named after Bryan's great-grandfather, a New York chef named James Calvert.) While Calvert's generous portions make it easy to skip dessert, don't. There are usually at least five or six choices, the ricotta beignets on page 160 often among them.

Spring Onion Soup with
Boar Lardon and Pecorino / JAMES

SERVES 6

For the soup

2 slices thick-cut boar bacon* or regular bacon, cut crosswise into ¼-inch cubes

1 bunch spring or summer onions with greens, about 1¾ pounds

2 ramps or 6 garlic chives

2 shallots

6 tablespoons (¾ stick) unsalted butter

1 cup chopped spinach leaves

¼ cup dry white wine

1 fresh thyme sprig

Coarse salt and freshly ground black pepper

¼ cup grated Pecorino Fiori Sardo or Pecorino Romano cheese

For the croutons

1 tablespoon unsalted butter

¼ cup small cubes sourdough or country bread

* Boar bacon, available in specialty groceries and online at dartagnan.com, is meatier and heartier than pork bacon; it also has one third less fat.

What better way to usher in the spring than with a spring onion soup? The onions have a fragrant, mellow flavor that goes well with the sharpness of the Pecorino and the richness of the lardon. "It's a simple soup that has straightforward flavors and is fairly easy to make," says chef Bryan Calvert. "And I think it really captures the essence of that spring freshness." The homemade croutons may seem like extra fuss, but they're worth the effort. They add crunch and somehow bring all the flavors together.

1. To make the soup, in a medium saucepan, cook the bacon over medium heat, stirring occasionally, until the fat is rendered and the bacon is crispy.

2. Meanwhile, clean the onions and ramps by separating the green tops from the white bulbs. Rinse thoroughly. Chop the onion bulbs, ramp bulbs, and shallots into medium dice. Coarsely chop the greens from the ramps, garlic, and onions.

3. Remove the bacon from the pot, leaving behind the rendered fat. Reduce the heat to medium low and add the butter. Add the diced onion bulbs, ramp bulbs, and shallots. Sauté, stirring occasionally, until tender but not brown, 10 to 15 minutes. Add the onion greens, ramp greens, and spinach and cook until tender, about 10 minutes.

4. Add the wine, increase the heat to medium high, and cook until the wine evaporates, 4 to 5 minutes. Add 4 cups water and the thyme sprig. Bring to a simmer and cook for 10 minutes more. Discard the thyme. Transfer the soup to a blender and puree until smooth. Return the soup to the pot over low heat and season with salt and pepper. Adjust the consistency with water and heat until warmed through.

5. To make the croutons, melt the butter in a small sauté pan over medium-high heat. Add the bread cubes, toss to coat, and cook until the bread is golden brown. Season with salt and pepper.

6. To serve, divide the soup among 6 soup bowls and top with lardon, grated cheese, and croutons.

Ricotta Beignets with
Red Wine Berry Coulis / JAMES

**MAKES 12 TO 14 BEIGNETS;
SERVES 4 OR 5**

For the beignet batter

3 tablespoons granulated sugar

3 tablespoons honey

½ pound cream cheese, at room temperature

¼ cup fresh sheep's-milk ricotta cheese or whole cow's-milk ricotta*

Grated zest of ½ lemon

3 large eggs

¼ cup whole milk

¼ cup heavy cream

*For the red wine berry coulis
(makes 1⅓ cups)*

½ cup dry red wine

½ cup granulated sugar

**1 pint fresh raspberries,
plus more for garnish**

**1 pint fresh blueberries,
plus more for garnish**

1 cup cornstarch

**1 cup confectioners' sugar,
plus more for garnish**

2 cups unsweetened shredded coconut

4 large eggs, lightly beaten

Vegetable oil, for frying

Fresh mint sprigs, for garnish

* *Try making your own ricotta.
See page 88 for directions.*

This dessert might sound like the product of some haute kitchen in New Orleans, but chef Bryan Calvert puts the inspiration much closer to home. "The cheesecake is so Brooklyn, it's a take on that," he says. Calvert's referring to what the beignets are, essentially, before the frying oil transforms them. Add the berry coulis, though, and this dessert becomes something wholly new. (You won't use all the coulis, but that's good; refrigerate and save for drizzling over vanilla ice cream.) The ideal time to make this dish is mid- to late summer, at the height of berry season.

1. Preheat the oven to 325°F. Grease an 8-inch round cake pan and set aside.

2. To make the beignet batter, combine the granulated sugar, honey, and cream cheese in a bowl with an electric mixer and cream until smooth. Add the ricotta and zest, and mix until combined. Add 1 egg at a time, incorporating each one fully before adding the next. Add the milk and cream.

3. Pour the mixture into the prepared cake pan and place it in a large shallow baking pan. Prepare a water bath by filling the baking pan with hot water so that it comes halfway up the side of the cake pan. Bake for 1 hour, or until a skewer inserted into the center of the cake comes out clean.

4. Remove the cake pan from the water bath, transfer to a rack, and cool, about 1 hour.

5. Meanwhile, to make the coulis, combine the wine, granulated sugar, 1 pint raspberries, and 1 pint blueberries in a nonreactive saucepan. Simmer and reduce until the mixture starts to thicken, about 30 minutes. Press through a fine-mesh strainer into a bowl, extracting as much liquid as possible with the back of a spoon or a spatula; discard the seeds and skins. Set aside to cool. The sauce will continue to thicken as it cools.

6. When the cake is cool, mix the cornstarch and confectioners' sugar in a bowl. Place the coconut in a separate small bowl and the eggs in a third bowl. Use a 2-ounce ice cream scoop to carefully form the beignets from the cake. Coat the beignets with the sugar mixture, then dip them in the egg and roll in the coconut.

7. Heat the vegetable oil in a deep fryer or deep pot until it registers 325°F on a deep-fry thermometer. Working in batches, fry the beignets, turning once, until golden brown, about 3 minutes. Remove the beignets with a slotted spoon and drain them on a paper towel.

8. To serve, place the sauce on a plate. Arrange 3 beignets on top of the sauce and garnish with the remaining raspberries, blueberries, or a mix of both, and the mint sprigs. Dust the beignets with confectioners' sugar.

THE GENERAL GREENE

FORT GREENE

We'll never fall out of love with diners, especially the Greek diners of Manhattan. The brusque service, the absurdly comprehensive menu (*shrimp scampi*?), the limp pickle that comes with your BLT—these sound like complaints, right? They're not. There's something timeless and reassuring about sliding into a booth, ordering a turkey club and black coffee, and flipping through the *Post*. If Greek diners disappeared on us, we'd mourn them. Hard.

But if the General Greene is the diner of the future, that would ease our suffering. This bright, convivial hangout in the heart of Fort Greene specializes in a fresher form of com-

fort—cheddar and smoked ham scramble, smoked trout melt with red onions, arugula, and Gruyère, and in a nod to its forebears, a "Greene Greek salad"—from early morning until late at night, all at prices that are no higher than traditional diners across the East River. Here's owner Nicholas Morgenstern, a former pastry chef and veteran of some of Manhattan's boldest-face kitchens (Daniel, Gilt, Five Ninth), on his restaurant's overarching philosophy: "What we put on the menu here is meant to be familiar. You should be able to say, Oh, I recognize *that*, and I want to eat that because it's something I remember. But then when you get your food, it should just exceed your expectation by being a little bit better and a little bit more interesting than what you

remember. It's like, *There's ten percent of something extra in there . . .*"

Robin Raisfeld and Rob Patronite, who write the excellent Underground Gourmet column for *New York* magazine, agreed he was succeeding. In August 2008, just a month after the General Greene opened, Raisfeld and Patronite gave the restaurant four stars out of five. Madness ensued. "We had all these people piling in from Manhattan, Town Cars parked outside," recalls Morgenstern, pictured (at right) with his chef, Julie Farias. "We're meant to be this neighborhood restaurant, but now the neighborhood can't get a seat. Waits for tables were exceeding an hour. I remember one night, there were girls from the Upper East Side who were *furious*." He sighs and grins, realizing plenty of restaurateurs would happily accept that problem. "It was just a difficult thing to manage."

Things eventually calmed down. The uptown girls headed back uptown, and the General Greene settled into the neighborhood restaurant it was designed to be. But somewhere along the way, the menu grew sprawling and unwieldy. Not quite Greek-diner unwieldy, but too big for Morgenstern's taste. So he brought in Farias, an old friend and colleague from Daniel and Five Ninth, to streamline and simplify things. She and Morgenstern both admit they've had to suppress their most experimental kitchen instincts and just give the people what they want. "Burgers and ribs sell," Morgenstern says. "So make really good burgers and ribs." Like the ribs on page 166.

Soft-Serve Raspberry Lime Frozen Yogurt

MAKES 1½ QUARTS

½ cup sugar

2 tablespoons nonfat dry milk powder

Pinch of salt

2 cups full-fat or low-fat Greek yogurt

1 cup whole milk

1 10-ounce package frozen raspberries or 10 ounces fresh raspberries

Grated zest of ½ lime plus 1 tablespoon freshly lime juice

General Greene owner Nicholas Morgenstern operates an ice cream business, Greene Ice Cream, and whenever weather permits he parks a cart with six rotating flavors right outside the restaurant.

1. Combine the sugar, milk powder, and salt in a mixing bowl. Add the yogurt and milk and whisk until completely incorporated. Fold in the raspberries and lime zest and juice.

2. Pour the mixture into the cylinder of an ice cream machine. Process and freeze according to the manufacturer's instructions.

3. Freeze for 1 hour, then serve; this timing is important to achieve that optimal soft-serve texture and flavor.

Soft Tofu with Broad Beans and Chile Bean Paste / THE GENERAL GREENE

Carnivores: You know that vaguely unsatisfied feeling you get after eating a vegetarian entrée, no matter how delicious and skillfully prepared? This tofu dish does not give you that feeling *at all*. In fact, it's the most viscerally satisfying vegetarian meal we've ever had. "It's kind of a bastardized version of *ma po* tofu," says chef Julie Farias, referring to the classic Szechuan dish. But whereas the Chinese-American version of that dish can be, in Farias's words, "a cornstarchy, thicky, gelatinous mess," this version is far more polished. It's *really* spicy, yes, but the fire brings flavor, not just heat.

SERVES 4

12 to 14 ounces soft tofu (Chef Farias likes Mori-No Silken Soft Tofu)

2 pounds fresh broad beans (fava beans), shelled (yields ½ pound), or 1½ cups frozen broad beans

¼ cup canola oil

2 garlic cloves, thinly sliced

½ cup chile bean paste (*toban djan*), such as Lee Kee Kum brand

1 celery stalk, sliced thin and the leaves reserved

½ cup fresh cilantro leaves

½ cup fried broad beans (available in Asian and Middle Eastern markets)

1. Cut the tofu into 4 equal pieces and place in 4 shallow serving bowls. Refrigerate while you prepare the broad beans.

2. Prepare an ice bath. Bring a large saucepan of salted water to a boil. Add the broad beans and cook for 2 minutes. Drain and transfer to the ice bath. Peel the skin off the beans and discard.

3. In a large sauté pan, heat the canola oil over medium heat. Add the garlic and cook until soft and translucent, 2 to 3 minutes. Add the chile bean paste and cook until aromatic, about 2 minutes. Add ½ cup water and bring to a boil. Cook until the sauce thickens slightly. Increase the heat to high and add the broad beans. Toss until the beans are heated through.

4. Combine the sliced celery, celery leaves, cilantro, and fried broad beans in a bowl. Set aside.

5. Top the bowls of cold tofu with the broad bean mixture. Garnish with the celery mixture.

Salt and Pepper Pork Ribs with
Spiced Yogurt Sauce / THE GENERAL GREENE

SERVES 4

For the rub

1 cup dark brown sugar

½ cup coarse salt

2 tablespoons coarsely ground black pepper

16 St. Louis–style pork ribs (about 2½ pounds)

For the spiced yogurt sauce

Coarse salt

2 garlic cloves, minced

1 pint Greek yogurt

2 tablespoons ground sumac,* plus more for garnish

Finely grated zest of ½ lemon

* Available in Middle Eastern markets

There's nothing magical or surprising about how these ribs are made: Shellac with a salt-pepper-sugar rub, refrigerate overnight, and slow-cook for 150 minutes. It's the sauce—Greek yogurt stained hot-pink with sumac, a Middle Eastern spice—that sets them apart. "It's a bright dish," says chef Julie Farias. "Not just boring old brown ribs." St. Louis–style ribs are cut from the spare ribs to form a neat rectangular stack, making them easier to cook and serve. Ask your butcher.

1. Combine the brown sugar, salt, and pepper in a medium bowl. Rub the ribs generously with the sugar mixture to completely coat the meat side. Cover with plastic wrap and refrigerate overnight.

2. **To cook the ribs,** place the ribs meat side up on a rimmed baking sheet and pour any liquid that has accumulated over the ribs.

3. Preheat the oven to 250°F. Position a rack in the lower third of the oven.

4. Place an empty deep 9 x 13-inch baking pan on the floor of the oven. Carefully pour boiling water into the pan—enough to fill it three-quarters full.

5. Place the baking sheet on the oven rack, above the pan of water, and cook the ribs, uncovered, for 2½ hours, or until the meat is very tender. Set the ribs aside until they are just cool enough to handle.

6. **Meanwhile, make the yogurt sauce.** Sprinkle a cutting board with a pinch of salt. Place the minced garlic on top. (The salt will help to break down the garlic.) Use the flat side of a large knife to form a paste.

7. Combine the yogurt, sumac, lemon zest, and garlic paste in a medium bowl and mix until combined. Season to taste with salt.

8. Turn the ribs over so that the meat faces down, and cut between the bones to separate the ribs.

9. **To serve,** spread a generous spoonful of yogurt sauce in the middle of each of 4 plates and place 4 ribs on each plate. Sprinkle with sumac and serve.

FIVE LEAVES

GREENPOINT

The Dark Knight and *The Imaginarium of Doctor Parnassus* aren't Heath Ledger's only gifts from the grave. Five Leaves is another. Ledger and Jud Mongell, the actor's friend and countryman, had been collaborating on the restaurant right up until Ledger died in January 2008. The Ledger family decided to honor their son's financial commitment to Five Leaves, and Mongell and his wife, Kathy Mecham, opened the restaurant in August that same year.

Located in a triangular building at the corner of Lorimer and Bedford, Five Leaves is an appealing mashup of French bistro, Australian café, and New England sailor's bar. The restaurant's prevailing personality depends on when you're there and where you're sitting. On a sunny summer day, it's all Paris—small round tables line the perimeter outside, the word OYSTERS etched in bistro font on the glass above your head. But when you sit down and scan the menu, Australia starts to assert itself. The Five Leaves Burger is a direct import, as is "The Big Breakkie," a gigantic breakfast of two organic eggs, hash browns, wheat toast, and any two of the following: grilled chorizo,

fried tomatoes, sautéed mushrooms, baked beans, avocado, and bacon. Five Leaves keeps going until late at night, when the bearded, flannel-shirted crowd slurps down Blue Point oysters and muscadet with cans of Dale's Pale Ale. The nautical theme is subtle—sea vistas on the tabletops, a porthole on the bathroom door, fishing weights dangling from the fixtures—but the clientele can definitely drink like sailors.

Five Leaves had been percolating in Mongell's mind for years. "I used to open his wardrobe and find bits of paper notes everywhere with ideas for the café he was someday going to do," says Mecham. The couple did a long stint at Café Gitane, and

that Nolita institution's influence is all over Five Leaves (not least in the customers, who seem to have mastered the art of devoting entire days to coffee and cigarettes). They worked at Moto in Williamsburg, too, another odd-shaped restaurant whose seemingly disjointed parts add up to a cohesive whole. (Moto's designer, John McCormick, consulted on Five Leaves's look and feel.) And Mongell was a waiter at DuMont (page 50), yet another neighborhood hangout built on the strength of an addictive burger. Actually, Five Leaves does two great burgers: a straight-up version with one modern twist (harissa mayo) and the hair-on-your-chest creation on page 170.

Five Leaves Burger with Grilled Pineapple, Pickled Beets, Sunny-Side-Up Egg, and Harissa Mayonnaise / FIVE LEAVES

SERVES 4

1 pineapple, peeled, cored, and cut into ½-inch-thick rings (you will need 4 rings for this recipe)

2 cups seasoned rice wine vinegar

2 tablespoons honey

1 teaspoon whole coriander seed

1 teaspoon whole black peppercorns

2 tablespoons extra-virgin olive oil

½ teaspoon dry mustard

2 heaping tablespoons peeled and thinly sliced fresh ginger

1 tablespoon prepared harissa (we like Dea Harissa Hot Sauce)

4 tablespoons prepared mayonnaise

Zest and juice of 1 lime

2 pounds ground beef chuck, preferably grass-fed, not too lean

Coarse salt and freshly ground black pepper

4 tablespoons (½ stick) unsalted butter, divided

4 ciabatta buns

4 slices prepared pickled beets

4 large eggs

Yes, this recipe sounds like the work of a drunk person, and it may have been. "It's an especially great hangover cure," says Kathy Mecham, an Aussie who owns Fives Leaves with her husband, Jud Mongell. But against all odds—*grilled pineapple ring?*—it totally works. "It's something we always missed, being in New York," Mecham says of the sloppy sandwich, an Australian import. "So we decided to do a similar burger, but using high-quality ingredients." Note that the pineapple should be prepared the night before.

1. Place 4 pineapple rings in a large heat-proof glass or stainless-steel bowl. In a medium nonreactive saucepan, combine the vinegar, honey, coriander seed, peppercorns, olive oil, mustard, and ginger. Bring to a boil and cook for 5 minutes. Pour the mixture over the pineapple, cover with plastic wrap, and refrigerate overnight.

2. Combine the harissa, mayonnaise, and lime zest and juice in a small bowl and set aside.

3. Prepare the grill for cooking or heat a ridged grill pan over medium-high heat until hot. Remove the pineapple from the marinade and grill for 2 minutes per side.

4. Season the beef with salt and pepper and form into 4 burgers. Grill the burgers, covered only if using a gas grill, turning once, about 5 minutes total for rare or 6 minutes for medium-rare.

5. Melt 2 tablespoons of the butter. Lightly brush the cut side of the buns with butter and grill for 1 or 2 minutes. Spread the harissa mayonnaise on the grilled buns.

6. In a nonstick pan, melt the remaining 2 tablespoons butter over medium-low heat. Break each egg into a small bowl and add it to the pan. Gently fry the eggs until the whites are set (sunny-side up), taking care not to break the yolk.

7. Place a burger on the bun and top each burger with a pickled beet slice, grilled pineapple slice, and sunny-side-up egg.

Roasted Beet and Blood Orange Salad with Arugula, Macadamia Nuts, and Goat's-Milk Yogurt Dressing / FIVE LEAVES

SERVES 4 TO 6 AS A FIRST COURSE

For the beets

3 medium red beets, about 4 ounces each, stems and root ends removed

2 medium golden beets, about 4 ounces each, stems and root ends removed

1 fresh thyme sprig

1 fresh rosemary sprig

2 garlic heads, broken into cloves, skins on, lightly crushed

2 tablespoons extra-virgin olive oil

2 cups coarse salt, plus more to taste

For the yogurt dressing

6 ounces goat's-milk yogurt

Grated zest of 1 orange

1 tablespoon honey

Pinch of cayenne pepper

For the vinaigrette

2 shallots, peeled

¼ cup sherry vinegar

1 tablespoon Dijon mustard

¾ cup extra-virgin olive oil

½ cup whole macadamia nuts

6 ounces baby arugula, about 4 cups

3 blood oranges (about 1 pound), peeled and sliced into rounds

Here's an alternate take on all those beet-and-goat-cheese salads that seemed to take over America in the past decade or so. This version has a goat's-milk yogurt dressing instead of goat cheese, a decadent crunchiness from the toasted macadamias, sliced blood oranges, and a beet vinaigrette (yes, there are two dressings) that turn the whole thing into the culinary equivalent of an Ellsworth Kelly painting—a color explosion that tastes as bright and vibrant as it looks.

1. Preheat the oven to 350°F.

2. Wash the beets and pat them dry. In a large bowl, toss the beets with the herbs, garlic, olive oil, and a pinch of salt. Cover the bottom of an 8 x 8-inch baking pan with the 2 cups salt. Set the beets, herbs, and garlic on top of the salt, cover the dish with foil, and bake until the beets are tender when pierced with a sharp knife, about 1 hour 15 minutes.

3. Set the pan aside to allow the beets to cool, then peel the beets and cut them into wedges, reserving half of 1 red beet for the vinaigrette. Keep the red beets and golden beets separate or their colors will bleed together.

4. Reduce the oven temperature to 325°F.

5. **To make the yogurt dressing,** combine the yogurt, zest, honey, and cayenne in a small bowl. Set aside.

6. **To make the vinaigrette,** in a blender or food processor, puree the shallots and the roasted red beet half with the vinegar and mustard. With the motor running, add the olive oil in a slow stream, blending until emulsified.

7. Place the macadamia nuts in a shallow baking dish in a single layer. Bake for 3 to 5 minutes, shaking the pan once halfway through to evenly brown. Allow to cool slightly, then roughly chop.

8. Combine the red and yellow beets with half the yogurt mixture in a medium bowl and toss to coat. In another bowl, toss the arugula with the beet vinaigrette to coat.

9. To serve, divide the beets and blood orange slices among 4 or 6 plates, top with the arugula, and garnish with the macadamias and a drizzle of the remaining yogurt dressing.

MAMA O'S PREMIUM KIMCHEE / CLINTON HILL

KHEEDIM OH

When he's not making kimchee or one of his other products (daikon kimchee, cucumber kimchee, and kimchee salsa), Kheedim Oh is making music. "I just do Mama O's for fun," says Oh, who deejays at a few clubs and is a member of the Beatards, a hip-hop trio. "I don't think there are too many kimchee-making deejays out there."

Were you especially into kimchee growing up?

Yeah. I've been really blessed that my mom—she is *super*-Korean—makes really good kimchee. Because whenever you go to a Korean restaurant, they bring out the kimchee, and it's *horrible*. That's what always surprised me when people say they actually like kimchee, because I'm like, *What kimchee are you eating?*

For the unititiated, how about a thirty-second primer on kimchee.

Sure. Kimchee is a traditional Korean pickled dish usually made with napa cabbage. It's the "seoul" of Korean food. Ha-ha. We eat it at breakfast, lunch, and dinner, typically as a side dish. Basically, there are two different ways to make it. The easy way is to cut the cabbage into bite-size pieces at the beginning, mix it all up, and then brine it. But the flavor doesn't get that intense, and it spoils faster. When you do it the old-fashioned way, which is the way I do it, you quarter or halve the cabbage heads, and then you brine 'em. And then the next day you stuff each individual leaf with a mixture of shredded daikon, salt, sugar, crushed red pepper flakes, watercress, ginger, and fish sauce. Then you pack it up tight and leave it to ferment.

What's in your kimchee salsa?

Tomatoes, two types of onions—red and white—cilantro, crushed red pepper flakes, daikon kimchee, and regular kimchee. So basically I just replaced the jalapeños in a typical salsa with diced-up pieces of daikon kimchee and regular kimchee.

Do you know if people have done this before, combining these two things?

I don't think so. Not that I've heard of, no. [*laughs*] But I think people love that, when you combine two cuisines. The Derek Jeterizing of food.

How'd you get your first retail account?

So there's this butcher, Jeffrey's, in Essex Market on the Lower East Side. And one day I was in there buying some ribs. The butcher says, "You get these ribs and some kimchee, you eat like a king." This is a Jewish guy from the Bronx. I'm like, *Who you tellin'?* I say, "You like kimchee?" He says, "Yeah, I love it." I'd been making my mom's kimchee for myself and my friends, so I brought some by. And he said, "I want to carry this."

Before moving your operations to Sweet Deliverance's kitchen in Clinton Hill, you were cooking out of a friend's place in Sunset Park. How'd the neighbors feel about the smell?

Yeah, that cabbagey smell will light up a building, from top to bottom. [*laughs*] Not high on people's favorite-smells list. But the thing about that building was, everyone was in the same family. So they had to just deal with it.

You seem like you're at a moment where you're happy that you're having success with Mama O's but a little worried that it's going to take over your life.

Well, if I make money, that's great, but it's not about the money. It's about making something that *I* want to eat. I have to make this decision, like, Oh man, they want all this kimchee, but I only have this much left, and that means I'm not gonna have any! Usually, though, I have too much. I'm a bachelor; I live by myself. [*He leans into the recorder.*] *Ladies.* And whenever I make a fresh batch, my fridge just turns into a kimchee locker. Ketchup and kimchee, that's all I got.

CHAR NO. 4

CARROLL GARDENS

Whenever we dine out alone, we sit at the bar. Sometimes, if we're feeling expansive, we'll chat with the bartender, sometimes not. Either way, it's a lot more fun than staring across the table at an empty chair. And in all of Brooklyn, there's no better place to eat at the bar than Char No. 4, a sleek but inviting restaurant built on pork and brown liquor.

Start with the view. Displayed behind the bar is an eye-popping selection of whiskeys: 150 bottles of single-malt Scotches, blended Scotches, ryes, Irish whiskeys, Japanese whiskeys, Tennessee whiskeys, Canadian whiskeys, weird corn whiskeys, esoteric American whiskeys, and bourbons—above all, bourbons—glowing like caramel-coated jewels against a wall of warm yellow light. Remember that scene in *Pulp Fiction* when Vincent Vega opens the briefcase and its mysterious contents bathe his face in a golden glow? It's kind of like that. Or maybe we just *really* like whiskey.

We like pork, too, especially smoked pork, and so does chef Matt Greco, who was sous chef at A Voce and Café Gray in Manhattan before Char No. 4 owners Michael Tsoumpas and Sean Josephs hired him to run their kitchen. (Many of the whiskeys on sale here are from Tsoumpas's personal collection.) There's a smoker on the premises and Greco makes full use of it, from the smoked and fried pork nuggets with hot sauce to the smoked bacon on the BLT with pickled tomatoes and chile mustard aioli to the home-made smoked stout and maple pork sausages with Brussels sprouts and bacon. Those who don't eat pork will find a smattering of chicken, beef, and seafood dishes, but vegetarians should probably go somewhere else.

Greco was planning to move to South Carolina when he met

Tsoumpas and Josephs and heard about their concept for a bourbon bar. "And I was like, 'Wow, I love bourbon,'" Greco says. "I'm not a wine person, I'm a beer and whiskey drinker. I'm from Texas, and that's just what I grew up on." They hired him in April 2008 and opened five months later.

Part of the appeal of Char No. 4—which is named for the stages of aging whiskey in charred oak barrels, the fourth stage being the highest and most intense—is that after a few visits, that whiskey list becomes a kind of challenge: *Can I get through the whole thing?* Anyone who tries will need some cash: Ten of these whiskeys, including the William Larue Weller 19 Year and the Macallan 14 Year Sherry Butt, cost a hundred bucks for a single ounce. But there are also about thirty whiskeys that sell for less than three dollars an ounce. Whatever your budget, Greco stands by, ready to serve up plenty of food to soak up all that booze.

Clam Potato Leek Soup / CHAR NO. 4

This is basically New England clam chowder, so why not just call it what it is? "To be totally honest," admits chef Matt Greco, "I thought I was making a pretty straightforward clam chowder, which I called, um, clam chowder. But I kept running into all these purists saying, '*This isn't chowder!* It's too thin, or it's too thick, or it has too much bacon in it,' or whatever. And I was like, 'You know, I'm just trying to make a nice bowl of chowder.' So I changed the name." Call it whatever you want, Matt, just keep it on the menu. This is a spectacular bowl of soup—smoky and rich and perfect with a loaf of airy bread in the heart of winter.

SERVES 4

20 Littleneck clams

⅓ cup dry white wine

¾ pound purple or red new potatoes (about 5 potatoes), unpeeled

3 ounces slab bacon, cut into ½-inch dice, or 4 slices bacon, cut into ¼-inch strips

1¼ cups thinly sliced leeks, white and tender green parts

1 teaspoon coarse salt

1 cup heavy cream

1 cup whole milk

Minced fresh chives, for garnish

1. Discard any clam with broken, cracked, or open shells that do not close when firmly tapped. Fill a large bowl with salted water. Add the clams and soak for 10 minutes. Drain, then scrub them with a brush to remove any remaining grit.

2. Place the clams and wine in a large pot or Dutch oven over medium-high heat. Cover and cook until the clams open, about 8 minutes. Strain the liquid through a fine-mesh strainer and reserve. Remove the clams from the shells, discarding any clams that did not open. Cut the clams in half and set aside.

3. Cut the potatoes into medium dice and place them in a bowl of cold water; set aside.

4. Cook the bacon in a large pot over medium heat until the fat is rendered, 7 or 8 minutes. Reduce the heat to low, drain the potatoes, and add them to the pot with the bacon. Stir in the leeks and salt. Cook, covered, stirring occasionally, until the potatoes are tender, about 15 minutes. Add the cream, milk, and reserved clam juice and cook for 5 minutes more. Blend 1 cup of the soup in a blender (make sure there are a good amount of potatoes in the blender). Return the pureed soup to the pot. Add the reserved chopped clams and cook until heated through. Adjust the seasonings, garnish with fresh chives, and serve.

Sugar Snap Peas with Minty Pea Pesto

/ CHAR NO. 4

SERVES 4 AS A SIDE DISH

3 tablespoons pine nuts

1 cup frozen peas

3 fresh mint leaves

1 teaspoon roasted garlic paste*
or 1 garlic clove, chopped

Grated zest of ½ lemon

¼ cup plus 2 tablespoons
extra-virgin olive oil

Coarse salt and freshly ground
black pepper

1 pound sugar snap peas,
trimmed and washed

2 tablespoons finely grated
Parmigiano-Reggiano, plus
more for garnish

To make roasted garlic paste, preheat the oven to 325°F. Cut the top off a head of garlic, wrap it in foil, and roast the garlic until golden brown, about 1½ hours. Allow the garlic to cool enough so you can handle it, then squeeze the garlic cloves out of the head and mash with a fork until it forms a smooth paste.

Chef Matt Greco's grandmother is an Italian immigrant who lived most of her life on a farm in Texas. She didn't invent this particular dish, but her cooking definitely inspired it. The pesto is a variation of a fava bean pesto Greco used to make when he worked for chef Andrew Carmellini at A Voce, the celebrated Italian restaurant in Manhattan. And the Italian theme continues with the pine nuts and Parmigiano-Reggiano (sprinkle generously), adding crunch and depth to the brightness of the snap peas.

1. Preheat the oven to 325°F. Place the pine nuts in a small ovenproof skillet and toast in the oven for 5 minutes, or until light brown. Transfer to a small bowl and allow to cool, then chop 1 tablespoon of the pine nuts. Set the chopped and whole pine nuts aside.

2. Prepare an ice bath. Bring a large pot of salted water to a boil. Add the peas and cook for 1 minute, or until tender. Using a slotted spoon, transfer the peas to the ice bath. (Keep the water boiling.) Use the slotted spoon to transfer the peas from the ice bath to a food processor. (Reserve the ice bath.)

3. To the food processor, add the mint, garlic paste or chopped garlic, lemon zest, the 2 tablespoons whole pine nuts, the ¼ cup olive oil, ¼ cup water, and salt and pepper to taste. Process until well combined but not completely smooth. Adjust the seasonings and reserve.

4. Add the snap peas to the boiling water and cook for 1 minute. Transfer to the ice bath. Drain and place in a medium bowl with the remaining 2 tablespoons olive oil, the Parmigiano-Reggiano, and the reserved chopped pine nuts. Season with salt and pepper.

5. Spread ¼ cup of the minty pea pesto on the center of each plate. Place the snap pea mixture on top. Garnish with additional grated cheese.

NO. 7

FORT GREENE

Tyler Kord doesn't quite disdain the local-seasonal-sustainable mantra of most new Brooklyn restaurants, but he certainly—well, okay, he kind of disdains it. "I've never been into, *Buy the most incredible ingredients and treat them as simply as possible*," says No. 7's chef and part-owner, the faux-reverence dripping from his voice. "I'd rather take those simple ingredients and treat them incredibly. I'd rather take a case of rotting artichokes and make the *craziest shit ever*. Put on a bigger show."

That's a provocative posture in Brooklyn, a.k.a. "Berkeley East." But it sure does differentiate him in the market. It's safe to say Kord is the only chef in the borough who would have come up with this: cinnamon-raisin shrimp toast with caviar, curried crème fraîche, and peanut butter. Or this: matzoh-crusted tofu with kale, lo mein, fried egg, and pico de gallo. Or this: catfish and braised pork cheeks with fried eggs, collard greens, and soggy Fritos. Yep, they go with brunch. At least at No. 7 they do.

This is high-risk, high-reward cooking, much closer in spirit to molecular gastronomists like Grant Achatz or Wylie Dufresne than farm-to-table preachers such as Dan Barber or Peter Hoffman. Sometimes Kord knocks it out of the park, sometimes he whiffs. But you gotta respect a guy who always swings for the fences.

An early hit was his fried broccoli with dill, grapefruit, and black beans,

which remains on the menu. Sounds dissonant as hell, right? A John Cage composition on a plate? It's not. The tempura-fried broccoli sings the lead here, but the chorus of supporting flavors follows right along.

Kord's culinary background is French. After graduating from the French Culinary Institute, he stayed on to work for chef Alain Sailhac, and his last job before opening No. 7 in October 2008 was sous chef to Jean-Georges Vongerichten at Perry Street. His plan was to open a small place, more bar than restaurant, where he'd serve "a couple of the coolest dishes" he could do. But he needed financial partners to make it happen, and one of them fell in love with a large vacant space on Greene Avenue, directly above the Lafayette stop on the C train. The partner said he'd only be involved if they used that space. "So I said, 'Okay, let's do that space,'" Kord says. "And it ended up being a much bigger beast than I envisioned. And now I have this huge goofy restaurant."

Seared Tuna with Korean Pear and Jalapeño Oil / NO. 7

SERVES 6

For the pears

¼ cup freshly squeezed lime juice

¼ cup distilled white vinegar

2½ tablespoons sugar

½ teaspoon coarse salt

½ teaspoon xanthan gum (such as Arrowhead Mills brand)

1 large Korean pear, also called Asian pear

For the jalapeño oil

4 large jalapeños, stems removed

½ cup canola oil

1¼ teaspoons coarse salt

For the tuna

1½ pounds sushi-grade tuna, cut into six pieces, 1 x 1 x 2 inches

Coarse salt

Extra-virgin olive oil

¼ cup micro basil or chiffonade-cut large leaf basil

No. 7's refreshingly blunt chef, Tyler Kord, sees no need to gussy up his recipes with a charming backstory. "I wanted to pair tuna with Korean pears because it sounded delicious," he says. "It just seemed like a good idea." The sauce, which Kord describes as "gloopy" in a good way, was inspired by the syrupy texture of canned peaches. (It also keeps the pears from oxidizing.) He's right: It *is* delicious. And it looks cool, too.

1. To make the pear and its syrup, in a medium bowl, whisk together the lime juice, vinegar, sugar, salt, xanthan gum, and 1⅔ cups water until completely dissolved. Peel, core, and cut the pear into thin half-moon slices. Place the pear slices in the bowl with the lime juice mixture and set aside.

2. Fill a large bowl with ice and place a metal bowl on top of the ice.

3. To make the jalapeño oil, combine the jalapeños, canola oil, and salt in a blender and puree on high until the sides of the blender heat up, about 3 minutes. Transfer the oil to the metal bowl over ice and allow to cool completely.

4. To prepare the fish, heat a grill pan or large sauté pan over high heat. Season the tuna with salt. Lightly coat the grill pan with olive oil or heat 2 tablespoons olive oil in the sauté pan. Grill the tuna on each side until it has grill marks but is still raw inside, or sauté the tuna for 1 minute on each side, about 4 minutes in all. Slice each tuna log into 5 even slices.

5. To serve, alternate the tuna and pear slices on serving plates. Generously drizzle with the pear syrup, jalapeño oil, and olive oil. Top with basil.

Butterscotch Pudding with Sautéed Pears and Turkish Coffee Shortbread / NO. 7

SERVES 6

For the sautéed pears

1 tablespoon extra-virgin olive oil

2 firm Bartlett pears, peeled and cut into ½-inch dice (about 2½ cups)

¼ cup sugar

2 teaspoons freshly squeezed lemon juice

2 tablespoons freshly squeezed orange juice

For the butterscotch pudding (makes 2½ cups)

3 large egg yolks

2 tablespoons cornstarch

1 tablespoon dark molasses

½ teaspoon kosher salt

1½ cups whole milk

1 cup heavy cream

1 vanilla bean, split, scraped, seeds discarded

½ cup sugar

2 teaspoons dark rum

4 tablespoons (½ stick) cold unsalted butter, cut into 4 pieces

Whipped cream

Freshly grated nutmeg

There's a good reason No. 7 always has a pudding on its dessert menu. "We don't have a freezer," says pastry chef Amanda Clark, who met chef Tyler Kord when both worked for Jean-Georges Vongerichten at Perry Street in Manhattan. "Pudding is kind of our sundae, and I treat it that way. It's great on its own, but after the third bite you're like, 'Okay, I'm eating a big bowl of pudding.' So I like to layer in fruits and have cookies and streusels and things for texture, and whipped cream to add another layer of flavor. I want different bites to have different things going on." The butterscotch is a lovely cool-weather flavor, and the lemon juice and orange juice in the pears keep the dish from becoming too sweet.

1. To make the pears, heat the oil in a sauté pan over medium heat. Add the pears and sugar and sauté until the sugar begins to caramelize and the pears begin to soften, 6 or 7 minutes. Add the lemon and orange juices and cook until the liquid is reduced to a glaze, about 7 minutes. Line a rimmed baking sheet with parchment paper and spread the pears in a single layer to cool. Place a heaping tablespoon of pears in the bottom of 6 individual serving bowls. Set aside.

2. To make the pudding, in a medium bowl, whisk the egg yolks and cornstarch until smooth. Add the molasses and salt and whisk to incorporate. Slowly whisk in ½ cup of the milk until the mixture is smooth; set aside.

3. Combine the heavy cream, the remaining 1 cup milk, and the vanilla bean in a medium saucepan over medium-low heat until the liquid begins to steam. Remove the vanilla bean and keep the mixture warm.

4. Spread the sugar evenly over the bottom of a heavy medium saucepan and sprinkle with 2 tablespoons water; place over medium heat and cook, without stirring, until the sugar has caramelized to an amber color, about 15 minutes. Slowly add the cream mixture in a thin stream. Stir well with a wooden spoon to thoroughly combine. Remove from the heat.

5. Prepare an ice bath in a large bowl and place a clean metal bowl on top of the ice.

6. Stir the egg yolk–cornstarch mixture, then temper by slowly pouring ¼ cup of the hot caramel-milk mixture into the eggs, whisking constantly. Whisk in another ¼ cup of the hot mixture. Pour the egg mixture into the pot with the remaining caramel milk and cook over medium heat, stirring constantly, until the mixture boils, 6 to 8 minutes. Cook for 1 more minute, stirring, until the mixture thickens. Immediately pour the pudding into the bowl over the ice bath. Stir in the rum. When the mixture has cooled slightly, transfer to a food processor or blender. Add the butter, 1 tablespoon at a time, and blend until smooth and emulsified. Pour into serving dishes over the sautéed pears to within ¼ inch of the top. Wrap tightly with plastic. Chill for at least 4 hours, or up to 3 days.

7. To serve, top the pudding with whipped cream and sprinkle with freshly grated nutmeg. Serve 3 shortbread cookies with each bowl of pudding.

Turkish Coffee Shortbread

1. In a large bowl, whisk together the flour, semolina, baking powder, salt, espresso, cocoa powder, cinnamon, and cardamom. Set aside.

2. In the bowl of a standing electric mixer, cream the butter and confectioners' sugar until blended. Add the egg yolks, one at a time, and beat until well incorporated. Add the flour mixture, mixing until the dough forms a stiff, well-combined ball. Roll the dough into two 13-inch-long logs (1½ inches in diameter). Roll the logs in the turbinado sugar, pressing as you roll so that the sugar adheres. Wrap the logs in parchment paper and plastic wrap, and refrigerate for at least 1½ hours, or overnight.

3. Preheat the oven to 350°F.

4. Using a serrated knife, gently slice one log into twenty-five ¼-inch-thick disks. Place the cookies on a baking sheet 1 inch apart and bake for about 15 minutes. Cool for 5 minutes, then transfer the cookies to a rack and cool completely.

You can bake all the cookies at once or freeze the second log for up to 2 weeks.

MAKES 50 COOKIES

1 cup all-purpose flour

⅓ cup semolina

¼ teaspoon baking powder

½ teaspoon coarse salt

3½ teaspoons finely ground espresso

1 tablespoon cocoa powder

¼ teaspoon ground cinnamon

¼ teaspoon ground cardamom

8 tablespoons (1 stick) unsalted butter, softened

1 cup confectioners' sugar

2 large egg yolks

2 tablespoons turbinado sugar

BUTTERMILK CHANNEL

CARROLL GARDENS

Practically every Brooklyn chef and restaurateur has worked in Manhattan, often in restaurants that are huge, hectic, or corporate. In Doug Crowell's case, it was all three. Before fleeing to the relative countryside of Carroll Gardens, Crowell was the general manager of Blue Water Grill in Union Square and Blue Fin in Times Square, a pair of cavernous culinary theme parks whose high-quality seafood doesn't make them any less impersonal. (Both are owned by a restaurant group called B. R. Guest.) So when he decided to set out on his own, he dreamed of opening a food business that was as far from those restaurants as possible. A little *too* far.

"I thought, I'm gonna open a sausage stand—a hole in the wall that sells nothing but sausages," he says now, as he proofreads tonight's menu at Buttermilk Channel, catching a typo. "But then I sort of came down to earth from there. I was like, *All right, I like wine, I like to serve people.* So then I was thinking I'd open more of a diner—a breakfast, lunch, and dinner place. But then you find the space, and you see what the neighborhood needs, and that's not what this neighborhood needed. This neighborhood needed a bistro, a neighborhood restaurant."

It would be hard to conceive of a more universally inviting menu than that of Buttermilk Channel, which is named for the stretch of water between Brooklyn and Governor's Island. (Legend has it that when farmers would cross the mile-long strait to sell their milk in Manhattan, the tidal rips were strong enough to churn the milk into butter.) Crowell's executive chef, Ryan Angulo, hits every note in the dining zeitgeist: house-made pickles and charcuterie, local cheeses, East Coast oysters (served raw with pomegranate, baked with chile mayonnaise and bread crumbs, or pan-roasted with buttered toasts), a kale and endive salad, a delicata squash tart, and entrées ranging from fried chicken with cheddar waffles and savoy cabbage slaw to brook trout wrapped with bacon to our favorite dish, the duck meat loaf crowned with a perfectly crisped onion ring (see page 192).

Unique? Not really. Satisfying? Hell yes. And the neighborhood responded emphatically. Despite opening into the teeth of the recession, in November 2008, Buttermilk Channel earned an instant reputation for two things: crowd-pleasing food and huge crowds to please. On some nights, the wait for a table exceeded two hours. It still didn't feel as chaotic and cacophonous as the pretheater rush at Blue Fin, but it was a little nuttier than Crowell expected. And a whole lot nuttier, presumably, than the sausage stand would have been.

Duck Meat Loaf with Creamed Spinach, Onion Ring, and Duck Jus / BUTTERMILK CHANNEL

SERVES 4

For the meat loaf

1 tablespoon extra-virgin olive oil

1 medium yellow onion, minced

1 pound duck breast meat, skin discarded, plus ¼ pound duck fat*

¼ cup chopped golden raisins

½ cup fresh unseasoned bread crumbs

2 tablespoons chopped fresh flat-leaf parsley

1½ teaspoons coarse salt, plus more to taste

1 large egg, lightly beaten

1 tablespoon chopped fresh thyme leaves

¼ cup dry white wine

2 cups homemade chicken stock or prepared low-sodium chicken broth

Freshly ground black pepper

* Ask the butcher to separate the fat from the breast meat, weigh the fat, and, if necessary, add more fat to total ¼ pound, then grind the meat and fat together.

You think the onion ring looks decadent? It's actually restrained compared to chef Ryan Angulo's original vision. "At first I put a big piece of crispy duck skin on top, but we felt like that might scare some people," he says. "It made the dish a little too fatty." True, the replacement ain't exactly spa food, but what the onion ring delivers is balance—the sweetness from the onion (and from the raisins in the meat loaf) works perfectly with the savory duck and creamy spinach.

1. To make the meat loaf, preheat the oven to 350°F. Heat the olive oil in a medium sauté pan over medium heat. Add the onion and cook until translucent, about 10 minutes. Remove from the heat and cool.

2. Combine the onion with the meat, raisins, bread crumbs, parsley, salt, egg, and thyme in a large bowl.

3. Form the mixture into four mini meat loaves and place on a rack in a 9 x 13-inch roasting pan. Bake for 35 minutes, or until the internal temperature registers 145°F on a meat thermometer. (You can also make one large meat loaf and bake it for 1 hour and 15 minutes.)

4. To make the jus, remove the meat loaves, drain the fat from the roasting pan, and deglaze immediately by adding the wine to the pan and scraping the brown bits off the bottom of the pan. Transfer the wine and brown bits to a medium saucepan and place over medium-high heat. Cook until almost all the liquid is evaporated, about 3 minutes. Add the stock, bring to a boil, and cook until the liquid is reduced by half, 8 to 10 minutes. Reduce the heat to low and season to taste with salt and pepper. Cover the pan and keep warm.

5. To make the creamed spinach, combine the celery root and heavy cream in a medium saucepan. Bring to a boil, then reduce to a gentle simmer, cover, and cook until tender, about 30 minutes. Strain the celery root and reserve the liquid. Transfer the celery root and ½ cup of the liquid to a food processor and puree until smooth. Set it aside in the processor.

6. Bring a large pot of salted water to a boil. Blanch the spinach until wilted, 1 to 2 minutes. Drain and rinse under cold water to stop the cooking. Squeeze the spinach to remove excess water. Finely chop the spinach and set aside.

7. Stick the pointed end of the clove into the onion half. Then combine the onion and milk in a saucepan and bring to a gentle simmer over medium heat. Remove from the heat and let steep for 5 minutes or so. Discard the onion and clove.

8. In a medium saucepan over medium heat, melt the butter and whisk in the flour. Cook for 4 minutes, whisking constantly. Slowly add the warm milk, whisking continuously, and simmer until the sauce thickens, about 1 minute. Add the reserved spinach and mix well to combine. Add the spinach mixture to the celery root mixture in the food processor and puree.

9. To make the onion rings, preheat the oven to 200°F. Separate the onion slices into rings and pick out 4 large rings for the meat loaf garnish. (Fry the rest and serve them in a bowl on the table, or reserve the onion for another use.)

10. Combine the flour, salt, and pepper in a shallow bowl. Pour the buttermilk into another shallow bowl. Line a rimmed baking sheet with parchment paper or wax paper and a plate with paper towels.

11. Dip the onion rings in the buttermilk and dredge in the flour, gently shaking off the excess. Repeat, first in the buttermilk, then the flour, and shake off the excess. Transfer to the baking sheet.

12. Heat 3 inches of vegetable oil in a 3-quart pot or deep 12-inch heavy skillet over medium-high heat until it registers 360°F on a deep-fry thermometer. (If you don't have a thermometer handy, preheat the oil, then drop a kernel of popcorn in the oil. It will pop as the temperature reaches 350 to 360°F.)

For the creamed spinach

¾ pound celery root (celeriac), scrubbed, peeled, and cut into 1-inch cubes

1½ cups heavy cream

1 pound spinach, thick stems removed and leaves rinsed

Coarse salt

½ medium yellow onion

1 whole clove

1 cup whole milk

2 tablespoons unsalted butter

2 tablespoons all-purpose flour

For the onion rings (makes 1 dozen large rings and lots of smaller rings)

1 large Spanish onion (about 1 pound), peeled and sliced ½-inch thick

1 cup all-purpose flour

½ teaspoon coarse salt, plus more to taste

¼ teaspoon freshly ground black pepper

1 cup buttermilk, well shaken

Vegetable oil, for frying

12. Working in batches, carefully place the battered onion rings in the hot oil and fry, turning as needed with a slotted spoon, until golden brown on all sides, 3 to 4 minutes per batch. Transfer to the paper-towel-lined plate and season to taste with salt. Transfer back to the baking sheet and place in the oven to keep warm.

13. To serve, spoon the creamed spinach in the center of 4 plates. Place the duck meat loaf on top of the puree and spoon the jus around the puree. Top each meat loaf with one onion ring.

Doug's Pecan Pie Sundae / BUTTERMILK CHANNEL

MAKES 6 SUNDAES

For the piecrust

1½ cups all-purpose flour

½ teaspoon salt

3 tablespoons sugar

8 tablespoons (1 stick) cold, unsalted butter, cut into ½-inch cubes and kept refrigerated until needed

3 to 4 tablespoons ice water

For the filling

1½ cups sugar

4 tablespoons (½ stick) unsalted butter, melted

3 large eggs

¾ cup light corn syrup

2 tablespoons molasses

1 tablespoon bourbon (optional)

1⅔ cups chopped pecans

2 pints vanilla ice cream

Whipped cream, for serving

It doesn't get much more satisfying than this: Start with the most hedonistic pie known to man, then atomize it and swirl it into a childhood nostalgia trip. "Doug kept talking about this pecan pie that he makes every year at Thanksgiving, and he thinks it's awesome," says chef Ryan Angulo of owner Doug Crowell. "He's the only one who eats it, because his family doesn't like pecan pie. At the same time, we were trying to come up with some fun desserts. I said to Doug, 'Why don't we make your pecan pie, crush it up, and stick it in a sundae?' We tried it, and there it is. It's our most popular dessert."

1. To make the piecrust, place the flour, salt, and sugar in a food processor fitted with a metal blade; pulse for a few seconds to combine. Add the butter and pulse until the butter is the size of peas. Add 3 or 4 tablespoons ice water, 1 tablespoon at a time, and pulse. Pinch a small amount of the mixture between your fingers; you need to add just enough water for the dough to hold. Turn the mixture out onto a clean surface and shape into a disk, handling as little as possible. Wrap the dough in plastic wrap and refrigerate for at least 45 minutes.

2. To make the filling, combine the sugar and melted butter in the bowl of a standing mixer. Add the eggs one at a time, incorporating each fully before adding the next. Add the corn syrup, molasses, and bourbon, if using, and mix to combine. Fold in the chopped pecans. Set aside.

3. On a lightly floured surface, use a floured rolling pin to roll the dough into a 12-inch round. Place in a 9-inch glass or metal pie plate. Gently press the dough against the bottom and up the sides of the plate. Trim the dough edge. Freeze the pie shell for 30 minutes.

4. Preheat the oven to 425°F. Line the pie shell with parchment paper and fill with dry beans or pie weights. Bake for 6 minutes, or until the shell begins to set. Remove the parchment and weights and bake for 3 minutes more. Lower the oven temperature to 350°F and set the pie shell aside to cool.

5. Pour the pecan filling into the shell. Place the pie on a rimmed baking sheet and bake for 65 to 70 minutes, or until the filling no longer looks liquid and it jiggles just slightly. Check the pie often after

50 minutes; if the crust is getting too brown, cover it with foil. Allow the pie to cool completely.

6. To assemble the sundaes, use a 2-ounce ice cream scoop and scoop some pie (including the crust) into the bottom of each of 6 tulip sundae glasses. Top with 1 scoop of ice cream, followed by another scoop of pie, then the ice cream and pie again. Finish with a dollop of whipped cream.

EARLY BIRD FOOD & CO. / RED HOOK

NEKISIA DAVIS

Nekisia Davis started out making granola as holiday gifts for her coworkers at Franny's (page 68); the next thing she knew, she was a mainstay at the Brooklyn Flea, turning out three different kinds of "tiny batch" granolas: Aloha, with mango and macadamia nuts; Jubilee, with cherry and pistachio; and Farmhand's Choice, with pecans.

What's your genesis story?

It's an absolute accidental business. I had no intention of starting a business at all.

Ha! That's a recurring theme in this book.

I wanted to try making granola, and so I did. I went to the food co-op, and I went around and got all of my favorite things: brown sugar, maple, coconut, pecans. And I just started kind of playing around with the recipe.

While working as a manager at Franny's, you also created the restaurant's liqueur program, concocting recipes for homemade amaro, limoncello, and other liqueurs. Not the most obvious path to granola-making. Is there a Proustian moment in your past that led to this business?

Well, I used to pick pecans out of my great-grandmother's tree in her backyard in Odessa, Texas, and we'd put them in our breakfast; she also had blackberries at her lake house, and we'd eat them with maple and milk. But no, it's not like granola has played some big role in my life up until now. It's just something that I love that I wanted to make myself. And I like experimenting in the kitchen.

What's the most distinctive thing about your granola?

I put olive oil and salt on it. Actually, I put olive oil and salt on pretty much everything I eat!

Are you consciously trying to change the perception of granola as a breakfast-only thing? Or *should* it be a breakfast only thing?

With the addition of the salt, it kind of opens it up to other parts of the day. Kind of like you would crave— well, I don't know how many people crave potato chips anymore, but I definitely do sometimes. So this can

kind of fill that craving for salt, but without ingesting a bunch of processed junk.

What's the best wine to drink with granola?

Probably something a little sweet and salty, maybe a nice nutty sherry. Or maybe an amaro. A little bitter, a little sweet and herbaceous at the same time.

I'm sure you've had some trying moments, being a one-woman show.

Oh yeah, all the time. I can't tell you how many batches I've pulled out of the oven and I was like, "Goddamn, I forgot to put the coconut in." Being all by myself, I don't have a check system, someone to say: Hey, did you put in the coconut? Hey, did

you already salt that? Hey, did you rent a Zipcar before they're all gone so you can do deliveries on Friday? But it's funny. It's really tempting to look toward the future. I keep thinking, I really want to enjoy, just . . . all of *this*. I'm trying to take it one day at a time and enjoy everything and have fun and laugh at myself when I do ridiculous things.

ROBERTA'S

BUSHWICK

Describing Roberta's in a book is tricky. We're typing these words six months before *The New Brooklyn Cookbook* even comes out; readers will come upon them many months and years later. By then, who knows what this ever-evolving place will be?

This much is probably still true: Roberta's is a fun, strange, and beloved restaurant in a raw neighborhood. Its clientele is heavy on tattooed kids with Swat Valley beards who love to gather around the picnic tables out back and swill Captain Lawrence Liquid Gold until closing time. Its staff, while friendly and warm, sometimes conveys the message that erratic service is the price one must pay for proximity to such immeasurable coolness. And it has two totally separate kitchens, both of which turn out bold and flavorful food that's more responsible to the environment than it is to your cholesterol.

Kitchen number one, in plain view on the left as you walk in, is built around a bright red wood-burning oven that bakes bubble-crusted thin pies ranging from the classic (a basic Margherita; the Rosso with tomato, oregano, and garlic) to the eccentric (the Cheeses Christ has black pepper, mozzarella, taleggio, Parmigiano, and heavy cream; the Axl Rosenberg goes over the top with mushrooms, jalapeño, sopressata picante, and the masterstroke, "double garlic"). Kitchen number two, hidden in the back and becoming more prolific and ambitious all the time, is a meat-centric laboratory for the creation of dishes like roasted marrow bones with sel gris, citrus, and parsley; pork belly with pineapple, Brussels sprouts, and chili flakes; and lamb saddle (the loin and breast) with butternut squash and mint. If you want to eat light at Roberta's, order pizza. Even the salads usually have at least one hit of unexpected decadence. The tongue salad on page 202 is a prime example, as is a recent special of perfectly dressed mustard greens with lightly grilled pears enriched by a big lovin' spoonful of creamy ricotta.

Of course, this being Roberta's, don't expect to see any of those specific dishes ever again.

"We were very flexible and open to the restaurant taking on its own life," says chef Carlo Mirarchi, one of Roberta's three operating partners. (There's a much larger group of financial partners, but Mirachi, Brandon Hoy, and Chris Parachini, whose mother is Roberta, are the three who work here every day.) "When we first opened [as a pizzeria, in January 2008], I had nothing. I had a crappy Fleischer that was sitting on top of a milk crate, two butane burners, and one frying pan. But we just did things slowly and that was it. It's kind of its own animal right now."

Calf's Tongue with Treviso Radicchio, Pistachios, and Smoked Ricotta / ROBERTA'S

SERVES 4

For the brine

1 cup coarse salt

½ cup sugar

1 teaspoon whole cloves

1 teaspoon whole allspice

1 navel orange, cut in half

1 calf's tongue, about 1 pound, preferably fresh, or thawed if frozen

2 blood oranges

½ cup plus 2 tablespoons good-quality red wine vinegar, divided

1 tablespoon sugar

1 head Treviso radicchio

2 tablespoons extra-virgin olive oil

¼ cup Salvatore Bklyn smoked ricotta or fresh ricotta

1 tablespoon chopped pistachios

Vincotto,* for garnish (optional)

* Vincotto, meaning cooked wine, is a sweet Italian condiment available at D. Coluccio's and gourmet food shops or online at www.buonitalia.com.

"Basically, we just wanted to showcase some tongue," says Carlo Mirarchi, the chef at Roberta's. "I don't think I can make it much more eloquent than that." He pauses, and you can guess at his thoughts: *How the hell do I articulate the pleasure and satisfaction of a well-made tongue salad?* "We just enjoy preparing food that takes a little focus and energy and skill to bring the best out of." No question, this salad is an undertaking. First you need to procure a calf's tongue from your butcher, then you brine it for at least three days. You can cook the tongue ahead of time if you like, then slice and warm when you're ready to assemble the salad. Just don't forget to save the cooking liquid for rewarming.

1. To make the brine, in a large pot, combine the salt, sugar, cloves, allspice, and orange halves with 1 gallon cold water. Bring to a boil over high heat, then remove the pot from the heat and strain the liquid. Cool the liquid completely, then pour it into a large container with a tight-fitting lid and add the tongue. Cover and refrigerate for at least 3 days and up to 2 weeks.

2. To cook the brined tongue, remove the tongue from the brining liquid and discard the liquid. Place the tongue in a large pot of cold water and bring to a simmer over medium-high heat, then reduce the heat to medium so that the water is just simmering. Slice one blood orange in half, squeeze the juice into the pot, and add the squeezed orange to the pot along with ½ cup of the vinegar and the sugar. Continue simmering for 2⅓ to 3 hours, or until the tip of the tongue is easily pierced with a paring knife, but not falling apart. Remove the tongue from the cooking liquid, reserve the liquid, and plunge the tongue into a bowl of cold water. Peel the tongue and remove the dark tissue and gristle at the base with a sharp knife. Set the tongue aside.

3. Strain the cooking liquid into a large saucepan. Boil the liquid over high heat until it is reduced by half, about 1 hour.

4. Meanwhile, prepare the Treviso. Discard the outer leaves and stem. Separate the remaining leaves and place them in a large bowl of ice water to soak, about 30 minutes. This will help to reduce the bitterness.

5. Slice the tongue as thinly as possible lengthwise into about 16 slices and add the slices to the cooking liquid until the tongue is warmed through.

6. Dry the Treviso well and season with salt and pepper. Heat the olive oil in a large sauté pan and, working in batches to avoid crowding the pan, add the Treviso. Add the remaining 2 tablespoons vinegar and cook for about 3 minutes, until the leaves begin to cook through. Remove the Treviso from the pan and drain on paper towels.

7. To plate the tongue, smear a tablespoon of smoked ricotta on the bottom of each of 4 plates. Toss the tongue and Treviso with the juice of the remaining blood orange and 2 tablespoons of the cooking liquid and mix well by hand. Place next to the ricotta, and garnish with crumbled pistachio. If using, drizzle the plate with vincotto.

VINEGAR HILL HOUSE

VINEGAR HILL

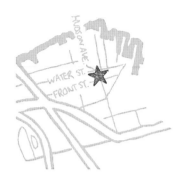

If they didn't seem like such natural partners, you might wonder whether Jean Adamson and Sam Buffa's personal union wasn't born of professional ambition. The couple met at Freemans, the self-described "rugged clandestine Colonial American tavern" located at the end of a preposterously atmospheric alley off the Bowery. Adamson was the chef, and Buffa owned the barbershop in Freemans Sporting Club, the affiliated men's boutique. Adamson is a full-throttle chef who loves pork, butter, and cast-iron skillets; Buffa is a décor-obsessed antiques freak addicted to Americana and found objects. Turns out they both dreamed of opening a restaurant that fused Adamson's culinary vision with Buffa's aesthetic taste. "I was looking for a chef girlfriend and I didn't even know it," says Buffa. He's sort of joking.

They had to gut-renovate the space they found on a residential block in the sleepy neighborhood of Vinegar Hill, but that was made easier by the fact that they lived in the carriage house out back. (They've since moved into the apartment above the restaurant and converted the carriage house to office space and wine storage.) The 750-degree heart of Vinegar Hill House is a wood-burning oven responsible for everything hot that comes out of the kitchen, save pastas and sauces. "When Sam and I conceptualized the restaurant, there was this kind of hand-built-house kind of thing," says Adamson. "With that, my idea was that everything would be cooked with fire, over an open flame, kind of communal-style." Adamson's most famous dish is probably her Red Wattle country chop, sliced porterhouse-style and

served over sauerkraut, though the cast-iron chicken (page 206) gives the chop a run for its money in terms of both richness and popularity. The delicata squash (page 208), a creation of chef de cuisine Brian Leth, has a following among vegetarians and meat-eaters alike.

As for Buffa's half of the equation: wow. Especially considering how much of the restaurant's charm was acquired on the cheap, from re-purposed materials. The bar is faced with wood salvaged from a barn in Virginia. Several tables were built with butcher block scavenged from a renovation upstairs. The old shutters from the front of the building now serve as decorative paneling in the bathroom. And the remarkable thing is, it doesn't feel old or kitschy. Somehow all these discarded objects blend together under Buffa's careful eye to become some-

thing fresh and vital. And the décor is always evolving. Jean has a thing for pottery from the seventies, so they're sprinkling pieces around the restaurant. An oil painting of John F. Kennedy seems to appear in a different location every time we come in. "My whole goal," says Buffa, "was I wanted it to be a continuation of the neighborhood, but then have a feeling that someone had lived there for a while and had taken pieces, found objects, and added onto it, added some layers."

Unless you're one of the regulars who live in Vinegar Hill, "it feels like an adventure to come here," Buffa adds. "At Freemans you feel like you're going on an adventure when you go down that alley, and I think there's a similar thing that happens here. Even though you're just going out to dinner, it feels like you're going on a little vacation."

Cast-Iron Chicken with Caramelized Shallots and Sherry Pan Sauce / VINEGAR HILL HOUSE

SERVES 4

10 shallots, peeled, 2 sliced and 8 whole

1 large yellow onion, sliced

Two 2- to 3-pound organic or Amish chickens*

3 tablespoons extra-virgin olive oil

2 cups dry white wine

1½ quarts (6 cups) homemade chicken stock or prepared low-sodium chicken broth

1 bay leaf

8 fresh thyme sprigs, divided

Coarse salt and freshly ground black pepper

10 tablespoons (1¼ sticks) unsalted butter, divided

4 teaspoons vegetable oil, divided

½ cup sherry vinegar

Ask your butcher to bone out the chickens and cut them in half, leaving leg and wing bones intact. Make sure to reserve the other bones for the jus.

Been looking for a good excuse to buy that Lodge cast-iron skillet you've had your eye on? Here's a fine reason to splurge on two (or buy one and borrow another). At Vinegar Hill House, chef and co-owner Jean Adamson serves this dish in small individual skillets, but you'll be able to achieve very similar results at home. The chicken comes out tender and juicy, and the rich sauce (enhanced by those yummy brown bits scraped from the skillet) demands a good bread for sopping.

1. Preheat the oven to 425°F.

2. **To make the jus,** combine the sliced shallots, onion, and reserved chicken bones on a rimmed baking sheet. Toss with the olive oil. Roast, stirring every 10 minutes, until all the ingredients are browned, about 30 minutes. Remove the bones from the tray, leaving any fat behind, and transfer the contents of the tray to a large stockpot over medium-high heat. Add the wine and cook until it is reduced by three quarters. Add the stock, bay leaf, and a few sprigs of thyme. Bring to a boil, then reduce the heat to medium low and simmer for 45 minutes. Strain the jus through a fine-mesh strainer. Refrigerate until chilled, then skim the fat and reserve the jus.

3. Place the 8 whole shallots in an 8 x 8-inch baking pan. Season with salt and pepper, add 2 tablespoons of the butter, and pour in ⅛ cup water. Cover with aluminum foil and roast for 20 minutes. Uncover and roast for 15 minutes more, or until the shallots are tender and golden. Set the pan aside.

4. **To roast the chickens,** place two 9-inch seasoned cast-iron skillets† in the oven for 15 minutes. Season the chickens generously on both sides with salt and pepper. When the skillets are hot, carefully remove them from the oven and add 2 teaspoons of the vegetable oil to each skillet.

Place 2 chicken halves in each skillet, skin side down. Roast for about 30 minutes, checking often, until the juices from the thigh run clear.

5. Remove the skillets from the oven and pour off any fat. Turn the chicken halves over, skin side up, and deglaze each pan with ¼ cup of the sherry vinegar, scraping the bottom to release any brown bits. Add 4 tablespoons of the butter, ¼ cup of the reserved chicken jus, and 4 shallots to each pan. Return to the oven and roast for 3 minutes.

6. To serve, place a chicken half, 2 shallots, and a bit of the pan sauce on each plate. Garnish with the remaining thyme sprigs.

† *At the restaurant, this dish is served in individual 6½-inch skillets. If you choose to do the same, cook ½ chicken in each pan, then add 2 tablespoons of the sherry vinegar to deglaze, 2 tablespoons of the butter, ⅛ cup of the reserved chicken jus, and 2 shallots per pan. Be careful because the skillets will be extremely hot. Use trivets under each pan when serving.*

Delicata Squash with Toasted Squash Seeds and Aleppo Pepper / VINEGAR HILL HOUSE

SERVES 6

Six delicata squash, 3 to 4 inches long, halved lengthwise

8 tablespoons (1 stick) unsalted butter, divided

Coarse salt

2 tablespoons pure maple syrup

Freshly ground black pepper

1 to 2 tablespoons extra-virgin olive oil, plus more for garnish

2 egg whites

Ground Aleppo pepper or paprika, for garnish

Sea salt, for garnish

Brian Leth, the chef de cuisine at Vinegar Hill House, came up with this easy-to-make dish one day at the height of summer, as he was fantasizing about what he'd like to eat when it got cold again. The squash gets even sweeter with the maple syrup, but both are balanced and reined in by the two types of pepper, toasted squash seeds, and sea salt. The result? A rich, buttery, deeply satisfying vegetarian entrée that's inspired by a cold-weather classic from your grandmother's recipe collection: the twice-baked potato.

1. Preheat the oven to 425°F.

2. Scrape the seeds from the squash and place them in a colander. Rinse under cold water to remove as much pulp as you can. Drain, then transfer the seeds to a plate lined with a paper towel and reserve.

3. Peel 6 of the squash halves (the least attractive ones) and cut them into 1-inch cubes. Place the cubed squash in a large saucepan with a tight-fitting lid. Add 6 tablespoons of the butter and season with salt. Cover and cook over low heat, stirring occasionally, until the squash is soft, 25 to 30 minutes. Transfer to a blender and, working in batches, puree the squash with the maple syrup. (You can also use an immersion blender to puree the squash.) Add the remaining 2 tablespoons butter, pureeing until the mixture is silky smooth and thick. Refrigerate until ready to use.

4. While the squash is cooking, line a rimmed baking sheet with parchment paper and lightly oil the paper. Season the remaining squash halves with salt and pepper and place them cut side down on the baking sheet. Bake for 20 minutes, or until tender.

5. Reduce the oven temperature to 375°F. Toss the reserved squash seeds with the olive oil, salt, and pepper and spread on a parchment-lined rimmed baking sheet. Toast the seeds in the oven until they are crispy and aromatic, 15 to 20 minutes. Stir the seeds halfway through the cooking time to break them apart.

6. Whip the egg whites to soft peaks and fold them into the cooled squash puree. Spoon the puree into the baked squash halves. Return them to the oven and bake for 15 minutes, or until the puree and the edges of the squash are golden brown.

7. To serve, drizzle each squash half with olive oil and garnish with the toasted seeds, Aleppo pepper or paprika, and sea salt.

PRIME MEATS

CARROLL GARDENS

Shortly before our sit-down with Frank Falcinelli and Frank Castronovo—known in Carroll Gardens and beyond as "the Franks"—Falcinelli canceled. Something had come up, which is no surprise given how busy these guys are these days. Okay, no sweat. Castronovo can tell the story: the Rise and Rise of the Frankies Empire. Over a few afternoon beers at Prime Meats, he recalls how they grew up together in Queens Village, Queens, then lost touch. How they both became chefs, Castronovo embarking on a nomadic global career and Falcinelli staying closer to home. And how they ran into each other eighteen years later, in 2003, at a fortuitous moment. Falcinelli had been thinking about opening an American-Italian restaurant (as opposed to an Italian-American restaurant) in his Carroll Gardens neighborhood, a casual place that would serve, in Castronovo's words, "the food we grew up on." That place was Frankies 457 Spuntino, which opened in September 2004. (We asked for recipes, but the Franks understandably declined because they just published their own fantastic cookbook, *The Frankies Spuntino Kitchen Companion & Cooking Manual*.) Then came another Frankies on Clinton Street in Manhattan. Then Café Pedlar, a coffee shop in Cobble Hill. And finally, in February 2009, following much hype and speculation on the food blogs—Would it be a pizzeria? A butcher shop? A steak house?—Prime Meats, a half block down Court Street from Frankies.

Inspired by their shared love of German-Austrian food and Castronovo's five-year stint cooking in the Black Forest, Prime Meats is both a labor of love and a calculated attempt to fill a neglected niche. "It *is* one of the world's great cuisines, and it's just not getting shown the way it should be shown," Castronovo says. "Why do something brand-new when there's something out there? And when you look at the dishes you realize, they reach out. They go across Germany, they go into Poland, they go into Russia, they go into the Czech Republic and Slovakia, into Hungary, Austria, Switzerland, and France."

But this isn't strictly purist cuisine. Yes, the sauerbraten on page 212 is a classic. So is the sürkrüt garnie, an irresistible but paralyzing medley of pork belly, bratwurst, calf's tongue, and knockwurst. And the weisswurst comes in the traditional bowl of scalding water, with a pretzel roll and sweet mustard on the side. But you'd be hard-pressed to find anything as bright and fresh as the celery salad (page 217) in the beer halls of Bavaria. "It's of the palate," he says. "But we invented it." He's talking about the salad, but it's true of the whole restaurant.

Beef Sauerbraten with Red Cabbage and Pretzel Dumplings / PRIME MEATS

SERVES 6

For the beef sauerbraten

2 pounds beef brisket

2 cups dry red wine

1 cup red wine vinegar

4 juniper berries

2 teaspoons white peppercorns

1 celery stalk, cut into large dice

2 carrots, cut into large dice

1 leek, sliced

2 garlic cloves, cut in half

4 yellow onions, 3 cut into ¼-inch slices and 1 diced

¼ cup canola oil

Coarse salt and freshly ground black pepper

2 Granny Smith apples, peeled and cut into ½-inch dice

1 cup golden raisins

1 bay leaf

1 teaspoon fresh or dried thyme

¾ cup homemade beef or chicken stock or prepared low-sodium beef or chicken stock

If the celery salad on page 217 represents the interpretive end of Prime Meats's menu, this sauerbraten stands for tradition. But co-owner Frank Castronovo admits it's not *exactly* like the kind you'd get in the motherland. "It's better!" he says, then backpedals slightly. "I'm not saying that to be—we have Germans who say that, Germans who come into the restaurant." Frank, you have reason to be proud. This is a straight-up recipe that enhances the rich flavors of every element of the dish. But plan ahead: Ideally, the meat should marinate for four days.

1. **To make the sauerbraten,** place the brisket in a deep pan or Dutch oven. Add the wine, vinegar, juniper berries, peppercorns, celery, carrot, leek, garlic, and 1 of the sliced onions. The brisket should be completely submerged. Cover and refrigerate for 4 days. Turn the meat once each day. After four days, remove the meat from the marinade and pat it dry. Strain and reserve the marinade.

2. Preheat the oven to 275°F. Heat the oil in a large Dutch oven over high heat until hot but not smoking. Add the brisket and brown it on all sides, about 10 minutes. Remove the meat, leaving the fat in the pan, and season with salt and pepper. Add the 2 remaining sliced onions. Reduce the heat to medium and cook, stirring occasionally, until the onions are tender and caramelized, about 15 minutes.

3. Deglaze the pan by adding the reserved marinade and scraping the bottom of the pan to release any browned bits. Add the apples, raisins, bay leaf, and thyme and stir to combine. Return the meat to the pan with any accumulated juices and bring to a simmer over medium heat. Cover the pot and transfer to the oven. Braise for 2½ hours, or until the meat is very tender, turning the meat halfway through.

4. **Prepare the pretzel dumplings** while the meat is braising. Warm the milk in a small saucepan over low heat. Place the pretzels in a large bowl and pour the warm milk over the top. Season lightly with salt and pepper. Cover the bowl with plastic wrap and let the pretzels soak for 30 minutes.

1 cup whole milk

**6 day-old soft pretzels,* about
2 ounces each, sliced ⅛-inch thick**

**Coarse salt and freshly ground
black pepper**

**3 to 4 tablespoons unsalted butter,
divided**

1 medium Spanish onion, finely diced

¼ cup chopped fresh flat-leaf parsley

1 large egg, lightly beaten

** Buy soft pretzels in your supermarket
freezer section. Bake them one day, then use
them to make the dumplings the next day.*

5. In a sauté pan, melt 1 tablespoon of the butter over medium heat. Add the onion and sauté until translucent. Season with salt and remove from the heat. Stir in the parsley, then add the seasoned onion to the dumpling mixture and, using your hands, mix to combine.

6. Bring a large pot of lightly salted water to a boil.

7. Add the egg to the dumpling mixture and incorporate well. Using your hands, squeeze the mixture through your fingers to break it up. With slightly wet hands, form 3 smooth logs that are 2 inches across. Wrap each log in plastic wrap and twist the ends to secure them. Then wrap them in aluminum foil and secure the ends. Drop the logs into the boiling water. Return to a boil, then reduce heat and simmer, partially covered, for 30 minutes. Remove from the water and open the foil and plastic wrap to allow the logs to cool.

8. Meanwhile, prepare the cabbage. In a Dutch oven or large skillet fitted with a lid, melt the butter over medium heat. Add the onions and apples and sauté until the onions are translucent, about 5 minutes. Add the cabbage, cherries, red wine, cloves, brown sugar, and bay leaf, stirring to combine. Increase the heat to medium high and bring to a boil.

9. Cover the pan, reduce the heat, and simmer, stirring occasionally, for 1 hour. Remove the bay leaf and stir in the cider vinegar and lemon juice. Cook for 1 minute.

10. When the brisket is tender, transfer it to a cutting board. Add the stock to the Dutch oven and reduce over medium heat, until the sauce is reduced by half, about 20 minutes. Season with salt and pepper to taste.

11. Slice the brisket against the grain and return to the pot with the sauce. Keep warm.

12. To finish the pretzel dumplings, discard the foil and plastic wrap and cut the logs into ½-inch-thick slices. Melt 1 tablespoon of the butter in a large sauté pan over medium-high heat. Working in batches and using more butter as needed, add the sliced dumplings to the pan and sauté until golden, 1 or 2 minutes. Turn and cook for 1 minute more.

13. To serve, place a cup of braised red cabbage on each of 6 plates and top with 3 slices of brisket. Spoon the sauce over the meat and serve with 3 pretzel dumplings on the side.

For the sweet-and-sour cabbage

5 tablespoons unsalted butter

½ cup diced red onion

1 medium white onion, diced

2 Granny Smith apples, peeled and cut into small dice

1 large red cabbage, about 3 pounds, cored and sliced thin

⅔ cup dried cherries

1½ cups dry red wine

2 whole cloves

⅓ cup brown sugar

1 bay leaf

⅛ cup apple cider vinegar

Freshly squeezed juice of ½ lemon

Celery Salad with Cider Vinegar and Sunflower Oil / PRIME MEATS

One night at Prime Meats we dined with a few friends and here's what we ordered: landjäger, sürkrüt garnie, steak frites, sautéed brown trout, weisswurst, herb mushroom spaetzle, and, to cut all that richness, a few celery salads. "You gotta have some palate-cleansing stuff, some light things," says co-owner Frank Castronovo. Definitely. This crisp salad is the perfect counterweight to the heavier half of the plate. The freshness of the celery is the prevailing flavor, but it's enhanced by the sharpness of the radish, the zing of the vinegar, and the rounding effect of the sunflower oil. You don't *have* to use a mandoline to slice the veggies, but if you want them to look like they do in this photo, you should.

1. To make the celery salad, in a large bowl, combine the celery root, celery, celery leaves, parsley leaves, and radish slices. Season to taste with salt and pepper.

2. To make the vinaigrette, in a small bowl, whisk the apple cider vinegar and sunflower oil.

3. To serve, drizzle the salad with a generous amount of the vinaigrette and toss to coat.

SERVES 4 (MAKES 5⅓ CUPS)

For the celery salad

1¼ cups celery root (celeriac), thinly sliced and julienned, preferably on a mandoline

1½ cups celery, thinly sliced, preferably on a mandoline

1¼ cups celery leaves

1 cup fresh flat-leaf parsley leaves

⅓ cup thinly sliced radishes, preferably sliced on a mandoline

Coarse salt and freshly ground black pepper

For the apple cider vinaigrette

2 tablespoons apple cider vinegar

½ cup sunflower oil

THE VANDERBILT

PROSPECT HEIGHTS

By Brooklyn standards, the Vanderbilt is a big restaurant. Big enough, in fact, to accommodate four distinct dining experiences. You can eat at the bar, as we did recently, starting with a dangerous cocktail called the Chase & Shade, which is basically apple juice for big kids: applejack, brandy, apple cider, molasses, black tea, and Regans' No. 6 orange bitters. You can snack at one of the high-stooled tables up front, an upscale version of the kind in airport lounges. Order a beer—there are usually about a dozen bottles and six or seven drafts to choose from—and the blistered *shisheto* peppers, which amount to gastronomic Russian roulette: One out of every seven or eight is freakishly spicy. You can sit in the back at a conventional table and choose from a flexible menu that allows for any ordering strategy—gussied-up bar snacks, charcuterie, and

regular entrées—so long as you're hungry. Or you can grab a counter seat facing the open kitchen, in which case you should close your menu and turn yourself over to the cooks performing directly in front of you. But please, be gentle with the chef and part-owner, Saul Bolton, who's still getting used to all this exposure after hiding in the kitchen of Saul (page 18) for the past decade. "Most people are very nice: 'Oh, this is *greeeaat*,'" Bolton says. "You smile at them, they smile at *you*. But then you get some people where you're like, *I swear to God, I have done something wrong. I'm being punished here*."

Bolton's not complaining *too* much, though. On the contrary, he seems like a man having a ridiculous amount of fun. ("Yesterday I made a buttload of boudin blanc, and it was the best batch yet!") Having played a key role in establishing the basic idea of high-end dining in Brooklyn, he's reveling in the Vanderbilt's the-only-rule-is-there-are-no-rules approach. Some dishes, like the pork loin with Parisian gnocchi and butternut squash puree (page 220), wouldn't

seem out of place at Saul. Others, like the spicy fried chicken wings, definitely would. "I'm just happy to be able to learn new stuff and do new things and work with new people," says Bolton. "The learning curve is huge and exhausting. It's freaking me out. That's why I'm so freaked out right now."

He can afford to be a little freaked out, because things seem to be running smoothly. The Vanderbilt's a slick operation. Of all the

restaurants in this book, only Dressler (page 114) feels as big-city-ish. Which doesn't mean it's formal. It's not. But it's airy and geometric, and the black-clad waiters look more Tribeca than Prospect Heights. Like No. 7 (page 182), whose experimental cooking feels like a deliberate rejection of the it's-all-about-the-ingredients zeitgeist, the Vanderbilt represents the expanding and casual confidence of fine dining in Brooklyn.

Pork Loin with Parisian Gnocchi and Butternut Squash Puree / THE VANDERBILT

SERVES 6

For the gnocchi (makes 5 dozen)

6 tablespoons (¾ stick) unsalted butter

1 teaspoon coarse salt

1 cup all-purpose flour, sifted

1 tablespoon grainy mustard

3 large eggs

1 tablespoon chopped fresh sage

Here's autumn on a plate: sliced pork over a puree of butternut squash with Brussels sprouts. And if chef Saul Bolton had stopped right there, we would not have complained. But the gnocchi is what elevates this dish and makes it one you'll remember (and crave). Inspired by a Parisian gnocchi dish Bolton had at Thomas Keller's Bouchon, these are made with *pâte à choux* (a light, versatile dough) and flavored with grainy mustard. "It's kind of a spaetzle idea," Bolton says. "You get the nice caramelized outside, and then they're kind of like fluffy little cakes on the inside." The gnocchi can be made ahead of time and frozen.

1. To make the gnocchi, combine the butter, salt, and ¾ cup water in a small saucepan and bring to a simmer over medium heat. Add the flour, stirring rapidly with a wooden spoon until the mixture pulls away from the sides of the pan. Reduce the heat to low and cook for 5 more minutes, stirring constantly, until the mixture looks smooth and moist.

2. Allow the mixture to cool slightly, then transfer the dough to a standing mixer fitted with a paddle. With the mixer on its lowest speed, add the mustard and mix until combined. Increase the speed to medium and add the eggs one at a time, making sure each is thoroughly incorporated before adding the next. Transfer the dough to a pastry bag fitted with a ⅝-inch tip. (If you don't have a pastry bag, fill a zip-top bag with the dough. Zip the bag closed, being sure to get as much air out of the bag as possible. Cut a ⅝-inch opening at the corner of the bag.)

3. Bring a large pot of salted water to a simmer. Prepare an ice bath in a large bowl and line a rimmed baking sheet with dish towels.

4. Pipe 2-inch-long gnocchi, cutting them off into the simmering water with a paring knife. Cook for 3 minutes, then transfer them to the ice bath. Drain the gnocchi and lay them on the baking sheet.

5. Place the baking sheet in the freezer until the gnocchi are completely frozen. Transfer the gnocchi to a clean zip-top bag until needed.

For the butternut squash puree
(makes about 4 cups)

1 large butternut squash
(about 3 pounds), cut lengthwise
and seeded

2 shallots, sliced

1 garlic clove, thinly sliced

2 tablespoons brown sugar

½ teaspoon ground cinnamon

1 Gala or golden delicious apple,
peeled, cored, and diced

1 teaspoon coarse salt

½ teaspoon freshly ground
black pepper

1½ tablespoons extra-virgin olive oil

For the pork

Two 1- to 1½-pound pork tenderloins,
cut into six 5- to 6-ounce pieces

Coarse salt and freshly ground
black pepper

3 tablespoons extra-virgin olive oil

2 tablespoons unsalted butter

For the Brussels sprouts

5 tablespoons extra-virgin olive oil,
divided

2 cups Brussels sprouts, trimmed
and quartered

¼ cup chopped shallots

3 tablespoons unsalted butter, divided

Coarse salt and freshly ground pepper

2 tablespoons grated Parmigiano-
Reggiano

6. To make the squash puree, preheat the oven to 450°F. Place the butternut squash cut side up on a rimmed baking sheet lined with parchment paper. Sprinkle with the shallots, garlic, brown sugar, cinnamon, apple, salt, and pepper, then drizzle with the olive oil. Cover each half with aluminum foil. Bake for 45 minutes, or until the squash is easily pierced with the tip of a knife. When the squash is cool enough to handle, scoop out the soft inside and transfer to a blender. Puree until smooth, adjust the seasoning, and set aside to cool.

7. To make the pork, heat a large sauté pan over medium-high heat. Season the pork loins with salt and pepper. Add the olive oil to the pan, increase the heat to high, and add the pork loins. Brown the pork loins on all sides, 2 to 3 minutes per side. Reduce the heat to medium, add the butter, and baste the pork. Cover and cook until the pork reaches an internal temperature of 138 to 140°F, about 8 minutes. Transfer to a plate, cover with foil, and set aside to rest in a warm place.

8. Place the butternut squash puree in a small saucepan and warm over low heat.

9. To make the Brussels sprouts, wipe out the sauté pan and place it over medium-high heat. Add 2 tablespoons of the olive oil and heat until shimmering. Add the Brussels sprouts and sauté until golden brown and almost cooked through. Reduce the heat to medium, add the chopped shallots and 1 tablespoon of the butter, and cook until the sprouts are completely cooked through, about 5 more minutes. Season to taste with salt and pepper. Transfer to a bowl and set aside.

10. To finish the gnocchi, wipe out the sauté pan and place it over medium heat. Add the remaining 3 tablespoons of olive oil, then the frozen gnocchi. Cook until the gnocchi are golden brown, about 5 minutes. Add the remaining 2 tablespoons of butter, allow the butter to brown (but not burn), about 5 minutes, then toss to coat the gnocchi. Remove the pan from the heat and add the sage—it will crisp up a bit off the heat. Transfer the gnocchi and sage to a large plate and sprinkle with the cheese.

11. To serve, warm 6 dinner plates and swish a spoonful of butternut squash puree on each one. Slice each piece of pork into 3 pieces, placing the slices on top of the squash puree. Scatter the Brussels sprouts and gnocchi on each plate and serve.

Spanish Ham Croquettes with Saffron Aioli / THE VANDERBILT

These classic croquettes—crispy on the outside, creamy on the inside—are basically just good ham and béchamel, rolled into balls and breaded twice in finely ground panko. "Make a buttload of 'em," urges chef Saul Bolton. Trust us, there won't be any left.

1. To make the croquettes, in a medium saucepan, melt the butter over medium heat. Add the onion and garlic and sauté until the onion is translucent, about 6 minutes. Add the flour and cook, stirring continuously, for 5 minutes. Add the warm milk, whisking until incorporated, and cook for 5 minutes, or until the mixture begins to thicken. Reduce the heat to low and cook until the sauce is thick and creamy. Add the ham and chives. Season to taste with salt and pepper.

2. Spread the mixture onto a lightly oiled rimmed baking sheet to cool, then cover and refrigerate for 2 to 4 hours or until well chilled.

3. In a small bowl, beat the eggs with 1 tablespoon water. Place the flour in a second bowl and the panko bread crumbs in a third bowl.

4. Working quickly with lightly wet hands, roll the croquette mixture into walnut-size pieces. Line the baking sheet with parchment paper.

5. Dredge the croquettes in the flour, coating evenly, and shake off any excess. Dip the croquettes in the egg wash, then roll in the panko crumbs. Dip again in the egg wash and coat once more with the panko (skip the flour in the second round of coating).

6. Place the breaded croquettes on the lined baking sheet and refrigerate for 30 minutes to 1 hour, or until firm.

7. Meanwhile, to make the saffron aioli, crush the saffron threads between your fingers into a small bowl. Add the hot water and soak for 5 minutes to infuse the water. Combine the egg yolks, salt, garlic, and saffron-infused water in a medium-size mixing bowl. Whisk until the mixture is well combined.

MAKES 14 TO 16 CROQUETTES

For the croquettes

4 tablespoons (½ stick) unsalted butter

⅓ cup minced Spanish onion

1 small garlic clove, minced

¼ cup all-purpose flour

1½ cups milk, warmed

2 ounces Serrano ham, finely diced

¼ cup chopped fresh chives

Coarse salt and freshly ground black pepper

2 large eggs

⅓ cup all-pupose flour

2 cups finely ground panko (Japanese bread crumbs)

Vegetable oil, for frying

For the saffron aioli (makes 1⅓ cups)

¼ teaspoon crushed saffron threads

2 tablespoons hot water

2 large egg yolks

¼ teaspoon coarse salt, plus more to taste

1 garlic clove, finely minced

½ cup canola oil

½ cup extra-virgin olive oil

Freshly squeezed juice of ½ lemon (about 1 tablespoon), or more to taste

8. Begin adding a small amount of the canola oil and olive oil, 1 to 2 tablespoons of each, in a slow, steady stream, whisking constantly, until the mixture is emulsified. Once the oil is completely combined, add the remaining oil in a slow, steady stream. Season to taste with salt, then add the lemon juice to taste. Set aside.*

9. In a large pot or deep fryer, pour enough vegetable oil to cover the croquettes while frying and heat the oil to 375°F on a deep-fry thermometer. Line a plate with paper towel. Working in batches, fry the croquettes until golden brown, 3 to 4 minutes. (Keep the uncooked croquettes refrigerated until ready to fry.) Remove the croquettes from the oil with a slotted spoon and set them on the plate to drain. Season to taste with salt and pepper.

10. To serve, as tapas, place the croquettes on a plate and drizzle with saffron aioli.

* *This recipe makes more aioli than you will need. Transfer leftover aioli to an airtight container and refrigerate for up to 2 days.*

EAGLE STREET ROOFTOP FARMS / GREENPOINT

ANNIE NOVAK

It's a crazy sight: a 6,000-square-foot organic vegetable farm spread like a striped green blanket across the roof of a squat, sprawling building in one of Brooklyn's grayest neighborhoods. Eagle Street Rooftop Farms is never going to feed the whole borough (or even the whole block), but it grows dozens of crops, hosts its own Sunday market, and sells to local restaurants including Marlow & Sons and Anella, who serves a Rooftop Farm salad recipe in season. Rooftop farmer Annie Novak squeezes in as much Eagle Street time as she can around her day job as the coordinator of the children's gardening program at the New York Botanical Garden. We talked to her as she did some light chores at the farm on an early summer Saturday.

Do you have any agriculture in your background?

I'm from the Midwest. It's in the blood! But no, not really.

How did you get interested in farming, that this could be a living?

When I was in college, I was focused on development studies—the intersection between people and commodities. I was really interested in stories—where do things come from, where do they go, what do they do. The only way to get people to care about things is to give them a full narrative. Otherwise, who cares about recycling?

So I was studying chocolate, and I ended up going to West Africa, to study at the University of Cape Coast, in Ghana. And I was walking around the fields with this woman, and she was explaining to me how the women's work fits into the chocolate cooperative that she was part of, and I was like *women's rights! Women's rights!* And then she says, "We should go look at some chocolate trees"—and I realized I didn't know what they looked like. I felt like such an idiot. I knew nothing about the thing that I was writing about. That was when I started teaching myself about agriculture.

Which crops are you most excited about?

Everything seems to be growing really, really well. We had really good spinach; that was exciting. We dedicated two solid rows to cucumbers—all these different varieties, like Japanese and lemon cucumbers. We're growing a lot of different things because if you grow a lot of different crops, you can tell by the end of the year what works. This is the first time anyone's ever done a project on this scale on a roof, and we're hoping to expand to other buildings in the neighborhood, so I want to know what will survive.

You have lots of volunteers helping out on the weekends. What do you have them do?

Harvest, compost, sow—anything you would do at a farm. But we try to give them only jobs that are instructive. It's, what can they learn from it? I mentored with seven or eight different farmers, and I learned a lot from their different styles. In one case I picked thistles out of a cow field for six weeks. And I was like, "This is bullshit, I'm not learning anything." So I've tried to give the best of what I've learned. It's important to me to make the most of the space, and of the volunteers' time. They've been keeping the farm well watered, pest-free, and full of an incredible energy.

Do you take compost contributions?

Yes! Everybody who comes to volunteer brings a little bag that they've been freezing all week.

COCKTAILS

If Brooklyn's new dining scene is an attempt to excavate the best parts of the past—locally grown food served in mom-and-pop restaurants that often double as neighborhood gathering spots—its cocktail culture is even more overtly retro. "It's an attempt to recover what there was before Prohibition, to reach back and fix a broken tradition," says David Wondrich, the author of *Imbibe!* (a history of tippling and a biography of legendary nineteenth-century bartender "Professor" Jerry Thomas) and the single most opinionated drinks expert in Brooklyn, if not on the entire planet. True, this mixological archeology—archealcohology?—is hardly unique to the borough. But it sure is thriving here. Following, recipes from seven Brooklyn bars that are especially committed to the mixing of a proper drink.

Nor'easter

/ CHAR NO. 4, CARROLL GARDENS

Here's a version of Bermuda's national drink, the Dark and Stormy, with bourbon swapped in for rum. But wait—why the "Nor'easter" if it features America's ultimate Southern spirit? Never mind, let's not overthink it. But don't overdrink it, either: Between the ginger beer and the maple syrup, these go down entirely too easy.

In a cocktail shaker, combine the bourbon, lime juice, and maple syrup with ice cubes. Shake vigorously. Strain into a rocks glass filled with ice. Top with the ginger beer and garnish with the lime.

MAKES 1 DRINK

1½ ounces Old Crow bourbon or any bourbon of your choice

½ ounce freshly squeezed lime juice

½ ounce pure maple syrup

1½ ounces ginger beer

1 lime slice, for garnish

Gin Blossom

/ THE CLOVER CLUB, CARROLL GARDENS

MAKES 1 DRINK

1½ ounces Plymouth gin

1½ ounces Martini Bianco

¾ ounce apricot eau-de-vie

2 dashes orange bitters

Orange twist

This is the Clover Club's "house martini," and it definitely looks like one: a crystal-clear drink served straight up in a cocktail glass. But the addition of the eau-de-vie and Martini Bianco (in place of vermouth) lends both fragrance and complexity. Like the classic that inspired it, the Gin Blossom will get you where you're going, and fast.

Stir the first four ingredients in a cocktail shaker with ice and strain into a cocktail glass. Garnish with an orange twist.

Greenwood Cooler

/ QUARTER BAR, GREENWOOD HEIGHTS

MAKES 1 DRINK

Two ⅛-inch-thick slices cucumber, one with a rim-cut for garnish

4 fresh mint leaves

Lemon wedge

1 teaspoon simple syrup*

¾ ounce premium grapefruit juice

1¾ ounces vodka, preferably potato

1 ounce soda water

* Mix equal parts sugar and boiling water. Stir until the sugar dissolves. Store any extra in the fridge. Many drinks call for simple syrup, so it'll come in handy.

This cocktail was inspired by a glass of water co-owner David Moo drank one hot summer day at a wine bar in Greenport, Long Island. The water was served from a pitcher that had mint leaves and slices of lemon and cucumber floating in it. Like that glass of water, the Greenwood Cooler—originally called the Greenport Cooler but later changed to honor the bar's neighborhood—is soft, bright, and refreshing. Feel free to use gin instead of vodka.

Muddle the uncut cucumber slice, mint, and lemon in a highball or other tall glass until the cucumber slice has been partially destroyed and the lemon wedge juiced. Add the simple syrup, grapefruit juice, and vodka. Stir. Add enough ice so that it sticks out above the surface of the liquid. Top with soda and slide the rim-cut cucumber slice onto the edge of the glass. Slip in a straw, if you've got one, and enjoy.

Brooklyn Rumble

/ THE JAKEWALK, CARROLL GARDENS

MAKES 1 DRINK

2 ounces Scarlet Ibis Aged Trinidad Rum or other aged rum

¾ ounce freshly squeezed lime juice

¾ ounce simple syrup (see note, page 231)

½ ounce framboise

Dash of Angostura bitters

Jeremy Swift, head bartender at "the Jake," based his Brooklyn Rumble on the Bramble, a popular British cocktail that uses gin (instead of rum), lemon juice (instead of lime), and blackberry liqueur (instead of framboise, which is raspberry-based). Other than that, they're identical.

In a cocktail shaker, shake the first three ingredients and strain into a lowball glass filled with crushed ice. Pour in the framboise (it will sink to the bottom) and top with a dash of Angostura bitters.

Corpse Reviver No. 1

/ WEATHER UP, PROSPECT HEIGHTS

Weather Up is one of the most historically correct cocktail lounges in Brooklyn—indeed, in all of New York. The Corpse Reviver is a hangover remedy (duh) and is generally served with a restorative glass of ice water.

Stir the cognac, applejack, Antica Formula, and bitters in a cocktail shaker filled with ice, then pour into a chilled cocktail glass. Twist and roll the lemon peel over the cocktail glass to extract some of the lemon oil. Float the peel in the cocktail glass.

MAKES 1 DRINK

1½ ounces cognac

¾ ounce applejack

¾ ounce Antica Formula

Dash of Angostura bitters

Lemon peel, cut into a finger-length strip using a fruit peeler

Riposto / BROOKLYN SOCIAL, CARROLL GARDENS

MAKES 1 DRINK

Leaves from a short sprig of fresh rosemary, plus a sprig for garnish

2 or 3 segments of peeled tangerine

Splash of Triple Sec

2 ounces vodka

Brooklyn Social is arguably the granddaddy of the borough's modern cocktail scene—and it only opened in 2004. This drink is named after Società Riposto, a social club that occupied the Smith Street space before the bar took over. Riposto was the Sicilian hometown of its members.

Muddle the rosemary leaves and tangerine with the Triple Sec in a cocktail shaker. Add the vodka and shake with ice. Serve on the rocks in an old-fashioned glass. Garnish with the sprig of rosemary.

Prescription Julep / FORT DEFIANCE, RED HOOK

This recipe goes back to 1857, if not earlier, when it appeared in the September issue of *Harper's Monthly*. According to that article, the original recipe was a prescription, written in medical Latin, to treat a man whose dyspepsia had been brought on by reading about politics in the newspaper.

MAKES 1 DRINK

4 or 5 small fresh mint sprigs (with no black spots)

1½ ounces cognac

½ ounce rye whiskey

½ ounce simple syrup (see note, page 231)

1 teaspoon overproof dark rum (such as Gosling's 151 or Lemon Hart)

1. In a silver julep cup or a small stainless-steel mixing cup (or, as a last resort, a highball glass), add one of the mint sprigs, the cognac, rye, and simple syrup. Using a muddler, gently press the mint several times to express the oils into the liquid.

2. Put about 2 cups ice into a cloth bag, or wrap well in a large dish towel. Using a wooden mallet or a rolling pin, smash the ice into tiny bits, the finer the better; do not leave any ice chunks larger than a dime.

3. Fill the cup three-quarters full with crushed ice and stir a few times to combine. Add more crushed ice until it's piled into a cone above the rim of the cup. Select three or four good mint sprigs and nestle them into the ice, together in a tight bunch. Insert a straw next to the mint. (You might want to trim it so that it doesn't stick up too high.) Carefully drizzle the rum over the crushed ice and serve.

RECIPES INDEX

EQUIPMENT

When you're cooking restaurant food, restaurant equipment can make things a bit easier. Here are a few kitchen tools and accessories that will help you get the most out of the recipes in this book.

Rimmed **baking sheets** in assorted sizes: Great for roasting and baking, and for your *mise en place* (organization of your uncooked and prepared ingredients).

Cast-iron **Dutch oven** or heavy casserole with tight-fitting lid: Perfect for slow cooking or braising, either in the oven or on the stovetop.

Food mill: The perfect tool for vegetable purees, mashes, sauces, and soups; it strains and purees at the same time.

Food processor with mini cup insert: Perfect for chopping garlic, herbs, onions, and nuts. Nested into the standard 10- to 14-cup work bowl, the mini cup is more space-efficient than having a food processor and a separate mini chopper.

Quality **knife set:** Must include a chef's knife, a boning knife with a flexible blade, a paring knife, and a serrated knife for bread and tomatoes.

Lodge cast-iron stovetop **grill/griddle:** This spans two burners and turns your stovetop into a grill and griddle. Sear your meats, poultry, and vegetables on the ridged grill and flip over to cook pancakes and eggs on the smooth griddle.

Ice cream maker or attachment for standing mixer: Look for a machine with self-contained refrigeration and 1- to 2-quart capacity.

Immersion blender: This tall and narrow handheld blender is very convenient and efficient for pureeing soups and sauces directly in the pot.

Microplane grater: Razor-sharp, these stainless-steel graters are ideal for grating citrus rinds, hard cheese, fresh nutmeg, fresh ginger, and more.

Parchment paper: To line baking sheets when roasting for easy cleanup or to cover a braise to prevent too much liquid from evaporating. Silicone coated, nonstick, and scorch-resistent up to about 400°F.

Roller **pasta cutter:** Helpful for crimping and cutting ravioli.

Pasta maker or pasta roller attachment for a stand mixer: Yes, it takes some time, but the thrill of making a beautiful dough and serving fresh handmade pasta justifies the effort.

Potato ricer: A must for making mashed potatoes.

Digital food **scale:** Ensures accuracy in measuring all kinds of ingredients, especially when baking with chocolate, butter, and nuts. Choose one that shows both grams and ounces.

Lodge cast-iron **skillets**, 6½-inch to 15-inch: Great for braising, frying, and baking. Cast iron heats up quickly, makes a rustic serving piece, and gets better with age.

Spice grinder: Essential for grinding whole spices to fine powders.

Conical **strainer** (also called a China cap) or fine-mesh strainer (also called a chinois): A must for straining sauces and soups. A chinois often comes with a dowel to help push the food through the holes.

Thermometers: deep-fry thermometer/candy thermometer: Gauges the temperature of oil for deep-frying, boiled syrups, sauces, and candy mixtures. Instant-read **meat thermometer:** Judges doneness quickly and eliminates the guesswork. Poke the needle end of the thermometer into the center of the meat or thick part of a poultry thigh, always taking care to avoid the bone, until the temperature stops rising. **Oven thermometer:** Assures that your oven is properly calibrated.

Tongs: Essential for turning, lifting, and tossing salads. For the most versatility, choose a 10- or 12-inch sturdy metal variety with scalloped tips to "bite" and hold food.

RESOURCES

Here's contact information for the restaurants in this book, plus a list of our favorite shops, markets, pizzerias, food trucks, and other food-related entities in the borough.

RESTAURANTS

Al Di Là
248 Fifth Avenue
Park Slope
718-783-4565
www.aldilatrattoria.com

Aliseo Osteria del Borgo
655 Vanderbilt Avenue
Prospect Heights
718-783-3400

applewood
501 Eleventh Street
Park Slope
718-788-1810
www.applewoodny.com

Beer Table
427B Seventh Avenue
Park Slope
718-965-1196
www.beertable.com

Buttermilk Channel
524 Court Street
Carroll Gardens
718-852-8490
www.buttermilkchannelnyc.com

Char No. 4
196 Smith Street
Cobble Hill
718-643-2106
www.charno4.com

Convivium Osteria
68 Fifth Avenue
Park Slope
718-857-1833
www.convivium-osteria.com

Dressler
149 Broadway
Williamsburg
718-384-6343
www.dresslernyc.com

DuMont
432 Union Avenue
Williamsburg
718-486-7717
www.dumontrestaurant.com

Egg
135 North Fifth Street
Williamsburg
718-302-5151
www.pigandegg.com

The Farm on Adderley
1108 Cortelyou Road
Ditmas Park
718-287-3101
www.thefarmonadderley.com

Five Leaves
18 Bedford Avenue
Greenpoint
718-383-5345
www.fiveleavesny.com

Flatbush Farm
76 St. Marks Avenue
Park Slope
718-622-3276
www.flatbushfarm.com

Franny's
295 Flatbush Avenue
Prospect Heights
718-230-0221
www.frannysbrooklyn.com

The General Greene
229 Dekalb Avenue
Fort Greene
718-222-1510
www.thegeneralgreene.com

The Good Fork
391 Van Brunt Street
Red Hook
718-643-6636
www.goodfork.com

The Grocery
288 Smith Street
Carroll Gardens
718-596-3335
www.thegroceryrestaurant.com

iCi
246 Dekalb Avenue
Fort Greene
718-789-2778
www.icirestaurant.com

James
605 Carlton Avenue
Prospect Heights
718-942-4255
www.jamesresturantny.com

Locanda Vini e Olii
129 Gates Avenue
Clinton Hill
718-622-9202
www.locandavinieolii.com

Lunetta
116 Smith Street
Cobble Hill
718-488-6269
www.lunetta-ny.com/brooklyn

Marlow & Sons
81 Broadway
Williamsburg
718-384-1441
www.marlowandsons.com

No. 7
7 Greene Avenue
Fort Greene
718-522-6370
www.no7restaurant.com

Northeast Kingdom
18 Wyckoff Avenue
Bushwick
718-386-3864
www.north-eastkingdom.com

Palo Santo
652 Union Street
Park Slope
718-636-6311
www.palosanto.us

Prime Meats
465 Court Street
Carroll Gardens
718-254-0327
www.frankspm.com

Roberta's
261 Moore Street
Bushwick
718-417-1118
www.robertaspizza.com

Rose Water
787 Union Street
Park Slope
718-783-3800
www.rosewaterrestaurant.com

Saul
140 Smith Street
Cobble Hill
718-935-9844
www.saulrestaurant.com

The Vanderbilt
570 Vanderbilt Avenue
Prospect Heights
718-623-0570
www.thevanderbiltnyc.com

Vinegar Hill House
72 Hudson Avenue
Vinegar Hill
718-522-1018
www.vinegarhillhouse.com

BAKERIES/PATISSERIES

Almondine Bakery
French pastries and baguettes
85 Water Street
DUMBO
718-797-5026
and
442 Ninth Street
Park Slope
718-832-4607
www.almondinebakery.com

Baked NYC
Cakes, cookies, pies, tarts, brownies, muffins, scones, marshmallows, and granola
359 Van Brunt Street
Red Hook
718-222-0345
www.bakednyc.com

Bakeri
Norwegian specialities like fjord bread and herring sandwiches
150 Wythe Avenue
Williamsburg
718-388-8037
www.bakeribrooklyn.com

Betty Bakery

Fruit tarts, cupcakes, and wedding cakes

448 Atlantic Avenue

Boerum Hill

718-246-2402

www.cherylkleinman.blogspot.com

Colson Patisserie

French pastries, soups, salads, sandwiches, and quiches

374 Ninth Avenue

Park Slope

718-965-6400

www.colsonpastries.com

Down Under Bakery (DUB) Pies

Australian and New Zealand–style gourmet meat pies and traditional sweet treats

211 Prospect Park West

Windsor Terrace

718-788-2448

www.dubpies.com

Joyce Bakeshop

Pastries, Gorilla coffee

646 Vanderbilt Avenue

Prospect Heights

718-623-7470

www.joycebakeshop.com

Kumquat Cupcakery

Exotic flavored bite-size cupcakes

www.kumquatcupcakery.com

Nine Cakes

Made-to-order cakes and cupcakes

155 Columbia Street

Red Hook

347-907-9632

www.ninecakes.com

One Girl Cookies

Petite tea cookies and other handmade sweets

68 Dean Street

Cobble Hill

212-675-4996

www.onegirlcookies.com

Saltie Bakery and Sandwich Shop

Sandwiches, whole-grain and olive oil–based pastries

378 Metropolitan Avenue

Williamsburg

718-387-4777

www.saltieny.com

Scratchbread

Artisanal bread, scones, brownies, and shortbread

www.scratchbread.com

Sugarbuilt Cookies

Iced cookies with decorative art object motifs

www.sugarbuilt.com

Sweet Melissa Pâtisserie

Full-service bakery and tea shop since 1998

276 Court Street

Carroll Gardens

718-855-3410

and

175 Seventh Avenue

Park Slope

718-788-2700

www.sweetmelissapatisserie.com

Trois Pommes Patisserie

Greenmarket-inspired fruit tarts and ice cream, classic American cakes and sweets

260 Fifth Avenue

Park Slope

718-230-3119

www.troispommespatisserie.com

Whimsy & Spice

Handmade sweets with a dash of spice

646-709-6659

www.whimsyandspice.com

BREWERIES/BEER STORES/ BEER GARDENS/BEVERAGES

Bierkraft

Beer, cheeses, charcuterie, made-to-order sandwiches

191 Fifth Avenue

Park Slope

718-230-7600

www.bierkraft.com

Brooklyn Brewery

Brewing in Brooklyn since 1996; brewery tours

79 North Eleventh Street

Williamsburg

718-486-7422

www.brooklynbrewery.com

Brooklyn Homebrew

Equipment and ingredients for making beer at home

163 Eighth Street

Sunset Park

718-369-0776

www.brooklyn-homebrew.com

Brouwerij Lane Beer Merchants

Craft brews, growlers

78 Greenpoint Avenue

Greenpoint

347-529-6133

www.brouwerijlane.com

Eagle Provisions

Extensive beer selection, Polish sausage

628 Fifth Avenue

South Slope

718-499-0026

Franklin Park

Beer garden owned by Joe Carroll, owner of Spuyten Duyvil Bar and Grocery

618 St. John's Place

Crown Heights

718-975-0196

www.franklinparkbrooklyn.com

Kelso of Brooklyn

Craft brewery making pale ale, pilsner, and lager year-round; plus small-batch seasonal brews

529 Waverly Avenue

Greenpoint

718-398-2731

www.kelsoofbrooklyn.com

Kombucha Brooklyn

Detoxifying Chinese fermented tea energy drink brewed from organic ingredients, home brew kits

www.kombuchabrooklyn.com

Radegast Hall & Biergarten

Austro-Hungarian beer hall

113 North Third Street

Williamsburg

718-963-3973

www.radegasthall.com

Sixpoint Craft Ales

See page 46

40 Van Dyke Street

Red Hook

www.sixpointcraftales.com

Spuyten Duyvil

Beer garden featuring Belgian beer and cask-pulled ale

359 Metropolitan Avenue

Williamsburg

718-963-4140

www.spuytenduyvilnyc.com

CHOCOLATE

Fine & Raw

Bars and bonbons

151 Kent Avenue, Suite 108

Williamsburg

646-894-2929

www.fineandraw.com

Jacques Torres Chocolate

Chocolate factory and shop since December 2000

66 Water Street

DUMBO

718-875-9772

www.mrchocolate.com

Mast Brothers Chocolate

See page 134

105A North Third Street

Williamsburg

718-388-2625

www.mastbrotherschocolate.com

Nunu Chocolates

Hand-dipped salt caramels and other handmade chocolates

529 Atlantic Avenue

Boerum Hill

917-776-7102

www.nunuchocolates.com

COFFEE AND TEA

Café Grumpy

Grinds and brews by the cup in the Clover coffee machine

383 Seventh Avenue

Park Slope

718-499-4404

and

193 Meserole Avenue

Williamsburg

718-349-7623

www.cafegrumpy.com

Café Pedlar

Brews Stumptown coffee roasted in Red Hook; serves Frankies' Olive Oil Bundt Cake

210 Court Street

Cobble Hill

718-855-7129

www.cafepedlar.com

Café Regular

Serve La Colombe coffee

318 Eleventh Street

Park Slope

718-768-4170

and

Café Regular du Nord

158 Berkeley Place

Park Slope

No phone

www.caferegular.com

Gimme! Coffee

Espresso bar and artisanal coffee roaster

495 Lorimer Street

Williamsburg

718-388-7771

www.gimmecoffee.com

Glass Shop

Cafe serving La Colombe coffee, from the owners of Weather Up

766 Classon Avenue

Crown Heights

www.glassshoplocal.com

Gorilla Coffee

See page 26

97 Fifth Avenue

Park Slope

718-230-3244

www.gorillacoffee.com

Oslo Coffee Company
Brews its own coffee roasted in Williamsburg
133-B Roebling Street
Williamsburg
718-782-0332
and
328 Bedford Street
Williamsburg
718-782-0332
www.oslocoffee.com

Root Hill Café
Single-cup brew in a Clover coffee machine
262 Fourth Avenue
718-797-0100
www.roothillcafe.com

Southside Coffee
Intelligentsia coffee and Balthazar pastries
652 6th Avenue
Windsor Terrace
347-599-0887

Tea Lounge
Café, tea shop, bar, music venue
837 Union Street
Park Slope
718-789-2762
www.tealoungeny.com

COOKWARE/COOKING CLASSES

The Brooklyn Kitchen /The Brooklyn Kitchen Labs /The Meat Hook
100 Frost Street
Williamsburg
www.thebrooklynkitchen.com

The Brooklyn Kitchen
Tools necessary to make good food
718-389-2982

The Brooklyn Kitchen Labs
7,000-square-foot warehouse space for cooking classes, culinary events, lectures

The Meat Hook
Housed inside the Labs; full-service butcher shop
718-349-5033

A Cook's Companion
Cookware, bakeware, tableware, knives
197 Atlantic Avenue
Brooklyn Heights
718-852-6901
www.acookscompanion.com

Creative Cooks
Culinary education center designed just for kids
298 Atlantic Avenue
Cobble Hill
718-237-2218
www.creativecooks.us

Cut Brooklyn
See page 154
Gowanus
646-247-9955
www.cutbrooklyn.com

Juguemos a Cantar Spanish Institute
Spanish immersion cooking classes for kids
Park Slope
718-788-6472
www.juguemos.org

Kids Cook Brooklyn
Cooking classes for kids ages 4 to 13; fresh, natural ingredients and seasonal produce
170 Hicks Street
Brooklyn Heights
www.kidscookbrooklyn.com

Mimi's Soup Spoon
"Mommy/Daddy and Me" cooking classes for preschoolers
Multiple locations
646-957-5439
www.mimissoupspoon.com

The Tum Tum Tree
Children ages 4 to 7 explore creativity through cooking
Brooklyn Society for Ethical Culture
53 Prospect Park West
Park Slope
646-479-6336
http://web.mac.com/thetum
tumtree/iWeb/thetumtumtree/
home.html

CSAS (COMMUNITY SUPPORTED AGRICULTURE)

Amantai Farm CSA
Third Root Community Center
380 Marlborough Road
Ditmas Park
www.ditmasparkcsa.org

Bay Ridge CSA
Fourth Avenue Presbyterian Church
6753 Fourth Avenue
Bay Ridge
www.bayridgecsa.org

Bed-Stuy Farm Share
Magnolia Tree Earth Center
677 Lafayette Avenue
Bedford-Stuyvesant
718-783-8443
www.bedstuyfarmshare.org

Brooklyn Beet CSA
YWCA
30 Third Avenue
Boerum Hill
brooklynbeetcsa.ning.com

Bushwick CSA
301 Grove Street
Bushwick
718-418-7690 x232
bushwickcsa.wordpress.com

Carroll Gardens CSA
The Transit Garden
Smith Street and Second Place
Carroll Gardens
www.gardenofevefarm.com/csa_
carroll.htm

Charcuterie CSA
The Brooklyn Kitchen
100 Frost Street
Williamsburg
718-389-2982
www.thepiggery.net
www.thebrooklynkitchen.com

Clinton Hill CSA
Public School 56
170 Gates Avenue
718-907-0616
Clinton Hill
www.clintonhillcsa.org

Cobble Hill CSA
Christ Church
326 Clinton Street
Cobble Hill
718-858-9009
www.cobblehillcsa.org

DUMBO/Vinegar Hill CSA
Phoenix House
50 Jay Street
DUMBO
www.dumbocsa.org

East Williamsburg CSA
Red Shed Community Garden
266 Skillman Avenue
East Williamsburg
845-943-8699
www.eastwilliamsburgcsa.org

Flatbush Farm Share
CAMBA Office at Flatbush
Reformed Church
2103 Kenmore Terrace
Flatbush
212-741-8192, ext. 7
www.flatbushfarmshare.com

Greene Harvest CSA
Habana Outpost
757 Fulton Street
Fort Greene
www.greeneharvestcsa.com

Greenpoint-Williamsburg CSA
McCarren Park, North Twelfth
Street and Driggs Avenue
Greenpoint
and
Lutheran Church of the Messiah
129 Russell Street
Greenpoint
www.greenpoint-williamsburgcsa
.org

Greenwood Heights CSA
Slope Park
Sixth Avenue and Nineteenth
Street
Greenwood Heights
www.greenwoodheightscsa.com

Kensington/Windsor Terrace CSA
Windsor Terrace Community
Garden
East Fourth Street and Fort
Hamilton Parkway
Windsor Terrace
www.kwtcsa.blogspot.com

Prospect Lefferts Gardens CSA
21 Lincoln Road
Prospect Lefferts Gardens
347-823-1076
www.plgcsa.org

Red Hook CSA
Red Hook Community Farm:
A Project of Added Value
Columbia Street and Halleck
Street
Red Hook
718-855-5531
www.added-value.org/the-csa

Southside CSA
Bridget
20 Broadway
Williamsburg
www.southsidecsa.wordpress.com

Sunset Park CSA
St. Michael's Church
4247 Fourth Avenue
Sunset Park
www.sunsetparkcsa.org

Sweet Pea CSA
First Unitarian Universalist
Church
50 Monroe Place
Brooklyn Heights
sites.google.com/site/sweetpeacsa/

FARMS
Added Value
On Wednesdays at:
Red Hook Senior Center
6 Walcott Street
Red Hook
and
on Saturdays at:
Red Hook Community Farm
590 Columbia Street
Red Hook
305 Van Brunt Avenue (office)
Red Hook
718-855-5531
www.added-value.org

BRM Bed-Stuy Farm
255 Bainbridge Street
Bedford-Stuyvesant
718-363-3085
www.brooklyrescuemission.org/
Bedstuyfarm.aspx

Brooklyn Grange Farm
37-18 Northern Boulevard
Long Island City, Queens
917-204-5644
Sunday market at:
Roberta's
261 Moore Street
Bushwick

Eagle Street Rooftop Farms
See page 226
Eagle and West Streets
Greenpoint
www.rooftopfarms.org

East New York Farms!
United Community Centers
613 New Lots Avenue
East New York
www.eastnewyorkfarms.org

FARMERS' MARKETS/
GREENMARKETS

Most greenmarkets do not have their own websites, but all details about each market are available on the Council of the Environment of New York City website (www.cenyc.org). Vendors and purveyors can change seasonally, so check the CENYC website for specific vendor lists.

Bay Ridge Greenmarket
Third Avenue at Ninety-Fifth Street in the parking lot of Walgreens Pharmacy
Saturdays, June–November, 8 A.M.–3 P.M.

Boro Park Greenmarket
Fourteenth Avenue at Fiftieth Street
Thursdays, July–November, 8 A.M.–3 P.M.

Brooklyn Borough Hall Greenmarket
Court Street at Montague Street
On the plaza at the intersection
Tuesdays and Saturdays year-round, 8 A.M.–6 P.M.
Thursdays, April–December, 8 A.M.–6 P.M.

Carroll Gardens Greenmarket
Carroll Street at Smith Street
Sundays, mid April–December, 8 A.M.–4 P.M.

Cortelyou Greenmarket
Cortelyou Road at Rugby Road
Sundays, year-round, 8 A.M.–4 P.M.

Fort Greene Park Greenmarket
Washington Park at Dekalb Avenue
Saturdays, year-round, 8 A.M.–5 P.M.

Grand Army Plaza Greenmarket
Prospect Park West and Flatbush Avenue
Northwest corner of Prospect Park
Saturdays, year-round, 8 A.M.–4 P.M.

Greenpoint/McCarren Park Greenmarket
Union Avenue between Driggs Avenue and North 12th Street
Saturdays, year-round, 8 A.M.–3 P.M.

Park Slope Indoor Farmers' Market
The Makers Market at Old American Can Factory
232 Third Street
Gowanus
January–May, 11 A.M.–5 P.M.
www.communitymarkets.biz/
market.php?market=34

Williamsburg Greenmarket
Broadway at Havemeyer Street
Thursdays, July–November, 8 A.M.–4 P.M.

Windsor Terrace Greenmarket
Prospect Park West at Fifteenth Street
Inside the entrance of Prospect Park
Wednesdays, May–November, 8 A.M.–3 P.M.

FOOD CO-OPS

Flatbush Food Coop
1415 Cortelyou Road
Ditmas Park
718-284-9717
www.flatbushfoodcoop.com

Greene Hill Food Co-op
Currently in development stage,
but accepting members
Fort Greene
718-208-4778
www.greenehillfoodcoop.com

Park Slope Food Coop
782 Union Street
Park Slope
718-622-0560
www.foodcoop.com

FOOD TRUCKS

Many of the trucks are only out in the warmer months but are available all year round for catering and special events. Find most NYC Food Trucks at any time via Twitter. Or track some at Google Maps; search "NYC Food Trucks."

Boiled in Brooklyn
Traditionally Southern fresh "green" boiled peanuts, also known as goober peas
www.boiledinbrooklyn.com

Choncho's Tacos
Beer-battered fish tacos with lime and hot sauces
www.chonchostacos.com
www.twitter.com/chonchostacos
And the restaurant:
The Loading Dock
170 Tillary Street
Downtown Brooklyn
646-355-7518

**El Diablo Taco Truck
inside Union Pool**
Tacos, chips, and guacamole
484 Union Avenue
Williamsburg
718-609-0484
www.eldiablotacos.com

The Empanada Lady
Chicken or beef empanadas
Thirteenth Street and Fifth
Avenue (Park Slope)
Carroll Street at Smith Street
(Cobble Hill)

Endless Summer Taco Truck
Fish tacos, burritos
Bedford Street at North Sixth
Street
Williamsburg
www.endlesssummertacos.com

Eurotrash Vending Truck
Swedish meatballs, fish and chips, fried Mars bars
106 North Third Street
Williamsburg
www.eurotrashtruck.com

Green Pirate Juice Truck
Freshly squeezed juices, healthy snacks
www.green-pirate.com
twitter.com/juicepirate

Milk Truck
Artisanal grilled cheese sandwiches
917-520-7415
www.milktruckgrilledcheese.com

NYC Cravings
Taiwanese-style fried chicken, fried pork, dumplings
nyccravings.com/twitter.com/
nyccravings

Pizza Moto Brooklyn
A mobile wood-fired brick-oven pizzeria
646-334-4456
www.pizzamotobklyn.com

Red Hook Food Vendors
Traditional dishes from all corners of Latin America
Red Hook Ball Fields
Clinton Street at Bay Street
Red Hook
www.redhookfoodvendors.com

Rickshaw Dumpling Bar
Dumplings, steamed buns, chocolate soup dumpling
www.rickshawdumplings.com
twitter.com/rickshawbar

Schnitzel & Things
Chicken, pork, and cod schnitzel
347-772-7341
www.schnitzelandthings.com

Van Leeuwen Artisan Ice Cream
Custard-based homemade ice cream
718-701-1630
www.vanleeuwenicecream.com
twitter.com/VLAIC

Van Leeuwen store:
632 Manhattan Avenue
Greenpoint

Wafels & Dinges

Traditional Belgian waffles with dinges (toppings) like strawberries, bananas, Nutella, and whipped cream
646-257-2592 for catering
866-429-7329 for truck location
www.wafelsanddinges.com

GROCERS/SPECIALTY MARKETS

Acme Smoked Fish

Open for retail sales Fridays only, 8 A.M.–1 P.M., cash only
30 Gem Street
Williamsburg
718-383-8585
www.acmesmokedfish.com

Back to the Land

Fresh, natural, organic, and whole foods, nutritional products, body-care products
142 Seventh Avenue
Park Slope
718-768-5654
www.backtothelandnaturalfoods
.com

The Bedford Cheese Shop

Old-fashioned cheesemongers, local artisanal products, cheese plate of the day, sandwich plate of the day
229 Bedford Avenue
Williamsburg
718-599-7588
www.bedfordcheeseshop.com

Blue Apron Foods

Artisanal cheeses, locally made products, imported and domestic specialty foods
814 Union Street
Park Slope
718-230-3180

Bklyn Larder

See page 70
228 Flatbush Avenue
718-783-1250
www.bklynlarder.com

Brooklyn Fare / Brooklyn's Kitchen at Brooklyn Fare

Gourmet grocery by day, after-hours private dining by night
200 Schermerhorn Street
Downtown Brooklyn
718-243-0050
www.brooklynfare.com

Brooklyn Standard Deli

The corner bodega meets natural-foods grocery and coffee bar
188 Nassau Avenue
Greenpoint
718-472-2150
www.thestandarddeli.com

Caputo's Fine Foods

Ciabatta sandwiches, homemade fresh mozzarella
460 Court Street
Carroll Gardens
718-855-8852

Choice Market

Café, bakery, market
318 Lafayette Avenue
Clinton Hill
718-230-5214

Choice Greene

Gourmet grocery in a general-store setting
214 Greene Avenue
Fort Greene
718-230-1243
and

Choice Market DUMBO

108 Jay Street
DUMBO
718-797-1695

D. Coluccio & Sons

Italian charcuterie, imported specialty foods
1214 Sixtieth Street
Borough Park
718-436-6700
www.dcoluccioandsons.com

D'Vine Taste

Homemade Lebanese dishes, imported specialty foods, bulk spices
150 Seventh Avenue
Park Slope
718-369-9548
www.dvine-taste.com

Fish Tales

Full-service fish market, prepared foods
191A Court Street
Cobble Hill
718-246-1346
www.fishtalesonline.com

Faicco's Pork Store

Homemade fresh sausages, Italian staples, heat-and-serve prepared foods
6511 Eleventh Avenue
Dyker Heights
718-236-0119

Fairway Market

One-stop shopping at this gastronomic mecca
480 Van Brunt Street
Red Hook
718-694-6868
www.fairwaymarket.com

Food Bazaar Supermarket
Specialty grocery chain catering to ethnic populations in the neighborhoods it serves
Multiple locations throughout Brooklyn
www.myfoodbazaar.com

Foragers Market
Full-service specialty grocery
56 Adams Street
DUMBO
718-801-8400
www.foragersmarket.com

G. Esposito and Sons Pork Store
Butcher shop, prepared foods, sandwiches
357 Court Street
Carroll Gardens
718-875-6863

Get Fresh Table and Market
Gourmet grocery, restaurant, homemade pickles and jams
370 Fifth Avenue
Park Slope
718-360-8469
www.getfreshnyc.com

Grab Specialty Foods
Cheese, charcuterie, local artisanal products, craft beer, growlers
438 Seventh Avenue
Park Slope
718-369-7595
www.grabspecialtyfoods.com

Greene Grape Provisions
Specialty gourmet market
753 Fulton Street
Fort Greene
718-233-2700
blog.greenegrape.com

Los Paisanos Meat Market
Old-school, full-service butcher shop
162 Smith Street
Cobble Hill
718-855-2641
www.lospaisanosmeatmarket.com

M & I International Foods Inc.
Slavic and Eastern European megastore, café
249 Brighton Beach Avenue
Brighton Beach
718-615-1011

Marlow & Daughters
Old-world butchering; grass-fed meat from regional farms; specialty foods
95 Broadway
Williamsburg
718-388-5700
www.marlowanddaughters.com

Perelandra Natural Food Center
Natural and organic grocer, juice bar, nutrition center
175 Remsen Street
Brooklyn Heights
718-855-6068
www.perelandranatural.com

Pomegranate
Kosher megastore
1507 Coney Island Avenue
Midwood
718-951-7112
www.thepompeople.com

Red Hook Lobster Pound
Six hours from the Maine lobster boats to Brooklyn
284 Van Brunt Street
Red Hook
646-326-7650
www.redhooklobsterpound.com

Rossman Fruit and Vegetable District
Huge selection, inexpensive, open 24 hours
770 Third Avenue
Greenwood Heights
718-788-3999

Russo's Mozzerella and Pasta
Old-style Italian provisions, homemade mozzerella and pasta
363 Seventh Avenue
Park Slope
718-369-2874

Sahadi's
Unique, gourmet products from the Far and Middle East, bulk nuts, dried fruit, candies, grains, and spices
187 Atlantic Avenue
Brooklyn Heights
718-624-4550
www.sahadis.com

Salvatore Bklyn
See page 90
347-225-2545
www.salvatorebklyn.com

Spuyten Duyvil Grocery
General store–style shop, domestic and imported beer, gourmet foods
132 North Fifth Street
Williamsburg
718-384-1520
www.spuytenduyvilnyc.com

Staubitz Market
Butcher shop since 1917, sawdust-covered floors and all
222 Court Street
Cobble Hill
718-624-0014
www.staubitz.com

Stinky Bklyn

Artisanal cheese shop from the owners of Smith & Vine, Brooklyn Wine Exchange, and the JakeWalk; a cheese-of-the-month club
261 Smith Street
Cobble Hill
718-522-7425
www.stinkybklyn.com

Union Market

Gourmet grocery, prepared foods
754–756 Union Street
718-230-5152
and
402–44 Seventh Avenue
Park Slope
718-499-4026
and
288 Court Street
Cobble Hill
718-709-5100
www.unionmarket.com

Urban Rustic

Grocery store emphasizing local produce and products
236 North Twelfth Street
Williamsburg
718-388-9444
www.urbanrusticnyc.com

HOT DOGS

Asiadog

Hot dogs with Asian-inspired toppings
718-594-3254
www.asiadognyc.com

Bark Hot Dogs

Austrian-style pork and beef hot dogs, Sixpoint beer
474 Bergen Street
Park Slope
718-789-1939
www.barkhotdogs.com

Willie's Dawgs

All-natural beef, chicken, turkey, or tofu hot dogs
351 Fifth Avenue
Park Slope
718-832-2941
www.williesdawgs.com

ICE CREAM

Blue Marble Ice Cream

Small-batch ice cream in classic flavors
420 Atlantic Avenue
Boerum Hill
718-858-1100
and
186 Underhill Avenue
Prospect Heights
718-399-6926
and
196 Court Street
Cobble Hill
718-858-0408
www.bluemarbleicecream.com

Brooklyn Ice Cream Factory

Eggless ice cream in eight signature flavors
1 Water Street
DUMBO
718-246-3963
and
97 Commercial Street
Greenpoint
718-349-2506

Greene Ice Cream

See page 163
299 Dekalb Avenue
Fort Greene
www.greeneicecream.com

People Pops

Popsicles made from fresh organic fruits and herbs
www.peoplespops.blogspot.com

Van Leeuwen Artisan Ice Cream

Custard-based homemade ice cream
632 Manhattan Avenue
Greenpoint
718-701-1630
www.vanleeuwenicecream.com

ORGANIZATIONS

BK Farmyards

Converts underutilized land in Brooklyn into tiny farms
www.bkfarmyards.com

The Brooklyn Food Coalition

Working to incorporate the principles of sustainable food production at the civic and governmental level
www.brooklynfoodcoalition.org

**Slow Food in Schools/
Slow Food USA New York**

Supports local youth food education projects (schoolyard gardens, cooking classes)
20 Jay Street, Suite M04
Downtown Brooklyn
718-260-8000
www.slowfoodusa.org/index.php/
programs/details/in_schools

PICKLES

Brooklyn Brine
Small-batch pickling company preserving locally grown vegetables in Tuthilltown Whiskey distillery Barrels
www.brooklynbrine.com

McClure's Pickles
Two brothers making pickles using their great-grandmother's recipe
www.mcclurespickles.com

Wheelhouse Pickles
See page 66
www.wheelhousepickles.com

PIZZA

Amorina
Roman-style thin-crust pizza and homemade pastas, from Albano Ballerini, owner of Aliseo Osteria del Borgo (see page 56)
624 Vanderbilt Avenue
Prospect Heights
718-230-3030
www.amorinapizza.com

Di Fara Pizza
Neapolitan round and square pies made solely by legendary owner Dom DeMarco in slow, old-world style with imported ingredients
1424 Avenue J
Midwood
718-258-1367
www.difara.com

L&B Spumoni Gardens
Since 1939, Sicilian pizza with mozzarella slices under a layer of San Marzano tomato sauce, homemade spumoni
2725 Eighty-sixth Street
Bensonhurst
718-449-1230
www.spumonigardens.com

Lucali
Thin-crust, brick-oven pizza and calzones prepared on a candlelit counter in an old candy store
575 Henry Street
Carroll Gardens
718-858-4086

Motorino
Modern pizza parlor serving wood-fired brick-oven Neopolitan-style pizza, antipasti
319 Graham Avenue
Williamsburg
718-599-8899
www.motorinopizza.com

Saraghina
Pizza, home-cooked antipasti and pasta, greenmarket produce, herbs from the Bed-Stuy Farm
435 Halsey Street
Bedford-Stuyvesant
718-574-0010
www.saraghinabrooklyn.com

Toby's Public House
New York– and Neapolitan-style individual pies
686 Sixth Avenue
Greenwood Heights
718-788-1186
www.tobyspublichouse.com

Totonno's Pizzeria Napolitano
Since 1924, the oldest continually operating pizzeria in the United States, coal-burning brick-oven thin-crust pizza
1524 Neptune Avenue
Coney Island
718-372-8606
www.totonnos.com

SUPPER CLUBS

A Razor, A Shiny Knife
Educational, social, and theatrical culinary events featuring modern and experimental cooking
Fort Greene
www.arazorashinyknife.com

Brooklyn Edible Social Club
Weekly five-course farm-to-table dinner parties for up to 12 guests
Prospect Lefferts Gardens
www.bkediblesocial.blogspot.com

Homunculus
This "Brooklyn Eat-Easy" serves weekly home-cooked dinners featuring elaborate preparations
Bushwick
www.homunculuseatez.blogspot.com

Studio Feast
Italian- and Asian-influenced five-course meals for 8 to 40 guests
www.studiofeast.com

The Ted and Amy Supper Club
Named for muses Ted Allen and Amy Sedaris, this supper club hosts three-course dinners for 8 to 12 people twice a month
Fort Greene
www.tedandamysupperclub.com

Whisk & Ladle
Weekly five-course dinner, cocktail hour, and wine in a loft somewhere in Brooklyn
Williamsburg
www.thewhiskandladle.com

WINERIES/SPIRIT SHOPS/ WINE BARS

Al Di Là Vino
See page 4
248 Fifth Avenue
Park Slope
718-783-4565
www.aldilatrattoria.com

Bar Olivino
Cozy wine bar serving wine, cheese, and accompaniments
899 Fulton Street
Clinton Hill
and

Olivino Wines
Boutique wine shop with well-priced selections
905 Fulton Street
Fort Greene
718-857-7952
www.olivinowines.com
and

Olivino Bed-Stuy
426D Marcus Garvey Boulevard
Bedford-Stuyvesant
718-249-0721

Big Nose Full Body
Neighborhood wineshop with a wide selection of both major and obscure varietals and producers
382 Seventh Avenue
Park Slope
718-369-4030
www.bignosefullbody.com
and

Brook-Vin
Big Nose Full Body's wine bar
381 Seventh Avenue
Park Slope
718-768-9463
www.brookvin.com

Blanc & Rouge
Wine shop serving DUMBO since 2000
81 Washington Street
DUMBO
718-858-9463
www.brwine.com
Website associated with Blanc & Rouge focusing on rare and hard-to-find wine

Blue Angel Wines
Specializing in organic wines
638 Grand Street
Williamsburg
718-388-2210
www.blueangelwines.com

Bridget
A satellite tasting room of Long Island's Bridge Vineyards selling and pouring New York State wines
20 Broadway
Williamsburg
718-324-2800
www.bridgevineyards.com

Brooklyn Oenology
Winery that showcases local artists on its labels
117 Dobbin Street #210
Greenpoint
917-582-3290
www.brooklynoenology.com

Brooklyn Wine Exchange
Big sister to Smith and Vine (see opposite), wine shop and learning center emphasizing New World wines, organic and biodynamic wines, New York State wines
138 Court Street
Cobble Hill
718-855-WINE
www.brooklynwineexhange.com

The Castello Plan
Wine bar owned by the proprietors of Mimi's Hummus and Market, featuring over 100 selections from small producers
1213 Cortelyou Road
Ditmas Park
718-856-8888
www.thecastelloplan.com

Dandelion Wine
Boutique wine shop with a come-and-hang-out kind of feel
153 Franklin Street
Greenpoint
347-689-4563
www.dandelionwinenyc.com

D.O.C. Wine Bar and D.O.C. Lounge
Sardinian enoteca and neighboring lounge featuring Italian wines, salami, cheeses, panini, pasta, and salads
85 North Seventh Street and
83 North Seventh Street
Williamsburg
718-963-1925
www.docwinebar.com

The Greene Grape

Wine store featuring affordable small-production selections
765 Fulton Street
Fort Greene
718-797-9463
www.brooklyn.greenegrape.com

Heights Chateau

Since 1986, over 2,000 wines and spirits
123 Atlantic Avenue
Brooklyn Heights
718-330-0963
www.heightschateau.com

Juice Box Wine and Spirits

Small neighborhood shop with a knowledgeable and enthusiastic staff
1289 Prospect Avenue
Windsor Terrace
718-871-1100

Long's Wines & Liquors

Neighborhood favorite featuring weekly wine tastings with wine makers and importers
7919 Fifth Avenue
Bay Ridge
718-748-6505
www.longswines.com

Picada y Vino Wine Shop

Specializing in pairing wine with food
327 Fifth Avenue
Park Slope
718-499-2392
www.picadayvino.com

Red White & Bubbly

Affordable wines, including a monthly featured selection of four wines under $10 plus their own label, Brooklyn Wine Company
211 Fifth Avenue
Park Slope
718-636-WINE
www.redwhiteandbubbly.com
www.brooklynwinecompany.net

SIP

Wine shop focusing on lesser-known vintages from small producers, private seminars
67 Fifth Avenue
Park Slope
718-638-6105
www.sipfinewine.com

Slope Cellars

Family-run neighborhood wine and spirits shop with a devoted following, "cheap and tasty" bottles for $10 or less
436 Seventh Avenue
Park Slope
718-369-7307
www.slopecellars.com

Smith and Vine

Excellent selection of small artisanal European vintners, 40 wines under $12
268 Smith Street
Cobble Hill
718-243-2864
www.smithandvine.com

Stonehome Wine Bar and Restaurant

Wine bar with a full dinner menu, dozens of wines by the glass, flights
87 Lafayette Avenue
Fort Greene
718-624-9443
www.stonehomewinebar.com

T.B. Ackerson Wine Merchants

Highly attentive service at this shop on Ditmas Park main drag
1205 Cortelyou Road
Ditmas Park
718-826-6600
www.tbackersonwine.com

Thirst Wine Merchants

Small-production Italian and French wines from sustainable, organic, or biodynamic vineyards
187 Dekalb Avenue
718-596-7643
www.thirstwinemerchants.com

Total Wine Bar

Casual space dominated by a U-shaped bar, serves wine in stemless tumblers, and small plates and cheeses
74 Fifth Avenue
Park Slope
718-783-5166
www.totalwinebar.com

MISCELLANEOUS

Brooklyn Honey

Honey foraged by more than 40,000 bees on a Greenpoint rooftop
www.brooklynhoney.com

Gerald Jerky

Made from Dickson's Farmstand Meats' grass-fed top round in two flavors, peppered and spicy Asian
www.facebook.com/people/
Gerald-Jerky/1828827516

Kings County Jerky Co.

Wood-smoked grass-fed jerky in flavors like classic, orange ginger, and Korean bulgogi
www.craftjerky.com

Mama O's Premium Kimchee

See page 174
www.kimcheerules.com

Sweet Deliverance NYC

Preparing organic meals in a wind-powered kitchen and delivering them right to your door
347-415-2994
www.sweetdeliverancenyc.com

The Brooklyn Bee

Unfiltered honey foraged by bees living in three hives in Fort Greene
www.thebrooklynbee.com

The Makers Market at The Old American Can Factory

Weekly gathering of local artisans and greenmarket vendors
The Old American Can Factory
232 Third Street
Gowanus
www.xoprojects.com/market/
home.html

Urban Organic

Home delivery service of organic produce and groceries
240 Sixth Street
Park Slope
718-499-4321
www.urbanorganic.com

ACKNOWLEDGMENTS

We'll start with Liz Garbus, a dear friend whose restless mind churns out five great ideas an hour. Luckily for us, one of them was the initial spark for *The New Brooklyn Cookbook* (on a walk with Melissa in Prospect Park). Thank you, Liz.

And thanks to our agents, Larry Weissman and Sascha Alper, who showed us how to write a proposal . . . and then how to ask for a deadline extension.

Thanks to Cassie Jones, our fabulous editor at William Morrow, for believing in this project and for shaping our raw material into a fully realized book. And thanks to Jessica Deputato, Cassie's talented assistant, for all of her effort and energy throughout the process.

Thanks to Michael Harlan Turkell, our gifted, tireless, and exceedingly well-connected photographer. Michael not only created every image in this book, he also introduced us to many of the chefs, restaurateurs, and producers. (Sixpoint Craft Ale's Mason's Black Wheat, a dark wheat beer, is named after Michael's cat.)

Thanks to Christine Schomer for hours of inspired brainstorming, days of exhaustive research on the resource guide, and years of devoted friendship and support. Thanks to Melissa Clark for showing us the ropes. And thanks to Amy Wallace, whose sharp and thoughtful edits added flavor and spice to the restaurant entries.

Thanks to Melissa's parents, Irma and Steve, in whose loving care we left our children for countless hours while we met with chefs, went to photo shoots, and toiled on the manuscript. And special thanks to Irma for her focused and meticulous recipe testing and editing.

Thanks to Brendan's parents, Bambi and Dan, who also offered hours and hours of support in Brooklyn and North Carolina, entertaining their grandkids so we could squeeze in a few hours of work.

Thanks to Brendan's brother, Kyle, and Melissa's sister, Jen, for all their love and encouragement.

Thanks to Roan and Dory, the two most precious things in our lives.

And finally, a gigantic thank you to each and every chef, cook, restaurateur, bartender, and food producer whose vision and drive created the Brooklyn food scene as we know it—and without whom *The New Brooklyn Cookbook* would (obviously) not exist. As authors and as eaters, we thank you from the bottom of our stomachs.

INDEX

Note: Page references in *italics* refer to recipe photographs.